T0305568

Cognitive Risk

Cognitive Risk is a book about the least understood but most pervasive risk to mankind – human decision-making. Cognitive risks are subconscious and unconscious influence factors on human decision-making: heuristics and biases. To understand the scope of cognitive risk, we look at case studies, corporate and organizational failure, and the science that explains why we systemically make errors in judgment and repeat the same errors.

The book takes a multidisciplinary and pedestrian stroll through behavioral science with a light touch, using stories to explain why we consistently make cognitive errors that not only increase risks but also simultaneously fail to recognize these errors in ourselves or our organizations. This science has deep roots in organizational behavior, psychology, human factors, cognitive science, and behavioral science all influenced by classic philosophers and enabled through advanced analytics and artificial intelligence. The point of the book is simple. Humans persist with bounded rationality, but as the speed of information, data, money, and life in general accelerates, we will need the right tools to not only keep pace but to survive and thrive.

In light of all these factors that complicate risk, the book offers a foundational solution. A cognitive risk framework for enterprise risk management and cyber security. There are five pillars in a cognitive risk framework with five levels of maturity, yet there is no universally prescribed maturity level. It is more a journey of different paths. Each organization will pursue its own path, but the goal is the same – minimize the errors that could have been avoided. We explain why risks are hard to discuss and why we systematically ignore the aggregation of these risks hidden in collective decision-making in an organization.

The cognitive risk framework is a framework designed to explore the two most complex risks organizations face: uncertainty and decision-making under uncertainty. The first pillar is cognitive governance, which is a structured approach for institutionalizing rational decision-making across the enterprise. Each pillar is complimentary and builds on the next in a succession of continuous learning. There is no endpoint because the pillars evolve with technology. Enterprise risk is a team effort in risk intelligence grounded in a framework for good decision-making. We close with a call to become designers of risk solutions enabled by the right technology and nurtured by collaboration.

We hope you enjoy the book with this context.

Security, Audit and Leadership Series

Series Editor: Dan Swanson, Dan Swanson and Associates, Ltd., Winnipeg, Manitoba, Canada.

The *Security, Audit and Leadership Series* publishes leading-edge books on critical subjects facing security and audit executives as well as business leaders. Key topics addressed include Leadership, Cybersecurity, Security Leadership, Privacy, Strategic Risk Management, Auditing IT, Audit Management and Leadership

Agile Enterprise Risk Management: Risk-Based Thinking, Multi-Disciplinary Management and Digital Transformation
Howard M. Wiener

Information System Audit: How to Control the Digital Disruption
Philippe Peret

Agile Audit Transformation and Beyond
Toby DeRoche

Mind the Tech Gap: Addressing the Conflicts between IT and Security Teams
Nikki Robinson

CyRM^{SM}: Mastering the Management of Cybersecurity
David X Martin

The Auditor's Guide to Blockchain Technology: Architecture, Use Cases, Security and Assurance
Shaun Aghili

Artificial Intelligence Perspective for Smart Cities
Vahap Tecim and Sezer Bozkus Kahyaoglu

Teaching Cybersecurity: A Handbook for Teaching the Cybersecurity Body of Knowledge in a Conventional Classroom
Daniel Shoemaker, Ken Sigler and Tamara Shoemaker

Cognitive Risk
James Bone and Jessie H Lee

Privacy in Practice: Establish and Operationalize a Holistic Data Privacy Program
Alan Tang

For more information about this series, please visit: https://www.routledge.com/Internal-Audit-and-IT-Audit/book-series/CRCINTAUDITA

Cognitive Risk

James Bone and Jessie H Lee

CRC Press
Taylor & Francis Group
Boca Raton London New York

CRC Press is an imprint of the
Taylor & Francis Group, an **informa** business

First edition published 2023
by CRC Press
6000 Broken Sound Parkway NW, Suite 300, Boca Raton, FL 33487-2742

and by CRC Press
4 Park Square, Milton Park, Abingdon, Oxon, OX14 4RN

CRC Press is an imprint of Taylor & Francis Group, LLC

© 2023 James Bone and Jessie H Lee

Library of Congress Cataloging–in–Publication Data

Names: Bone, James (Risk advisory consultant), author.
Title: Cognitive risk / James Bone and Jessie Lee.
Description: Boca Raton, FL : CRC Press, 2023. | Series: Security, Audit and Leadership Series | Includes bibliographical references and index.
Identifiers: LCCN 2022034775 (print) | LCCN 2022034776 (ebook) | ISBN 9781032039091 (hbk) | ISBN 9781032039114 (pbk) | ISBN 9781003189657 (ebk)
Subjects: LCSH: Organizational behavior. | Risk management. | Subconsciousness.
Classification: LCC HD58.7 .B655 2023 (print) | LCC HD58.7 (ebook) | DDC 658--dc23/eng/20221122
LC record available at https://lccn.loc.gov/2022034775
LC ebook record available at https://lccn.loc.gov/2022034776

ISBN: 978-1-032-03909-1 (hbk)
ISBN: 978-1-032-03911-4 (pbk)
ISBN: 978-1-003-18965-7 (ebk)

DOI: 10.1201/9781003189657

Typeset in Sabon
by Deanta Global Publishing Services, Chennai, India

Contents

About the authors

JAMES BONE

James Bone is the president of Global Compliance Associates, LLC, an enterprise risk researcher, and the first cognitive risk consultant. Since the publication of his first book *Cognitive Hack*, James has promoted the idea of a cognitive risk framework in several publications and has developed a following on social media as a thought leader in this space. James has also served as lecturer in discipline in Enterprise Risk Management at Columbia University School of Professional Studies. *Cognitive Risk* will be the first book of its kind to apply additional research and experience through case studies to formulate a more complete cognitive risk framework for cybersecurity and enterprise risk management. James has two websites, globalcomplianceassociates.com and thegrcbluebook.com, as well as 5,000–8,000 fellow global risk professionals seeking thought leadership in risk best practices.

JESSIE H LEE

Jessie H Lee has 20+ years of leadership experience in financial, government, higher education, and nonprofit sectors. Jessie is a strategic and insightful leader who enables organizations to transform and grow through innovative and inclusive approaches integrating enterprise risk management, technology, and data to strengthen financial and operational sustainability and flexibility. She employs data-driven approaches and builds collaborative and trusted relationships with boards, executive leaders, staff, strategic partners, and industry leaders. She founded Better Future Strategies LLC to enable the nonprofit and social enterprise organizations to achieve their visions. She is the Director of Operations at Statement Arts, a nonprofit providing arts education to young people in New York City. She teaches in both Enterprise Risk Management and Nonprofit Management Masters degree programs at Columbia University.

Introduction

WHAT IS COGNITIVE RISK AND WHY IT IS RELEVANT AS WE ENTER THE DIGITAL REVOLUTION?

Cognitive risk originated in healthcare to describe cognitive decline in dementia but has become a buzzword in technology in the digital age. This book is one of the first of its kind to define the role of cognitive risks in its many manifestations in organizational behavior. Cognition is defined as "the mental action or process of acquiring knowledge and understanding through thought, experience, and the senses." Cognition encompasses many aspects of intellectual functions and processes such as attention, the formation of knowledge, memory and working memory, judgment and evaluation, reasoning and computation, problem-solving and decision making, comprehension, and production of language.[1]

Cognitive processes have been studied by researchers in a broad range of disciplines from healthcare, psychiatry, cognitive psychology, neuroscience, philosophy, education, computer science, and many others. The human mind is central to how we perceive the world, imagine new ideas, and shape our perception of danger, joy, love, and life, but it also leads us astray. This book is about the risk factors that lead to errors in judgment when we least expect it. Daniel Kahneman, an applied psychologist, popularized these risks of the human mind in *Thinking, Fast and Slow*.

Daniel Kahneman and Amos Tversky's research, *Prospect Theory*, won the Nobel Prize in Economics in 1979, a first for the applied cognitive and mathematical psychologists. Kahneman and Tversky focused on the psychology of prediction and probability judgment and formed a foundation for behavioral economics as a new discipline of study in economic research and political thought. Daniel and Amos's work popularized heuristics and bias as risks that lead to errors in judgment under uncertainty. Kahneman and Tversky were not the first to make these observations. Prospect theory emerged from rational choice theory in economics.[2] Daniel Bernoulli is credited with being the first to recognize the contradictions in the notion of *expected value* as far back as 1738.

Bernoulli was the first to introduce the concept of systemic bias in decision-making based on a "psychophysical" world. As the world transitions from a psychophysical world to a "digital" one, the rise of misinformation, conspiracy theories, social media, and the current public discourse. Cognitive risks becomes increasingly more problematic where "truth" is harder to distinguish from subjective values. Bernoulli used a simple coin toss to demonstrate the limitations of "expected value" as a normative decision rule. Bernoulli's findings are still being violated by financial analysts in insurance, market analysts, enterprise risk management, healthcare diagnoses, and prediction in political campaigns. When I use the term, "violated," in this context, what I mean is the subjective value of a payoff is not always based on the absolute amount of the payoff. Bernoulli found that the "value a person attaches to an outcome can be influenced by subjective factors such as the likelihood of winning, or probability."

Kahneman and Tversky's attention to heuristics is instructive, which are the short-cuts that we learn over time in problem-solving and self-discovery, are not optimal, but do satisfy an approximation of a correct answer, which explains why "to err is inherently human." Heuristics are the underlying cause of error, but bias is the weight we apply in favor of or against choices we make in everyday life which can magnify the error in certain circumstances. When Kahneman and Tversky are mentioned, many observers primarily focus on bias in prospect theory, when in fact, heuristics is the headliner and biases are the bit-players in decision-making. Prospect theory provides a fresh perspective on the philosophical underpinnings that trace its roots to influential thought leaders as far back as Zoroastrian-Persian and Greek scientists and philosophers.

The term "cognitive risk" is coined by the authors, not as science but as an umbrella term to describe a multidisciplinary body of research and emerging disciplines that include human factors, behavioral science, cognitive science, linguistics, choice theory, decision science, and risk management, among others. Each of these disciplines explores how humans behave, make choices, and explain the influencing factors that shape our beliefs. The goal of this book is to examine cognitive risks through case studies to begin a journey of reflection on why we have failed to learn the lessons of the past and continue to repeat the mistakes of our ancient forefathers.

Cognitive risk is introduced at a critical inflection point in history, as we transition from a work environment largely made up of manual labor, knowledge work, and eventually to a new digital operating environment. The lessons learned in the physical world must be expanded to include a whole new set of digital risks in cyberspace at the intersection of human and machine interactions. In other words, risks in a digital economy require a different way of managing and a new set of tools to assess and evaluate digital risk. Traditional risk and governance models are still rooted in 19th-century subjective assessments of risk that are ineffective and do not fully account for cognitive risks or incorporate scientific rigor. The very reason we are "surprised" by events like the Covid-19 pandemic is because people have a hard time intuitively comprehending and evaluating the meaning of probability as defined by extremely improbable, the long tails of the bell curve.

The authors have coined the term *homo periculum* to describe a new category of risks related to cognitive blind spots. Homo periculum is similar to the concept of homo economicus, or rational man theory. Homo economicus is the portrayal of humans as agents who are consistently rational and narrowly self-interested, and who pursue their subjectively-defined ends optimally. It is a word play on *Homo sapiens*, used in neoclassical economic theories and in pedagogy.[345]

Homo periculum is presented to describe similar errors of judgment in enterprise risk and corporate governance that inhibit the mitigation of complex risks in strategic objectives. Homo periculum is the fallacy that humans possess an innate ability to consistently calculate probabilistic outcomes in managing risks in complex organizations. Luck and risk aversion play a bigger role than leadership is willing to acknowledge. Cognitive risk is a new risk practice for the digital age to examine the presence of *homo periculum* to better understand the role of human behavior as the largest contributor to organizational dysfunction and to help explain why we fail to see the onset of major risk events. Herbert Simon called this phenomenon *bounded rationality.*

Lots of books have been written on similar topics; *The Gray Rhino, The Black Swan, MoneyBall, Predictably Irrational, The Drunkard's Walk,* and hundreds more. Each time the authors have seemingly covered new ground when, in fact, each of the authors have all described the same problem that Herbert Simon, Dan Kahneman, Amos Tversky, Paul Slovic, Frank Knight, Adam Smith, and many others have explored earlier the inability to anticipate uncertainty.

This book takes a different approach. We accept that uncertainty is the wildcard that creates both opportunity and disaster. The opportunity is to harness uncertainty while minimizing the impacts. However, to do so we must understand that each of us have cognitive blind spots that may obscure risks that we do not see. If you get nothing more from this book than a better understanding of your own bounded rationality, you have begun the journey of understanding cognitive risk. Cognitive blind spots should no longer be seen as a personal weakness. Instead, this new understanding should empower readers that cognitive risks are inherent in everyone and allows leaders in all organizations to develop strategies to build resilience in organizations that technology alone cannot.

In general, we are aware of the importance of human behavior, yet we lack a yardstick for measuring its importance or the risks associated with behavior. The understanding of human behavior is subjective, at best, but it is broadly understood that some form of heuristics and bias is inherent in all decisions we make. Now we have science as a guide.

The goal of this book is to create a new way of thinking about uncertainty and human behavior that allows for better communication and coordination of strategic goals in an uncertain operating environment. More importantly, instead of focusing solely on technology, data analytics, and the next wave of machine learning, we put the human at the center of the solution.

This book intends to delve deeper into the questions we either fail to ask or are afraid to, such as, will a singular focus on digital technologies create risks that leave us more vulnerable and fragile? As the world transitions from technology that enables productivity gains to technology that enables entertainment, collaboration, and social interaction, are we becoming temporarily sustainable and less resilient to change and disruption? As the world builds reliance on global logistics and third-party providers, global trade has become robust in economic terms but more fragile to catastrophic and minor business disruption.

The World Economic Forum describes this era in time as the *Third Industrial Revolution*, a $200 trillion digital revolution. The world is moving forward with one foot still firmly planted in a 19th century analog world, and the other foot racing toward a new digital world, but are we simply straddling risks that are being ignored or we fail to see? *YES!* The symptoms are telling and wrought with the seeds of future impacts that take a toll on the human psyche and disrupt business models. There are more questions than answers which seem fitting. The rise of artificial intelligence, cyber risk, Internet of Things, and social and political upheaval creates anxiety and unease about the future.

As the world approaches the third anniversary of the COVID-19 pandemic, social media has been implicated as one example of these emerging digital risks but not the only one. This book is important if you are attempting to navigate the massive upheaval of the Digital Revolution. More importantly, this book is about understanding how to empower yourself and associates as global citizens interested in improving how your family, organization, or peer group evolves during this Third Industrial Revolution.

The idea for this book germinated in 2016, during the writing of another book, *Cognitive Hack: The New Battleground in Cybersecurity and Enterprise Risk Management*. In my search for metrics to quantify risk in cybersecurity, I discovered the biggest vulnerability is actually human error and judgment. Stunned at this finding, I was driven to learn more about the role of human error and judgment.

When considering the challenges mankind has faced over many millennia, the focus has primarily been on mankind's quest to conquer the physical elements of land, sea, space, and weather. The quest to contain the elements is still not complete, yet humans have learned to adjust and improvise. The greatest challenges we now face are increasingly caused by humans. Humans are directly and indirectly responsible for creating some of the largest systemic risks faced by mankind: global pandemics, cyber risks and privacy, hunger, poverty, climate change, pollution, corporate failure, racism and bigotry, war, and the list is getting longer each decade.

This book is written in the hopes that a more thoughtful conversation will begin with humility, *that what we think we know may not be all there is*. The lessons of the past were hard fought through trial and error but are easily forgotten by the next generation. This is the frailty of the human mind. Sir Isaac Newton is credited with many sayings but there are two that are most relevant here. The first is, "I can calculate the motion of the heavenly bodies but not the madness of people." This quote is still as prescient today as it was in Newton's time and is the basis for this book.

The second quote is the opportunity that lies before us: "Truth is ever to be found in the simplicity [of things], and not in the multiplicity and confusion of things."

NOTES

1. https://en.wikipedia.org/wiki/Cognition.
2. https://www.press.umich.edu/pdf/0472108670-02.pdf.
3. https://www.city-journal.org/html/not-quite-rational-man-15130.html.
4. https://en.wikipedia.org/wiki/Rational_choice_theory.
5. https://www.jstor.org/stable/223329?seq=1.

Chapter 1

Reimagining the organization

Homo periculum (Human risk)

This book is about how to enhance organizational performance by avoiding massive risk failure, especially when risks are hiding in plain sight. To illustrate this point, each chapter will be divided into three parts. Part 1 will describe the problem using failure in a case study format; part 2 will create a cognitive map of the inflection points that led to failure; and part 3 will decode the cognitive risk failure and propose loosely structured approaches with intentional control design to influence behavior. The three parts are designed to encourage thinking about how to apply the lessons from the case studies to improve organizational performance, risk governance, and complex risks like cybersecurity.

Reimagining the organization requires a human-centered approach and tools to keep pace with complexity. A human-centered approach is a process of discovery in performance-hindering risks. Risk professionals aren't asking the right questions. What are the risks that hinder performance? How well do we really know our risks? Am I investing in the right risk technology? Is the work process efficient? What does risk governance look like? How do we build scale in people.

Performance-based risk analysis is an enterprise-wide approach. The ESG movement is changing how organizations perceived their impact on the environment. ESG is paving a way forward, not ERM, but something is missing in both. Metrics are being gathered to demonstrate sustainable processes across the organizational footprint but what metrics are being gathered for the impacts on people? Few of the ESG goals will be met without proactivity influencing the right behaviors in employees, customers, suppliers, and more. The common denominator in all organizations is people, and governance plays the biggest role in driving the right behaviors and influencing good decision-making to achieve corporate and environmental goals for sustainable operations. But are we asking the right questions?

Where are the biggest pain points to people – employees and customers? How can we reduce or remove friction and costs in the back office? What are the strategies to enhance uncertainty management through better people management? Do we invest in the right skills and expertise to retain top talent who know how to build high-performing teams? How best to create

DOI: 10.1201/9781003189657-1

an environment of competitiveness in excellence and support for growth? The two biggest organizational risks are performance and expectations. The tools for managing performance and expectations require a human-centered approach.

Tone at the top is often mentioned as the key to successful outcomes, but really, a positive tone is needed at all levels of the organization in order to drive positive organizational culture. Business leaders often quote sports analogies focused on individual talent, such as "Best athlete" and "Team player." Yet many fail to create an environment that allows all people to succeed. Teams, win or lose in team sports, not individuals, and teams with talent disappoint when the "chemistry" created by management is poorly managed. Teams have both superstars and position players all who contribute to success. When organizations underappreciate the role position players contribute to success, the wrong kind of tone is set. Setting the right tone across an organization enhances performance in profound ways.

Setting the right tone is about creating an environment of excellence in execution and the right tools to solve problems. One of the key tools is organizational behavior. However organizational behavior is in flux today. The Great Resignation is signaling trouble in organizational behavior that has been ignored for decades.[1] Part of the problem is organizational hierarchy and 19th-century risk governance practices that have made organizations risk averse, less innovative, and bureaucratic.[2] To examine how organizations became rigid and inflexible, we must first consider corporate governance.

CONFUSION IN ENTERPRISE RISK PRACTICE

In 1985, the Committee of Sponsoring Organizations was formed to sponsor the National Fraudulent Financial Information Commission (the Treadway Commission). The Treadway Commission was sponsored and jointly funded by five major professional accounting associations and institutes based in the US: American Institute of Certified Public Accountants (AICPA), American Accounting Association (AAA), Financial Executives International (FEI), Institute of Internal Auditors (IIA), and Institute of Management Accountants (IMA).

The Treadway Commission recommended that the sponsoring organizations of the Commission work together to develop an integrated guidance on internal control. These five organizations formed what is now called the Committee of Sponsoring Organizations (COSO) of the Treadway Commission.[3,4,5]

In the mid-1970s, the US experienced widespread questionable corporate campaign finance and corrupt foreign practices which caused the Securities and Exchange Commission to enact the Foreign Corrupt Practices Act (FCPA) of 1977.[6] FCPA was enacted for the purpose of making it unlawful for certain classes of persons and entities to make payments to foreign government officials to assist in obtaining or retaining business. The anti-bribery provisions of the FCPA have applied to all US persons and certain foreign issuers of securities. With the enactment of certain amendments in 1998, the anti-bribery provisions of the FCPA now also apply to foreign firms and persons who cause, directly or through agents, an act in furtherance of such to take place within the territory of the US.

The FCPA also requires companies whose securities are listed in the US to meet its accounting provisions. These accounting provisions, which were designed to operate in tandem with the anti-bribery provisions of the FCPA, require corporations covered by the provisions to (a) make and keep books and records that accurately and fairly reflect the transactions of the corporation and (b) devise and maintain an adequate system of internal accounting controls. Congress never requested a risk standard to be added.

Congressional hearings on the causes of the failures focused on what could have been avoided by, among other things, *better audit practice*. Concerns about independent public accounting and audit practice are a recurring theme in corporate financial malfeasance, a topic to be returned to later. David S. Ruder, the Chairman of the Securities and Exchange Commission, emphasized "the role of internal audit in deterring, detecting, and reporting financial frauds"; however, the Commission Report went further.

The Treadway Commission set forth three major objectives: (excerpts are summarized here)

(1) To understand the extent to which fraudulent financial reporting damages the integrity of financial reporting, determine how fraud can be prevented, deterred, or detected sooner, and assess whether fraud is a product of a decline in professionalism of corporate financial officers and internal auditors; and whether the regulatory and law enforcement environment unwittingly tolerated or contributed to these types of fraud.
(2) Examine whether the role of the independent public accountant in detecting fraud had been negligent or lacked sufficient focus and determine whether changes to independent public accounting and internal audit practices can be enhanced through changes in audit standards and procedures to reduce the extent of fraudulent financial reporting.
(3) Identify attributes of corporate structure that contribute to fraudulent financial reporting or to the failure to detect such acts promptly.

The Treadway Commission recommendations targeted three groups: (a) public companies; (b) independent public accountants, and (c) the SEC.

(1) Public companies were recognized as accountable for preparing accurate financial statements, setting tone at the top, oversight of internal accounting and audit, establishment of a board audit committee, preparing management and audit committee reports, seeking out second

opinions from independent public accountants, and preparing quarterly reporting.

(2) Independent public accounting was recognized for playing a "crucial" role in detecting and deterring fraud, improving the effectiveness of the independent public accountant, and recommended changes in auditing standards, changes in procedures that enhance audit quality, improving communications about the role of independent public accountant, and changes in the process of setting audit standards.

(3) The Treadway Commission suggested to the SEC that improvements could be made in the area of fraudulent financial reporting including:
  a)   increased deterrence using new SEC sanctions,
  b)   greater criminal prosecution,
  c)   improvements in regulation of the public accounting profession, and
  d)   improvements by state boards of accountancy

The Treadway Commission also referenced two final recommendations related to the perceived liability and insurance crisis to be addressed. Additional recommendations suggested that individuals involved in the financial reporting process could benefit from "education to enhance the knowledge, skills, and ethical values that potentially may prevent, detect and defer fraudulent financial reporting." Accordingly, the report recommended changes in business and accounting curricula, professional certification examinations, and continuing professional education to achieve the goals of the Commission.

The final report is only 37 pages long which included 49 specific recommendations by the Treadway Commission.[7] The Treadway Commission study was published in 1987, and in the fall of 1992, a four-volume report entitled "Internal Control: Integrated Framework" was completed. The Treadway report presented a common definition of internal control and provided a framework against which internal control systems can be evaluated and improved. This report is guidance that US companies use to assess their compliance with the FCPA. This last statement is instructive and confirms the narrow scope of the COSO internal control integrated framework (ICIF). However, according to a survey conducted by online magazine *CFO* published in 2006, *82% of respondents said they used the COSO framework for internal controls, supposedly to comply with FCPA.*

It is reasonable to assume that expanding internal controls more broadly beyond FCPA would occur to include other areas of financial reporting as well. COSO's audit and internal controls guidance has remained fundamentally unchanged for 36 years, a focus on financial reporting and gathering evidence to attest to management's statements in financial reports. However, a 2020 study found that only 20% of respondents used COSO's guidance, and of those firms, only partial implementation is conducted.[8]

COSO published an addendum to the Reporting to External Parties volume of the COSO report. The addendum discusses the issue of, and provides a vehicle for, expanding the scope of a public management report on internal control to address additional controls pertaining to safeguarding of assets. In 1996, COSO issued a supplement to its original framework to address the application of internal control over financial derivative activities.

The COSO framework defined internal control as "a process, effected by an entity's board of directors, management and other personnel, designed to provide reasonable assurance regarding the achievement of objectives" in three categories – effectiveness and efficiency of operations; reliability of financial reporting; and compliance with applicable laws and regulations. COSO's integrated internal controls framework includes the following components –

> the control environment, risk assessment, control activities, information and communication, and monitoring. The scope of internal control therefore extends to policies, plans, procedures, processes, systems, activities, functions, projects, initiatives, and endeavors of all types at all levels of a company.

The COSO ICIF is definitional in nature, neither procedural nor prescriptive, which leads to confusion and disparate results in implementation. There was vigorous debate and confusion surrounding the definition of internal control over financial reporting. The guidance COSO issued on ICIF was clarification to assist with the scope of compliance. Notwithstanding the confusion, management has sole responsibility for adhering to this interpretation and public accountants are responsible for audit attestations in evidence to management's statements in financial statements.

A source of confusion has been the use of the term "risk assessment" in the COSO definition of internal controls over financial reporting. COSO's guidance includes risk language but fails to clarify the meaning of the term. For example, risk assessment as defined by COSO, "risks are analyzed, considering likelihood and impact, as a basis for determining how they should be managed. Risk are assessed on an inherent and residual basis." The definition leaves room for wide and varied interpretation which is a weakness of the COSO framework.

How should internal control risks be analyzed? Who should analyze the risks? What methods are most effective at analyzing the risk of internal control failure? What is an acceptable level of risk in internal controls? COSO fails to address these relevant questions nor define what is an "ineffective" or "effective" control. As a result, no training or expertise is needed to follow the guidance leading to disparate and varied results. Some risk professionals like the vagueness of COSO's guidance; however, a troubling increase in fraudulent financial reporting and corporate failure is the ultimate legacy of its framework.

A statutory requirement did not come into effect until 2002, after another series of financial accounting scandals in the late 1990s and early 2000s, in the Sarbanes–Oxley (SOX) Act of 2002. SOX holds both registered public accounting firms and management of public companies ultimately accountable for the accuracy of financial statement reporting.[9] Section 404 of the Sarbanes–Oxley Act established a new rule that required management to include in their annual reports a certification of management's assessment of the effectiveness of the company's internal control over financial reporting.[10]

The annual report of management on the company's internal control over financial reporting has several key requirements (only summaries provided): (a) a statement of management's responsibility to establish and maintain adequate internal controls; (b) a statement of management's assessment of the effectiveness of internal controls; (c) a statement identifying the framework used by management to assess the effectiveness of internal controls; and (d) a statement that the registered public accounting firm that audited the firm's financial statements include in management's annual report an attestation report on management's assessment of the company's internal controls over financial reporting. The COSO framework is not a standard, it guidance for management, and many executives are not aware of the type of framework used to assess the effectiveness of internal controls.

The Treadway Commission recognized the root cause of fraud as the behavior of independent public accountants, internal audit, and corporate executives in fraudulent financial reporting. The final Treadway report documented the debates and finger-point that ensued afterward ensuring that many of the recommendations were delayed or watered down until 2002 when Congress enacted the Sarbanes–Oxley Act. Many of the Treadway Commission's recommendations were codified into new legislation in SOX 2002. Ten years after the Treadway Commission, fraud grew exponentially worse, not better! Counterintuitively, COSO has benefited from the increasing frequency of fraud by pivoting to consulting on failure in internal controls over financial reporting.

COSO's member firms began promoting integrated internal controls as a *risk* framework with other Big Four Accounting firms, selectively chosen academics, and external consultants to promote risk-based audits. The risk communication has always been troublesome and fraught with a variety of conflicting definitions and meanings. Depending upon one's point of view, one person's perception of risks can mean different things to different people. COSO's generic risk language means that anything can be a risk without rigorous probabilistic confidence levels or rules-based guidance. Subjectively defined assessments of risk has led unintended rigidity under the guise of risk management leading to a culture of risk aversion as opposed to a culture of compliance.

Auditors are responsible for managing *audit risks*, not business risks. The biggest risk to registered independent public auditors is a failed audit; fraud, misstatements of financial reports, and failure to identify accounting malfeasance. The AICPA defines an auditor's role in assessing audit risk.[11]

This Audit Risk Assessment Tool (ARAT) is designed to provide illustrative information with respect to the subject matter covered and is recommended for use on audit engagements that are generally smaller in size and have less complex auditing and accounting issues. It is designed to help identify risks, including significant risks, and document the planned response to those risks. The Audit Risk Assessment Tool should be used as a supplement to a firm's existing planning module whether in a firm-based or commercially provided methodology. The Audit Risk Assessment Tool is not a complete planning module.

The AICPA recommends the Audit Risk Assessment Tool be completed by audit professionals with substantial accounting, auditing and specific industry experience and knowledge. For a firm to be successful in improving audit quality and efficiencies, it is recommended that an auditor with at least five years of experience complete the Audit Risk Assessment Tool, or the engagement team member with the most knowledge of the industry and client (often Partner in small or medium firms) provide insight to whomever is completing the Audit Risk Assessment Tool. The AICPA recommends this should not be delegated to lower-level staff and just reviewed—it should be completed under the direction of the experienced auditor (if you delegate to inexperienced auditor, you will be at risk for less effectiveness and efficiencies because the tool is intended to be completed by an experienced auditor).

The Audit Risk Assessment Tool does not establish standards or preferred practices and is not a substitute for the original authoritative auditing guidance. In applying the auditing guidance included in this Audit Risk Assessment Tool, the auditor should, using professional judgment, assess the relevance and appropriateness of such guidance to the circumstances of the audit. This document has not been approved, disapproved, or otherwise acted on by a senior committee of the AICPA. It is provided with the understanding that the staff and publisher are not engaged in rendering legal, accounting, or other professional service. All such information is provided without warranty of any kind.

The AICPA is clear that audit risks are the primary role of auditors and only "experienced" auditors should use the Audit Risk Assessment Tool. The ARAT is not a rigorous risk assessment tool to be used beyond the scope of an audit and guided by experienced senior auditors. It is however easy to see why there has been confusion about the role of audit in risk assessment and risk management as the scope of work auditors are asked to do has expanded. The problem is that the tools auditors have at their disposal are inadequate for an effective risk assessment and are recognized in the AICPA guidance above. Misinterpretations of this guidance and the misuse of risk language have resulted in unnecessary costs and poorly inadequate risk programs.

SOX added further confusion in its requirement on the formation of an audit committee on corporate boards. The Sarbanes–Oxley Act of 2002 mandates that audit committees be directly responsible for the oversight of the engagement of the company's independent auditor. Securities and Exchange Commission (the Commission) rules were designed to ensure that auditors are independent of their audit clients.[12] Guidance from the Securities and Exchange Commission is clear cut:

> The Commission's general standard of auditor independence is that an auditor's independence is impaired if the auditor is not, or a reasonable investor with knowledge of all the facts and circumstances would conclude that the auditor is not, capable of exercising objective and impartial judgment on all issues encompassed within the audit engagement. To determine whether an auditor is independent under this standard an audit committee needs to consider all of the relationships between the auditor and the company, the company's management, and directors, not just those relationships related to reports filed with the Commission. The audit committee should consider whether a relationship with or service provided by an auditor:
> (a) creates a mutual or conflicting interest with their audit client.
> (b) places them in the position of auditing their own work.
> (c) results in their acting as management or an employee of the audit client; or
> (d) places them in a position of being an advocate for the audit client.

Confusion in the interpretation of the guidance above has extended to the role of the audit committee. The SEC guidance for the audit committee did not intend it to become a de facto "risk committee." The role outlined by the SEC, as described above, is to ensure independence in the auditor's duty.[13] However, the audit committee's role is impaired by an increase in advisory and consulting relationships between the auditor and the company. The lines have been blurred to the extent that conflicts in the relationship between external auditors and the firm have become difficult to untangle.

The risk of "mutual and conflicting interests" is widespread when independent auditors are consulting on risk management, the sole responsibility of management, or providing other services that lend themselves to place the audit firm in a position of being an advocate for the audit client. The rules are intended to limit and prevent conflicts, yet these same conflicts continue to be the cause of financial fraud and business failure. The extent of the damage in misaligned interpretations of the rules created by auditor role expansion has become substantial in material loss in shareholder value and jobs when companies fail and litigation ensues.[14]

The original mandate given to the Treadway Commission was completed in 1992 when its report was issued. The report was designed to ensure *compliance* with the Foreign Corrupt Practices Act, a very narrow remit. Typically, when a Blue Chip panel has completed its task, the group is dissolved; however, the COSO group has persisted for 36 years. A detailed review of deliberate actions taken by the COSO board will demonstrate how the nonprofit remains a platform for generating consulting fees for independent public accounting firms.

The role of corporate risk functions was nonexistent or newly forming in the early-1990s and 2000s. Large financial services firms implemented market, financial, and credit risk departments, but operational risk management did not take shape until much later in the Basel Capital Accord formulated by Central Bankers. Many of these risk functions operate as silos without active engagement between the different disciplines, but recent changes have shown that enterprise risk functions are slowly evolving. Enterprise-wide risk management (ERM) is a process of coordinated risk management that places greater emphasis on co-operation among departments to manage an organization's range of risks as a whole. Enterprise-wide risk management is still an aspirational goal for most organizations with some progress noted. While COSO's ERM integrated framework (IF) has captured public attention as the most popular, the reality is that few organizations adhere to COSO's guidance and instead use a hybrid of risk practices to achieve an enterprise view of risks.

Several industries still do not have formal risk programs. Public accounting firms benefit from covering a broad swath of industries and internal operations. This perspective gives its members a ringside view of risk practice across diverse firms along with insights on management's expectations about the lack of leadership in risk practice broadly. COSO filled a gap in uncoordinated efforts in risk practice given its position on the audit committee of corporate boards.

Congressional legislation in Sarbanes–Oxley was designed to clarify the narrow scope of audit and public accounting firms after Enron, WorldCom, and Tyco revealed the complicity of audit behavior in fraudulent financial reporting.[15] Title I of Sarbanes–Oxley established the Public Company Accounting Oversight Board to monitor and inspect registered public accounting firms, evaluate audit quality, and administer discipline if necessary. Title II of SOX mandated auditor independence to avoid conflicts of interest, among many other requirements.

Fraud, executed through the manipulations of systems, people, and processes, is a significant risk to organizational survival, but it is one risk among many shared in all organizations. A financial risk exists if the principals of a firm choose to commit fraud. The risk of not detecting, deterring, preventing, and correcting this one risk, which can take many forms, is a significant business risk. However, fraud is a business risk the Treadway Commission and the SEC delegated to management, internal audit, independent public accountants, and the SEC to address. COSO's framework works only when people are committed to ethical behavior and follow acceptable accounting practice. One of the key concepts in the COSO integrated internal control framework is, internal control is carried out by people. It is not simply about policies, manuals, and forms, but about people at all levels of an organization.

However, in the same guidance, the limitations of COSO's framework are described here: Internal control involves human action, which introduces the possibility of errors in prosecution or trial. Internal control can also be overridden by collusion among employees (separation of duties) or coercion by senior management.

The magazine *CFO* reported that companies are struggling to apply the complex model provided by COSO. "One of the biggest problems: limiting internal audits to one of the three key objectives of the framework. In the COSO model, these objectives apply to five key components (control environment, risk assessment, control activities, information and communication, and monitoring "Given the number of possible matrices, it is not surprising that the number of audits can get out of control." CFO magazine continued to state that many organizations are creating their own risk and control matrix by taking the COSO model and modifying it to focus on the components that relate directly to Section 404 of the Sarbanes–Oxley Act."

In fact, a 20-year COSO study of fraud, since the enactment of COSO's ICIF, found that the occurrence and magnitude of fraud exploded over the 20 years since the enactment of COSO's ICIF.[16] In fact, the detection of fraud is more likely than not from an internal whistleblower than from internal audit or independent public accounting firms. Fraud risk is one of many financial risks inherent in all for-profit and nonprofit organizations alike. Human behavior is the risk not internal controls.

The fact that COSO's framework is not a risk management framework does not minimize the importance of this work. Naming ICIF a risk framework has created significant confusion in the emphasis placed on compliance versus the analysis of risk in the business broadly. The confusion created in audit's role should be settled to allow for advancements in both regulatory compliance and business risk analysis, separately and in collaboration. The attention and resources spent on compliance risks have created organizational rigidity, bureaucracy, and risk aversion.

It is important to understand how COSO and public accounting firms grew into a dual role: on the one hand, providing assurance services to external stakeholder on the accuracy of financial reporting; and on the other hand, acting as advisers and consultants on enterprise risk and other advisory services. These dual roles create inherent conflicts the SEC warns boards to be cognizant of and proactively address. Confusion, complexity, and complacency have led to the adoption of a framework designed to address a very narrow compliance mandate (bribery) became adopted as a *"one-size-fits all"* risk solution without any substantive evidence of efficacy in risk mitigation.

COSO's guidance points out these weaknesses:

> although business risk management provides significant benefits, there are limitations. Business risk management depends on human judgment and, therefore, is susceptible to decision making. Human failures, such as simple errors or errors, can lead to inadequate risk responses. In addition, controls can be voided by collusion of two or more people, and management can override business risk management decisions. These limitations prevent a board and management from having absolute security regarding the achievement of the entity's objectives.[17]

Philosophically, COSO is more oriented toward controls [compliance]. Therefore, it has a *bias* toward risks that could have a negative impact instead of the risk of missed opportunities.[18] The bias of negative outcomes creates risk-averse behavior while ignoring upside opportunities in informed risk-seeking behavior. To better understand the performance of COSO's guidance on the mitigation of fraudulent financial reporting, I reviewed the results from internal studies COSO published in 2010.[19,20]

In 2010, COSO published a nine-year study called "Fraudulent Financial Reporting – 1998-2007: An Analysis of US Public Companies."[21,22] A summary of the 2010 report was published by the North Carolina State Poole College of Management. The 2010 study was the last of only two studies conducted by COSO. The first study covered the years 1987–1997 and included a small sample of 294 cases of fraud. The 2010 study sample size included 347 cases of alleged fraudulent financial reporting.

Excerpts of the summary are presented here:

- The dollar magnitude of fraudulent financial reporting soared in the last decade, with total cumulative misstatement or misappropriation of nearly $120 billion across 300 fraud cases with available information (mean of nearly $400 million per case) This compares to a mean of $25 million per sample fraud in COSO's 1999 study. While the largest frauds of the early 2000s skewed the 1998-2007 total and mean cumulative misstatement or misappropriation upward, the median fraud of $12.05 million in the present study also was nearly three times larger than the median fraud of $4.1 million in the 1999 COSO study.
- Companies allegedly engaging in financial statement fraud had median assets and revenues just under $100 million. These companies were much larger than fraud companies in the 1999 COSO study, which had median assets and revenues under $16 million.
- The SEC named the CEO and/or CFO for some level of involvement in 89 percent of the fraud cases, up from 83 percent of cases in

1987–1997. Within two years of the completion of the SEC's investigation, about 20 percent of CEOs/CFOs had been indicted and over 60 percent of those indicted were convicted.

- The most common fraud technique involved improper revenue recognition, followed by the overstatement of existing assets or capitalization of expenses. Revenue frauds accounted for over 60 percent of the cases, versus 50 percent in 1987–1997.
- Relatively few differences in board of director characteristics existed between firms engaging in fraud and similar firms not engaging in fraud. Also, in some instances, noted differences were in directions opposite of what might be expected. These results suggest the importance of research on governance processes and the interaction of various governance mechanisms.
- Twenty-six percent of the fraud firms changed auditors between the last clean financial statements and the last fraudulent financial statements, whereas only 12 percent of no-fraud firms switched auditors during that same time. Sixty percent of the fraud firms that changed auditors did so during the fraud period, while the remaining 40 percent changed in the fiscal period just before the fraud began.
- Initial news in the press of an alleged fraud resulted in an average 16.7 percent abnormal stock price decline in the two days surrounding the news announcement. In addition, news of an SEC or Department of Justice investigation resulted in an average 7.3 percent abnormal stock price decline.
- Long-term negative consequences of fraud were apparent. Companies engaged in fraud often experienced bankruptcy, delisting from a stock exchange, or material asset sales following discovery of fraud – at rates much higher than those experienced by no-fraud firms.

The term *evidence-based* is used by research analysts to describe efficacious outcomes in studies to determine the effectiveness of methodology or practice. Using the above outcomes as evidence, COSO's ICIF would be referred to as the *null hypothesis* of financial fraud or risk mitigation.[23] In the 20 years after the formation of the Treadway Commission, financial fraud was materially worse. Considering the small sample size, the results were likely gross understatements of fraud. The COSO report did not break out which public accounting firm fared worse than other firms, but the aggregated nature of the findings suggests the weakness was broad.

COSO has never published follow-up reports after the 2010 study; however, more recent headlines provide further evidence that fraudulent financial reporting has gone global.[24,25,26]

In the 20 years that followed, after the Enron fraud faded into history, the Big Four Accounting firms rebuilt their consulting empires, advising on everything from insolvency to cybersecurity. But now a fresh stream of scandals has again raised concerns that firms selling services like merger advice cannot also function effectively as auditors.

(Michael O'Dywer and Kaye Wiggings, London, Financial Times,
"Insurgents take on the scandal-hit Big Four")[27]

"That has forced Deloitte, EY, KPMG and PwC to rein in the cross-selling that helped bring them a combined \$157 billion in annual revenues last year – opening the door for nimble competitors to lure away star performers with generous pay cheques."

"Smaller insurgents, many of them private equity-backed, are bidding for the most lucrative divisions of the Big Four's business without the drag of the low margin, highly regulated and potentially reputation-damaging audit operations."

In an odd twist of irony, independent public accounting firms have benefited from fraud by raking in billions in consulting fees. When a company fails because of financial malfeasance, one of the other big four firms takes over to clean up the mess. Due to the lack of competition and the global reach of the largest public accounting firms, audit has become too *Big to Fail*, or has it?

COGNITIVE MAP: THE UNINTENTIONAL CONSEQUENCES OF A GLOBAL ERM FRAMEWORK

The COSO ERM integrated framework has garnered global acceptance as a standard in some circles by leveraging confusion in the public. So how did public accounting firms and internal auditors who use COSO's guidance to leverage the credibility of the five participating organizations make billions in consulting fees? We can find clues to the answer in COSO's own research.

In a research study commissioned by COSO, we can begin to see how the organization orchestrated ERM IF into an international phenomenon. The findings were presented in a 2013 Alternative Accounts Conference. The COSO board participated in a set of workshops sponsored by the Queen's School of Business and the University of New South Wales with financial support provided by the CPA-Queen's Centre for Governance. The title of the study is "Hybridized Professional Groups and Institutional Work: COSO and the Rise of Enterprise Risk Management." The authors of the report were Christie Hayne, School of Business, Goodes Hall, Queen's University, Kingston, ON, Canada, and Clinton Free, Australian School of Business, University of New South Wales, Sydney, Australia.

Excerpts from the report are presented below:

> This study specifically aims to examine the emergence and institutional-
> ization of COSO's ERM-IF. Adopting a qualitative research design, we
> interviewed a range of individuals directly involved in COSO's Board
> and Project Advisory Council at the time the ERM-IF framework was
> devised, as well as the principal authors of the framework. We also
> interviewed individuals outside of the COSO groups (e.g., consultants,
> executives) that we felt would offer valuable insights into the process of
> diffusion. In total, we conducted 15 interviews with individuals impor-
> tant to COSO and the ERM-IF. We also consulted a large body of sec-
> ondary materials to provide further evidence and substantiate findings.

This study makes two key contributions. First, it presents an account of the
mechanisms and processes that gave rise to the formation of COSO's ERM
model, which has become the dominant risk management model in North
America and beyond. We detail how COSO engaged in a comprehensive
project of institutional work comprised of political, cultural, and technical activities (Lawrence & Suddaby, 2006)[28]; (Corbett, Kirsch, 2001)[29],
(Davila, 2009)[30], Perkmann & Spicer, 2008).[31] Drawing upon taxonomies
developed in the area of institutional work, we illustrate the varied and
overlapping forms of agency that enabled COSO's ERM-IF to successfully
institutionalize.

Recent research in the area of institutional work augments and extends
institutional theory, a perspective which has wide currency in accounting
research. While others have focused on categories of institutional work (e.g.,
Goretzki, Strauss & Weber 2013)[32], we adopt a holistic approach to illustrate
the wide ambit of work required to successfully diffuse a new managerial
technology. We demonstrate that COSO's institutional work was marked by
non-sequential, often serendipitous, actions that acted to overlap and rein-
force each other. To the best of our knowledge, this article is the first to fully
elaborate the notion of institutional work in accounting research.

Second, we present a more fully articulated conception of the actors
involved in the supply side of a management innovation. Specifically, we
draw attention to the notion of *hybridized professional groups*, reflect-
ing the way that COSO was able to draw importantly from the social and
cultural capital, networks, and resources of its members in disseminating
the emerging model. Miller, Kurunmaki and O'Leary (2008)[33] argue that
existing literature has largely neglected the hybrid practices, processes, and
expertise that make possible lateral information flows and coordination
across the boundaries of organizations, firms, and groups of experts or
professionals.

COSO's research suggests that its ERM integrated framework did not
emerge from the rigors of scientific testing or statistical analysis but instead
was an orchestrated effort coordinated by its Board members who leveraged

the "cultural capital" of its five professional organizations reinforcing credibility through its members in accounting, auditing, academics, researchers, and select consultants. The actions taken by the COSO Board were deliberate efforts undergirded by the credibility of forming a nonprofit group of professional associations which grew out of the Treadway Commission. Notwithstanding the fact that its framework is not designed to withstand the rigors of a robust risk framework.

> Scarbrough (2002[34]) argues that professional groups tend to fulfill theorization roles in the shaping of a management fashion while consultants fulfill the diffusion side), we demonstrate that a more distributed but cohesive group of actors – comprised of accountants, auditors, academics, researchers, and consultants – was able to perform multiple roles and effectively support both the development and preservation of the concept.

The researchers compared the emergence of COSO's ERM to past fads in management.

> Many researchers have observed that management innovations – including ISO standards (Corbett & Kirsch, 2001)[35], product development management control systems (Davila et al., 2009)[36], activity-based costing (Malmi, 1999), total quality management[37] (Sharma et al., 2010[38]), performance-based incentives (Bol & Moers, 2010) and the balanced scorecard (Busco & Quattrone, 2009; Qu & Cooper, 2011) – have swept across a broad range of industrial sectors in the past two decades (Abrahamson & Fairchild, 1999; Alcouffe, Berland & Levant, 2008; Bort & Keiser, 2011; Jackson, 2001).
>
> The diaspora of associated entities provided a key platform for advocating and promoting the ERM technology and provided a stable and influential network of support. Our analysis suggests that, as a large, multi-faceted hybridized professional group, COSO was able to bridge conventional diffusion categories of disruption, creation, and maintenance.

This study sheds light on the deliberate steps COSO took to create a platform for commercial growth under the auspices of an independent nonprofit to reap billions in consulting fees for public accounting firms. The study is interesting in what is not included in its analysis:

(1) There is no due diligence provided on other existing risk frameworks for comparison to their own ERM IF.
(2) None of the academics or consultants provided detailed empirical evidence of the effectiveness of COSO's principles or guidance in real-life settings even though it had been in use for approximately 12 years after the Treadway Commission's report had been issued.

(3) The public accounting firms had 12 years to gather extensive data on the performance of COSO's ICIF to help inform how to extend its framework at the enterprise level and chose not to do so.

(4) If COSO had conducted such an analysis, the findings were not shared with researchers who conducted an extensive literature review in preparation for the study.

(5) Why did COSO not address the initial gap (human failures) identified in its own guidance? Extensive academic literature from Paul Slovic, Dan Kahneman, Amos Tversky, Frank Knight, Herbert Simon, and many other giants in psychology and economic theory was available to provide guidance for human behavior and decision-making under uncertainty.

Ultimately, the study was not conducted to determine if COSO's ERM integrated framework was effective in its mission. The study was designed simply to determine how effective COSO had been at creating a facade of legitimacy as a risk management framework with no efficacious outcomes from its guidance.

Many risk professionals and business executives are still surprised to learn that COSO ERM IF is not a risk standard and not required by legal mandate. COSO has been effective at "socializing" its principles as a best practice; however, COSO provides no metrics from which to measure the performance of its guidance. In other words, COSO simply filled a vacuum in risk management leadership that continues to prevail and created the appearance of a standard through the force of cohesion of its members collectively advocating for its guidance. Comments from researchers and participants on the COSO board exemplify their awareness of how confusion in organizational risk practice created opportunities for its integrated internal control framework.

> As it [COSO ERM IF] emerged, it became apparent that risk management was a canvass with a host of aspiring artists. Within the broad area of financial management, management accountants, internal auditors, external auditors, management consultants as well as a new and increasingly visible body of risk managers (see Aabo, Fraser & Simkins, 2005[39]; Hall, Mikes & Millo, 2013[40]) all sought to stake a claim as the concept opened up opportunities for applied use.
>
> In effect, this made risk management different from other innovations in accounting such as activity-based costing, the balanced scorecard or risk-based auditing, which have generally been circumscribed to particular areas of management accounting, auditing, or financial accounting. In this sense, COSO's ERM-IF is an innovation that is remarkable in its breadth (contested by a range of sub-disciplines) and commercial penetration (applied throughout the world).

While there is no legal mandate for its use, it nevertheless has attracted normative force. While Olson and Wu (2008) claim that there are over 80 risk management standards across the globe[41], research has consistently identified COSO ERM-IF as the best known (Fraser et al., 2008) and most widely diffused risk management standard (COSO, 2010b). The institutional work that has facilitated this rise is thus an important object of scholarly attention.

COSO ERM, like other subjectively defined risk management frameworks, is a prime example of the *rational man theory*, homo economicus, at play in enterprise risk practice. Economic theory of a rational man posits that humans innately possess all the skills and capabilities to always make rational choices. Research in economic theory and behavioral science has soundly refuted the fallacy in rational man theory by pointing out obvious examples of contradictions in rational behavior expressed in contemporary society. Homo periculum (*human risks or risk wo/man*) is a play on words like *homo economicus* in economics.[42] *Homo periculum* is introduced to define the fallacy of using subjectively defined risk processes; a fallacy in judgment that an organization's subjectively defined pursuits in risk management are conducted optimally. The persistence of the fallacy in *homo economicus* continues in risk practice today leading to failed performance and expectations in risk governance. This is a cognitive risk, a blindness to heuristics and biases, that limits our ability to recognize errors in judgment. A more detailed explanation of homo periculum will follow in part 3.

The critique is not all negative. COSO was instrumental in focusing attention on the basic elements of a risk program for compliance. COSO's ICIF is foundational yet as we enter a digital age of innovation, smart systems, and hybrid work we must move forward with risk tools and technology equal to the task of a new digital operating environment. The "E" in ERM is no longer relevant. Risks are not contained by physical walls. Digital business models create digital risks that are not addressed or even contemplated in COSO's guidance.

COSO's research study also contained warnings about the dual role COSO has created as a trusted agent and an adviser on risk management. "For some, however, accounts of institutional entrepreneurship have tended to be hagiographic and represent a bridge too far in asserting the heroic influence of individual agents" (Delmestri 2006;[43] Lawrence, Suddaby and Leca 2009;[44] Suddaby 2010[45]). As Lawrence, Suddaby and Leca (2011, pp. 52–53[46]) put it:

> Missing from such grand accounts of institutions and agency are the myriad, day-to-day equivocal instances of agency that, although aimed at affecting the institutional order, represent a complex mélange of forms of agency – successful or not, simultaneously radical and conservative,

strategic and emotional, full of compromises, and rife with unintended consequences.

A wide range of studies have examined the factors that support the demand for management innovations. The phenomenon of management "fads" and "fashions" has inspired a large body of research, prompting some commentators to question whether management fashions research itself has become the next academic fad (Clark, 2004[47]). The social and organizational functions of management innovations are generally related to reducing uncertainty, insecurity, ambiguity, and imperfection (Mazza & Alvarez, 2000[48]) and providing managers with an image of innovativeness (Kieser, 1997[49]) or even heroism (Clark & Salaman 1998[50]). Somewhat paradoxically, this is often achieved through the use of concepts that are of high linguistic ambiguity. (Benders & Van Veen 2001[51])

The warnings are prophetic and capture the risk of using COSO's ERM framework to address even mundane risks. The AICPA guidance above succinctly points out the risk of untrained auditors using their own audit risk tool inappropriately. Many risk and compliance professionals erroneously believe that the process of implementing COSO's framework is an act of risk management. The goal of risk management is *actively seeking to learn what you don't know about risks*. The real nature of risk management is reductions in ignorance about risk writ large. Knowledge of a risk is the first step of discovery followed by an understanding of root cause analysis in risk origination and finally risk treatments.

Researchers in the study provided extraordinary insights from participant's comments in individual interviews. The following commentaries from board members, consultants, and academics provide an intimate perspective in how COSO ERM was conceived and promoted as a risk management framework from an insiders' perspective:

> COSO is kind of an odd organization, not just in terms of being a virtual organization but, you know, what is it? It's not really a standard setter and yet it is kind of a standard setter. It's not a company; it's not a for-profit organization. And so, I think, when COSO comes out with guidance, it carries a pretty unique credibility because you can't attribute their actions to a profit motive per se.

> (Douglas Prawitt, Interview 5)

The cipher COSO itself is noteworthy. Described as "disarmingly mundane" by Consultant 3, COSO leaves unspecified the identity of the involved organizations and imparts an almost faceless proceduralism to COSO's activities.

Members of the COSO Board describe how confusion in public perception in COSO's not-for-profit status creates a shield from scrutiny into public accounting firm's profit motives.

What followed from these discussions was a recognition of the failure COSO's integrated internal controls framework and the need to move on to the next approach of promoting an enterprise-wide framework to replace ICIF.

> Oliverio (2001) pointed to a number of failings including the absence of implementation guidance and clear allocations of responsibility as well as the imperative of an enterprise-wide approach. Furthermore, the competing frameworks were all motivated in some part by observations that COSO's IC-IF was no longer adequate in managing against diverse and growing risks. Where internal control was once seen as a valuable process for assuring the achievement of an organization's goals, it was seen to come under increasing scrutiny.[52]

> There were some people who were looking ahead and saying "Okay, what's the next step?" We [COSO] have this internal control framework out here and now companies are using it, auditors are looking at internal controls.... What's the next step in the evolution of things? What are outside parties interested in? They are interested in how you're controlling things, but what's at the core of that control framework? First, it's identifying risk and then implementing controls to mitigate and control those risks.... So, in a way, the COSO internal control framework was a rudimentary risk management framework.

> (Douglas Prawitt, Interview 5)

> In effect, what PwC was able to do was to position itself to roll out its framework as the international benchmark. Under the COSO badge, PwC was able to take the lead in consulting in the area.

> (Consultant, Interview 3)

> What the profession needed was a comprehensive way to talk about risk. There are many ways of looking at risk but what we found is that people were talking and using the same terms in different fashions and so forth. And our view was that we needed a comprehensive framework on enterprise risk management, and it had to be across the enterprise and that if we could introduce the framework, it could get more people talking about enterprise risk management-management and therefore moving to manage risk in a much more effective way. So that was the motivation behind starting with the ERM framework.

> (Larry Rittenberg, Interview 7)

Because of that lack of a mandate [from a regulator, for example], organizations can sort of pick and choose pieces of it that work and not feel like they have to do a full blown implementation. We're in the early phases of ERM where people are just out there picking, there's no mandate for anything and so I think people have found it helpful, but I guess it's good that they're not being forced into it at this point. ERM is so complex to really do, companies have realized if they try to go from A to Z, it will stall.

(Mark Beasley, Interview 3)

I think part of it is because of the COSO consortium of organizations and frankly PricewaterhouseCoopers having been the author of the COSO ERM report – the names attached and the fact that COSO's internal control became a standard. The background and expertise of those organizations, and if I may say so also PwC, has caused people to look to it as the place to go in gaining insight, in gaining direction on how to build an ERM architecture in their organizations.

(Rick Steinberg, Interview 9)

This is an excellent time to introduce cognitive mapping.[53] The term was generalized by some researchers, especially in the field of operations research, to refer to a kind of semantic network representing an individual's personal knowledge or schemas. The cognitive map above provides a look into the "mind's eye" of participants as they deliberate the merits of adopting COSO ERM IF.[54]

Part of it is probably, just the fact that it's a US framework, to be honest with you. I think that carries a lot of clout, probably decreasingly so the way the world is moving, but I think that it still does carry some impact.

(Douglas Prawitt, Interview 5)

The whole US thing; it's what I call the McDonald effect: it's American, it's big, and it's what the New York Stock Exchange will accept.

(John Fraser, Interview 1)

I was invited to speak in Tokyo, and I remember talking to the Minister of Economy … he said, "But you also have to understand that many Japanese businesses are already New York Stock Exchange traded and so whatever they hear is happening in the US, they want to do it". He said, "Many others are New York Stock Exchange wannabes. So, they're not on the New York Stock Exchange yet, but they want to figure out what the best practices are in the US and then get ready and say that they're already doing those practices ... so that division is going to implement enterprise risk management or some COSO framework to make it look more relevant."

(Paul Walker, Interview 8)

Some accounting firms were fairly responsive to it [COSO's ERM-IF] and kind of did similar to us [PwC], kind of developed methodologies and things to go deliver services around it. There was also some who felt that they could build a better mousetrap or already had a better mousetrap.

(Frank Martens, Interview 14)

Most consulting firms want to have tools and frameworks that are branded their own so they can use them, even if it's just a slight change. I think everybody tries to come up with their own little process wheel, everybody tries to come up with their own framework for looking at it, everybody tries to come up with their own common risk language, it's just the way it is.

(Consultant 1, Interview 10)

There are a lot of mouths to feed, and we were out hawking for work like everyone else. And COSO was a name that people knew ... Sure most of the big players refined this to develop their own proprietorial tools, but the COSO model opened the door if you like.

(Consultant 3, Interview 12)

The comments from board members, consultants, and public accountants give you a real sense of the genesis of COSO ERM. There clearly was recognition that a singular focus on internal controls was no longer sufficient and a new approach was needed. One interviewee noted, "ERM is so complex to really do." ERM is hard because the methods for analyzing disparate risks in aggregate requires different approaches than subjectively defined audit risk tools. It is unlikely that measures of "likelihood" and "impact" are sufficient analytical predictors of enterprise-wide risks such as cyber, operational, human, technological, and strategic risks in aggregate.

On the one hand, there is no longer a regulatory justification for COSO to continue to exist 36 years after the conclusion of the Treadway Commission. The Sarbanes–Oxley Act of 2002 has still not materially reduced fraudulent financial reporting. On the other hand, neither the SEC nor the Public Company Accounting Oversight Board has fully addressed the inherent conflicts of interest in the dual role of consulting and audit advisory work.

The firewalls that should exist have proven to be made of paper mâché, if they exist at all. Corporate boards and management must take back control of the audit committee's clearly defined scope to ensure audit independence. There is now a robust and thriving community of risk professionals and risk advisory firms to provide organizations with independent risk guidance or to supplement existing risk departments.

Auditors and public accounts have a value role to play in advancing internal controls over financial statements. More advanced guidance is needed on digital controls, connected devices, external third-party controls in the cloud, and on vendor site inspections. As organizations continue the transition to digital strategies, support to strengthen internal controls over financial reporting provides ample opportunity for public accounting firms to consult and advise. The SEC should also ensure and encourage an expansion of regulated public audit firms' eligibility and regulate independent risk advisory firms to enable competition for access to the global marketplace of ideas in financial accounting and risk management.

Researchers demonstrate the challenges in creating a competitive market in public accounting.[55]

Because public accounting is a regulated practice, the profession actively manages its relationship with the state. While prior studies have analyzed the profession's efforts to shape its regulatory environment, few studies have examined the profession's pointed attempts to influence a specific regulatory policy that affects the practice of auditing in the United States. Drawing on extant theories of regulation and political economy, this study investigates the rationality and effectiveness of political action committee (PAC) contributions paid to members of the US Congress by the US public accounting profession during the policy formulation period of the Sarbanes–Oxley Act of 2002.

Based on the results of empirical tests, we conclude that the US profession strategically manages its relationship with the federal government, in part, through direct involvement in the financing of political campaigns. Furthermore, the profession's pattern of contributions implies an ideologically conservative as well as a professional regulatory motivation for providing financial support to federal legislators. Thus, although the US profession continues to proclaim the primacy of its public interest orientation, it does not appear to be politically neutral when attempting to influence public policy.

DECODING THE FAILURE IN AUDIT AND CONFUSION IN ENTERPRISE RISK MANAGEMENT

The unintentional *noise* in public accounting and auditing has cost financial markets trillions of dollars in real and potential losses on a global scale – creating a massive cognitive risk and one that could have been mitigated had Congress, the SEC, and the public understood the need to focus on the root cause of risk (human behavior) instead of internal controls over financial reporting. Herbert Simon pointed out this risk in 1947 in *Administrative Behavior* and introduced the concept of "bounded rationality."[56] Simon recognized that a theory of administration is largely a theory of human decision making, and as such must be based on both economics and on psychology.

Simon presented arguments against the then prevalent theory that "humans as agents who are consistently rational and narrowly self-interested, pursue their subjectively-defined ends optimally." Even though academics have settled the fallacy of belief in perfect rationality, remnants of these beliefs and practices still operate in corporate boards, government, and other institutions whether we consciously realize it or not. Our inability to recognize these risks is what I call cognitive risks.

Cognitive risks exist in many forms but primarily manifest in inattentional blindness to risk in judgment, bias, and impacts in human error.[57] Inattentional blindness

> occurs when an individual fails to perceive an unexpected stimulus in plain sight, purely as a result of a lack of attention rather than any vision defects or deficits. When it becomes impossible to attend to all the stimuli in a given situation, a temporary "blindness" effect can occur, as individuals fail to see unexpected but often salient objects or stimuli.

Examples include texting while driving, or decision-making while distracted by calls or deadlines. While we value multitasking, we are lousy at doing it well. Counterintuitively, inattentional blindness occurs by blindly following what other organizations have adopted as "best practice."

Why is cognitive risk relevant? Behavioral economists and researchers have already identified similar risks in heuristics, bias, health, and safety issues; however, to date, their insights have not been applied to risk governance specifically. The idea became obvious to me as an area in need of attention and research after reading the insightful examples provided in the book, *Noise*. An entirely new and unexplored approach to thinking about risk has been revealed in the precepts in *Noise*. Kahneman et al. present a simple approach, *decision audits*, to detect the presence and the magnitude of this hidden risk.

As an example, the global adoption of COSO ICIF and COSO ERM IF is noisy and biased on several fronts. Let me explain further. The process of implementing COSO ICIF is both *noisy* and *biased* in that no two organizations adopt the processes and principles in the same way. The definition of "noise" is variability (dispersion) in judgment(s). What that means in practical terms is two-fold: a) COSO lacks a verifiable target of performance for risk mitigation when a partial implementation is as satisfactory as a full implementation. b) COSO lacks any predictive value in how effective the framework would perform as evidenced by the variability in disparate implementation outcomes.

The second major problem with COSO's two frameworks is they are biased toward a focus on internal controls over financial reporting. This point was made clear by COSO itself in the creation and explanation of the ICIF. A biased framework is systemically incorrect in that no matter the means of implementation, users will view risks in one way limiting one's view of the spectrum of risks that exist. This is a classic cognitive risk in inattentional blindness!

There are two kinds of error: *Noise and Bias*. Consider a group of friends at their favorite pub playing a game of darts. The group is made up of four teams who play every Friday night. Team 1's darts consistently hits near the bullseye. The team 1's tightly clustered darts represent a perfect pattern. Team 2 is consistently off target to the left, but also in a tightly clustered pattern of darts (*biased*). Team 3's darts are widely scattered with no discernable pattern (*noisy*), and Team 4's darts are off target but also widely scattered (*both noisy and biased*). Now convert the darts into business decisions. Bias has gotten more attention, but noise is a hidden culprit in the flaw of judgment and more than expected.

A layman's explanation may also be helpful. Here is a practical example: If two dozen firms of the same size and risk profile adopt COSO's ICIF or its ERM IF in disparate ways, there is no way to determine if COSO's framework is an effective tool to mitigate risks because of inherent noise and bias in how the framework is implemented. In practical terms, inconsistency in how COSO's framework is implemented creates a regulatory lottery. If a regulator finds deficiencies in one firm, the same deficiencies or greater may exist in other firms creating a systemic risk within the industry. The evidence of this lottery effect has played out in fraudulent financial reporting across different industries after the partial adoption of different components of COSO's two main frameworks.

Fundamentally, COSO's ICIF and its ERM IF are flawed risk frameworks and the billions spent on implementation are the costs of error in judgment. COSO's own research is evidence of inherent flaws in its framework, but the real damage in corporate governance is the expectation that COSO's framework is a best practice in risk management.

Over-reliance on subjectively defined risk management programs is an example of the fallacy I call, cognitive risk, or *homo periculum*. *Homo periculum* is a fallacy in assuming frameworks like COSO's ERM IF are optimal approaches to achieving maturity in risk management programs. Compliance-oriented frameworks are helpful to ensure consistency in institutional behavior but are only the first step in a multidisciplinary process toward building a robust risk practice. This concept may be hard to grasp initially because many risk professionals are not familiar with the science of risk. But consider that all buildings rely on a good foundation based on ground and weather conditions the architect must consider for long-term sustainability, including maintenance and upkeep.

Or consider the analogy one senior executive frequently used. A race car needs good brakes, suspension system, and tires for different weather and road conditions to allow the race car driver to perform optimally to win while remaining safe. Weakness in any of the foundational areas of design create inherent vulnerability to the entire system. That is why the World Trade Center towers held after the planes hit allowing most of the participants to escape unharmed versus the catastrophic failure of the Condo towers on the beach in Florida. Attention to details matter because the details allow you to take informed risks after you have addressed the fundamentals.

Risk management is not solely about following someone else's script for what a risk program is, it is about understanding the proper design of a risk program to address your unique and specific risk needs.

Reimagining the organization is about designing new solutions for the needs of your firm not following the leader, especially when the self-anointed leaders know less about your risks than you do.

The merging of psychology and economics has resulted in a more robust understanding of judgment and decision-making under uncertainty and helps explain why this flaw has gone undetected and underrepresented in traditional risk frameworks like COSO ERM, ISO 31000, and most existing risk programs. It is premature to call any traditional risk framework "mature" without an extensive grounding in the science of risk whose root and branch is informed in psychology, behavioral economics, behavioral science, and decision science. Economists dubbed the rational man theory "homo economicus." I have dubbed the rational risk theory in traditional risk practice "homo periculum," a fallacy I call cognitive risk, a fallacy that organizations' subjectively defined pursuit of risk management is conducted optimally.

The noise in public accounting and audit that I referred to earlier is the same as those referenced in the prologue: "wherever there is judgment, there is noise – and more of it than you think" (*Noise*, p.12, Kahneman, Sibony, and Sunstein 2021). Public accounting and audit are predicated on judgment. Judgment is required in response to accounting for the complexity of today's business environment. A problem arises when attempting to overly rely on subjective judgment in the application of complex risk analysis without appropriate rules-based guidance.

We now know that noise is the variability of judgment. When business leaders and auditors differ on "the risk" of a course of action or the outcome of certain business practices, these disagreements create bias and noise in judgment. When organizations lack the tools to minimize bias and noise, the resulting residual risk is costly whether known or not. This risk is largely undetected until the accumulation of these unresolved judgments add up to an unexpected failure or operational inefficiencies.

Now that we have established the context for why corporate failure and fraud continues to grow unabated, let us turn our attention to other examples of failure in case studies to demonstrate how cognitive risk thrives in a variety of circumstances.

NOTES

1. https://www.cbsnews.com/news/great-resignation-60-minutes-2022-01-10/.
2. https://www.cnbc.com/2022/01/14/the-great-resignation-expert-shares-the -biggest-work-trends-of-2022.html.
3. https://en.wikipedia.org/wiki/Committee_of_Sponsoring_Organizations_of _the_Treadway_Commission.
4. https://www.sec.gov/news/speech/1989/012689grundfest.pdf.
5. https://www.sec.gov/rules/final/33-8238.htm.
6. https://www.justice.gov/criminal-fraud/foreign-corrupt-practices-act.
7. See COSO, "Internal Control-Integrated Framework" (1992) ("COSO Report"). In 1994, COSO published an addendum to the Reporting to External Parties volume of the COSO Report. The addendum discusses the issue of, and provides a vehicle for, expanding the scope of a public management report on internal control to address additional controls pertaining to safeguarding of assets. In 1996, COSO issued a supplement to its original framework to address the application of internal control over financial derivative activities.
8. https://www.academia.edu/45682001/The_Future_of_Risk_Management.
9. https://corporatefinanceinstitute.com/resources/knowledge/other/top -accounting-scandals/.
10. https://www.sec.gov/rules/final/33-8238.htm.
11. https://www.aicpa.org/resources/download/aicpa-audit-risk-assessment-tool.
12. https://www.sec.gov/info/accountants/audit042707.htm.
13. https://www.sec.gov/info/accountants/audit042707.htm.
14. https://www.telegraph.co.uk/business/2022/01/12/kpmg-auditor-uses -minority-ethnicity-defence-forged-carillion/.
15. https://corporatefinanceinstitute.com/resources/knowledge/other/top -accounting-scandals/.
16. https://www.coso.org/documents/FraudStudyOverview_000.pdf.
17. https://en.wikipedia.org/wiki/Committee_of_Sponsoring_Organizations_of _the_Treadway_Commission.
18. https://en.wikipedia.org/wiki/Committee_of_Sponsoring_Organizations_of _the_Treadway_Commission.
19. https://corporatefinanceinstitute.com/resources/knowledge/finance/financial -engineering/.
20. http://guide.berkeley.edu/graduate/degree-programs/financial-engineering/.
21. https://erm.ncsu.edu/library/article/coso-fraud-study/.
22. https://pcaobus.org/oversight/inspections/firm-inspection-reports.

23. https://en.wikipedia.org/wiki/Null_hypothesis.
24. https://amp.ft.com/content/a8c60322-3e56-4889-b346-e34d3c5f1e97.
25. https://www.ft.com/content/57e0ff80-de17-48b1-9da7-5bdbaaad8898.
26. https://amp-ft-com.cdn.ampproject.org/c/s/amp.ft.com/content/548f99ff
    -1815-4af1-a7ef-e631cf9c720a.
27. https://www.ft.com/content/57e0ff80-de17-48b1-9da7-5bdbaaad8898.
28. T. Lawrence and R. Suddaby (2006), Institutions and institutional work, in: S.
    Clegg, C. Hardy, W. Nord, and T. Lawrence, eds., *Handbook of Organization
    Studies*, London: Sage, 215–254. https://doi.org/10.4135/9781848608030.n7.
29. C.J. Corbett and Kirsch, D.A., INTERNATIONAL DIFFUSION OF ISO
    14000 CERTIFICATION, 05 January 2009, https://doi.org/10.1111/j.1937
    -5956.2001.tb00378.x
30. Davila, et al, framework 48, Management Control Systems and Open, pps.
    55-59.
31. M. Perkmann and A. Spicer (2008). How are management fashions institu-
    tionalized? The role of institutional work. *Human Relations*, 61(6), 811–844.
    https://doi.org/10.1177/0018726708092406
32. L. Goretzki, E. Strauss, and J. Weber (2013), An institutional perspective
    on the changes in management accountants' professional role, *Management
    Accounting Research*, 24(1), 41–63.
33. P. Miller, L. Kurunmaki, and T. O'Leary (2008), Accounting, hybrids and
    the management of risk, *Accounting Organization and Society*, 1 October.
    https://doi.org/10.1016/J.AOS.2007.02.05.
34. H. Scarbrough (2002). The role of intermediary groups in shaping manage-
    ment fashion: The case of knowledge management. *International Studies of
    Management and Organization*, 32(4), 87-103.
35. C. J. Corbett and D. A. Kirsch (2009), International diffusion of ISO 14000
    certification, *Operations Management*, 5 January 2009. https://doi.org/10
    .1111/j.1937-5956.2001.tb00378.x.
36. Y. Lievens, W. van den Bogaert, and K. Kesteloot (2003), Activity-based cost-
    ing: A practical model for cost calculation in radiotherapy, *International
    Journal of Radiation Oncology, Biology, Physics*, 57(2), 522–535. https://doi
    .org/10.1016/s0360-3016(03)00579-0. PMID: 12957266.
37. Teemu Malmi (1999), Activity-based costing diffusion across organiza-
    tions: An exploratory empirical analysis of Finnish firms, *Accounting,
    Organizations and Society*, 24(8), 649–672, ISSN 0361-3682. https://doi.org
    /10.1016/S0361-3682(99)00011-2, https://www.sciencedirect.com/science/
    article/pii/S0361368299000112.
38. S. D. Levitt, J. A. List, and S. Sadoff.
39. Tom Aabo, John R. S. Fraser, and Betty J. Simkins (2005), The rise and evolu-
    tion of the chief risk officer: Enterprise risk management at hydro one, *Journal
    of Applied Corporate Finance*, 17(3), 62–75, Available at SSRN: https://ssrn
    .com/abstract=622744.
40. Matthew Hall, Anette Mikes, and Yuval Millo (2013), How do risk managers
    become influential?: A field study in two financial institutions, Revision, 2013
    October 17.
41. Indeed, several international risk management standards pre-date the COSO
    framework including CAN/CSA-Q850-97: *Risk Management: Guideline for
    Decision*-Makers issued by the Canadian Standards Association in 1997 (62

pages); BS 6079-3:2000 *Project Management: Guide to the Management of Business-related Project Risk* issued by the British Standards Institution in 2000 (22 pages); JIS Q2001: 2001(E) *Guidelines for Development and Importance of Risk Management* Systems issued by the Japanese Standards Association in 2001 (20 pages); IEEE Standard 1540-2001: *Standard for Software Life Cycle Processes – Risk Management Standard for Software Life Cycle Processes – Risk Management* issued by the American Institute of Electrical and Electronic Engineers in 2001 (24 pages); and AS/NZS 4360:2004: *Risk Management* issued jointly by Standards Australia/ Standards New Zealand in 2004 (24 pages). Based on a wide-ranging analysis of several standards, Raz and Hillson (2005) conclude that there is "wide consensus regarding the main steps and activities of a generic risk management process" (p. 65) and that "where there are apparent differences in process, these are largely attributable to variations in terminology" (p. 64).

42. https://en.wikipedia.org/wiki/Homo_economicus.
43. G. Delmestri (2006), Streams of inconsistent institutional influences: Middle managers as carries of multiple identities, *Human Relations*, 59(11), 1515–1541.
44. T. B. Lawrence, R. Suddaby and B. Leca (2009), Introduction: Theorizing and studying institutional work, in: T. B. Lawrence, R. Suddaby, and B. Leca, eds., *Institutional Work: Actors and Agency in Institutional Studies of Organizations*, Cambridge: Cambridge University Press. https://doi.org/10 .1017/CBO9780511596605.
45. R. Suddaby (2010), Construct clarity in theories of management and organization, *Academy of Management Review*, 35(3), 346–357.
46. T. Lawrence, R. Suddaby, and B. Leca (2011), Institutional work: Refocusing institutional studies of organization, *Journal of Management Inquiry*, 20(I), 52–58. Sagepub.com/journal/Permissions.nav. https://doi.org/10.1177 /1056492610387222.
47. T. Clark (2004), The fashion of management fashion: A surge too far? *Organization*. https://en.wikipedia.org/wiki/Homo_economicus.
48. C. Mazza and J. L. Alvarez (2000), Haute couture and Prêt-à-Porter: The popular press and the diffusion of management practices, *Organization Studies*, 21, 567–588. http://dx.doi.org/10.1177/0170840600213004.
49. A. Kieser (1997), Rhetoric and myth in management fashion, *Organization*, 4(1), 49–74. https://doi.org/10.1177/135050849741004.
50. Timothy Adrian Robert Clark and Graeme Salaman (1998), Creating the 'right' impression: Towards a dramaturgy of management consultancy, *Service Industries Journal*, 18(1), 18–38. Research Collection Lee Kong Chian School of Business. Available at: https://ink.library.smu.edu.sg/lkcsb _research/6284.
51. Jos Benders and Kees Van VeenView all authors and affiliations 8(1). https:// doi.org/10.1177/135050840181.
52. Clark, T. (2004). The fashion of management fashion: A surge too far? Organization, 11(2), 297-306.
53. Simon Ungar (2005), Cognitive maps, in: Roger W. Caves, ed., *Encyclopedia of the City*, Abingdon; New York: Routledge, 79. https://doi.org/10.4324 /9780203484234. ISBN 9780415252256. OCLC 55948158.

54. https://en.wikipedia.org/wiki/Cognitive_map.
55. https://www.researchgate.net/publication/223239550_Money_politics
_and_the_regulation_of_public_accounting_services_Evidence_from_the
_Sarbanes-Oxley_Act_of_2002.
56. https://en.wikipedia.org/wiki/Herbert_A._Simon.
57. https://en.wikipedia.org/wiki/Inattentional_blindness.

Chapter 2

Complexity in risk and risk perceptions

Cognitive risks – errors in judgment obscure our ability to detect risk

Cyber risk is one of the greatest risks to society in every country. Ransomware, malicious viruses, and disinformation are used to disrupt business and democracy alike. Cyber-attackers have breached national credit bureaus, agencies in the federal government, and businesses, small and large, but surprisingly these threats have not slowed online shopping or investments in Silicon Valley for tech Unicorns. Studies have shown differences by gender in perceptions of risk while shopping online.[1] Other studies have shown that while millions of people visit sites, only 3% make a purchase, and 65% of shopping carts are abandoned.

This raises many questions about perceptions of risks in the real world and in cyberspace.[2,3] Cyber risks are asymmetric meaning; the attacker has an advantage in choosing the timing, method, and frequency in launching an attack. Attackers have also learned that soft targets (humans) yield the best results at the lowest cost. Vulnerabilities in cybersecurity at the human–machine intersection is understood yet, paradoxically human factors in cyber risk continue to be underappreciated?[4]

THE SCIENCE OF RISK VERSUS SUBJECTIVELY DEFINED RISKS

I use the term "science of risk" to refer to an exhaustive body of research that has been explored for centuries and evolved along parallel paths with different reference points. At the risk of oversimplification, I will attempt to summarize different schools of thought on risk, and risk perception, to provide context for the remainder of this chapter, and the book in general. The concept of risk perception is still an evolving one for reasons that will become clear in the following paragraphs.

A caveat is offered before I delve into a summary of risk and risk perceptions. I will not offer a definition of risk. There are many definitions of risk with many points of view and varying definitions of controversy which I intend to avoid. Why avoid defining risk? Each of us perceives risks

DOI: 10.1201/9781003189657-2

differently; therefore, "just as the color of an eye plays no part in deciding whether something is or is not an eye, these 'accidental attributes' of a risk do not provide criteria in themselves for deciding whether, or not, something is, or is not, a risk" (Allum, Gaskell, and Jackson 2005).[5] A risk is or is not a risk, in the eye of the beholder ... therein lies the challenge in definitions of risk!

Over the last 20 years, risk has become a buzzword: risk-based audits, risk-based assessments, and risk-based cybersecurity are recent terms that have become part of the lexicon in social science and corporate risk programs. Many of these terms are either under-defined or carry a generic connotation. The term suggests an individual's self-assessment of risk in a specific domain. Typically, the assessment assumes that the risks are known in advance or the person conducting the assessment will know the risk when they see it. Both assumptions represent the "naïve" assessment of risks. The term risk and control self-assessments (RCSAs) falls into this category.

A naïve assessment of risk is a method used by many risk professionals, laypersons, and executives alike. This method of assessment is either conducted in a survey, interview, or group setting involving subject-matter experts (SMEs) answering questions like "what keeps you up at night?" or "what are the risks and what controls are in place to mitigate risks?" The answer(s) that follow produce a scale of high, medium, and low (with or without a numerical score). The final results are input in a risk assessment matrix in 3 × 3 or 4 × 4 grids and published as a dashboard for review with leadership. Upon completion, the assessments are put on a shelf until the next scheduled round of risk assessments. Some version of this exercise happens in hospitals, business, government, etc., and may involve risk training or education. Does that sound familiar?

These types of risk assessments are naïve in that what is being assessed is one's perceptions of risk, not actual risks, per se. This is particularly true due to the frailties of memory.[6] Few people possess the ability to recall past events in detail with great accuracy. Researchers have found that memory recall is somewhat more effective when people see an emotional event rather than simply hearing about it. Scholars recognize that memory is a fluid process that involves reconstruction of events and details rather than exact reproductions of events. Instead of exact recall, memories are often stitched together into plausible narratives based on beliefs, feelings, intuitions, guesses, and memory fragments (Loftus 1993, 2005)[7,8]. In other words, a picture of risks collected in RCSAs is incomplete, at best, and may even be somewhat misleading. Nonetheless, trustworthiness is given to one's recall of events in courtrooms, medical settings, and risk assessment.

Judges allow jurors to weigh the validity of a defendant's or witness's memory to determine culpability. Doctors assess pain level on a scale of 1–10. And risk professionals conduct subjective risk assessments. These assessments are imprecise; however, they are an important measure of one's perception of an event, pain, or risk. Risk perceptions are an important starting point for asking more in-depth questions about why a risk is perceived as a risk. A well-designed interview of one's risk perceptions combined with actual risk data is an excellent approach for reframing risks to understand conflicting heuristics and biases in risk perception.

Memory recall in the RCSA process falls into two primary categories: a) high-frequency, low-impact events, or b) low-frequency, high-impact events. In both cases, most of the salient details about the root cause and steps taken in remediation are lost. The recall of these events is subject to availability bias or heuristics. Availability bias is a mental shortcut that relies on immediate examples that come to a given person's mind when evaluating a specific topic, concept, method, or decision.[9,10,11]

Tools like RCSAs are the product of public accounting firms which have been adopted by risk professionals to conduct Sarbanes–Oxley internal control reviews. Accountants and auditors are *not* required to provide statistical analysis in audit sampling or risk analysis. Public accountants and auditors have devised their own "rules of thumb" in determining reasonable sampling for tests of audit attestation, not stochastic levels of confidence intervals.[12] Audit sampling recognizes "some degree of uncertainty is implicit in the concept of 'a reasonable basis for an opinion' referred to as the third standard of field work." The problem with reasonable assurance is we don't know what an auditor's degree of uncertainty exists in any opinion nor how much one auditor will differ in their opinion when looking at the same risk or issues. Auditors do not provide 99.9% confidence levels in attestations of internal controls over financial reporting. Auditors provide "reasonable assurance."[13] Reasonable assurance is a subjective judgment, and as we now know, where there is judgment there is error... and more than we think!

According to the Public Company Accounting Oversight Board (PCABO), "reasonable assurance refers to the auditor's degree of satisfaction that the evidence obtained during the performance of the audit supports the assertions embodied in the financial statements." Most auditors are not trained in statistical analysis as risk professionals, nor is it their role to do so. Audits attempt to replicate sufficient evidence in independent sampling to support management's assertions in financial statements. Attempting to describe the role of an auditor as a risk professional creates confusion and is a misrepresentation of the scope of an audit and the capability of auditors. Experienced auditors may provide an expert opinion about risk, and those opinions may be valid; however, opinions must be distinguished from statistically valid confidence intervals. Depending on the risk, the difference really does matter!

A small but growing generation of auditors is being trained in statistical methods which may change how audits are performed in the future as well as prompt changes in audit standards. More confidence and accountability would be instilled in financial statement reporting if independent public accountants and internal audit were required to provide "statistical confidence levels" as opposed to "reasonable assurance." However, until those changes are made, there should be no expectation that auditors provide more than reasonable assurance. The way to obtain confidence levels is not through a test of controls; confidence levels are derived from testing a stochastic pool of *risks* with time intervals.[14]

Pseudo-risk practices have created confusion and a lack of confidence in risk management with the executive suite, the board, and in cybersecurity risk practice as well. Instead of providing guidance to evaluate and inform on strategic planning and risk mitigation, risk management is relegated to "check-the-box" exercises that fail to add value. This confusion has been created by an unhealthy competition between internal audit, public accountants, and risk management to gain the attention of senior executives and the board of directors.

Management must have confidence in the role that each oversight discipline plays in corporate governance. Understanding how the role of each discipline contributes to risk governance is equally important in setting the right expectations for accountability. The annual process of creating risk inventories and RCSAs has become wholly inefficient because of role confusion. A board-level risk committee should be established and led by an executive with the requisite analytical skills, or a team of analysts, who are responsible for risk intelligence and defining automated risk solutions. Today's suite of technology offers a host of decision-support opportunities to inform the executive suite. More on this later in a discussion about cognitive governance.

WASTE IN SUBJECTIVELY DEFINED RISK PRACTICE

Let's examine the inefficiencies in traditional risk practice.[15] There is growing evidence of duplicative waste in risk work product. The annual audit plan is frequently deemed a risk-based audit and is either driven solely by internal audit or in collaboration with public accounting firms based on an auditor's view of risks. The internal risk department also conducts an annual risk assessment of the risks they deem important. And the chief compliance officer will also conduct a risk assessment of key compliance risks. This is the "first layer of duplicative risk waste" – uncoordinated and misaligned risk assessments that are subjectively defined by different oversight departments. Apologies to risk professionals who have mastered these next steps. Studies show however you are a minority. Two-thirds of risk management programs are rudimentary subjectively defined risk programs.[16]

Risk waste is both layered and duplicative. The process of defining key risks is layered when there are conflicting and redundant definitions of key risks. Identifying key risks is a collaborative process that requires agreement on the methodology for defining a risk key to the organization. Once defined, there should be agreement on the mitigation steps for each key risk. Criteria for periodic reassessment of key risks should be based on the materiality of the impact of failure. Key risk monitoring should be the lever for recognizing the change in the efficacy of controls to prevent, detect, or correct risks. Audit, compliance, risk management, and senior executives must agree on these processes to reduce waste in oversight.

If key risks change regularly, this may be a sign the risk has been misidentified as key. What is a key risk? Key risks must be defined for each organization. A generalized description is any risk that creates a material disruption in operations, material loss, material misstatement of financial performance, fraud and/or agency mismanagement, patient care, threats to competitive relevance, a cyber breach that impacts customer and intellectual property, or business continuity.

These examples are not exhaustive and should be specific in order to design processes to detect, prevent, and correct them as early as possible. The list should be short to allow for secondary and tertiary risk identification and subsequent mitigations. Risks have a shape and key risks should represent the top of the pyramid (or tail of the distribution) as low-probability, high-impact risks with the base of the pyramid filled with risks consistent with high-probability, low-impact risk (mean of the distribution). A normal distribution of risks is seldom the shape of organizational risks. The convention is used for illustrative purposes only.

The purpose of risk identification is not to put them on in an inventory to reassess annually. Risks must be addressed to a level that does not require frequent reassessment. Effective risk monitoring must be designed to detect a change in key risk materiality. Real risk data is needed, not subjective assessments of key risks. Data analysis provides the levers to understand change the source of surprise in risk behavior. Some key risks may be hard to quantify or have been determined to be subjective in nature. A metric is important for monitoring value-based key risks.

Measures such as patient care or customer satisfaction can be quantified by developing minimum and maximum thresholds that should not be breached. The importance of assigning values is not to rank risks. Too often, risk professionals assume the job is done when a risk inventory is complete. A risk assessment is not a project. Risk assessments should lead to a decision to mitigate, transfer (contracts), control design, share (insurance), and otherwise resolve the risk. Don't keep them in an inventory, act! A decision audit is a helpful tool for performing a cost–benefit analysis for risk mitigation.

Lastly, no matter how thorough the risk assessment process is, residual risks still exist in all organizations. You may not know what they are, but residual risks are simply the risks that have not been discovered, are ignored, or are hidden from sight. The reason you must act on key risks you know is because residual risks may be greater than you realize and not doing so adds to residual risks. Most risk programs have never developed risk assessments for hidden, residual risks buried in every organization. More on this in subsequent chapters.

The *1st layer of duplicative risk waste* is a crisis in staffing. Staffing in audit, risk, and compliance has increased five-fold or higher in oversight over the last 10–15 years. Senior executives have delegated its role in risk selection to a cadre of oversight functions creating a hidden layer of duplicative risk waste. If operational efficiency is important, resolving duplicative risk waste in oversight must become a high priority in every organization. Overlapping and redundant oversight hinders innovation and creativity and causes risk aversion. The opportunity costs of duplicative risk waste costs billions in risk capital and loss reserves in the financial services industry alone.

Line executives must be accountable for good risk practice and compliance in achieving organizational goals. A small expert team of risk advisers and control designers should provide line management with guidance to address day-to-day regulatory risks. Organizations must develop risk practice and compliance as a core muscle at the line management level. Bonuses, promotion, incentives, and rewards should be aligned with organizational objectives including risk mitigation. This will encourage smart automation of appropriate controls and cost management.

The *2nd layer of duplicative risk waste* is insufficient capital expenditure (CapEx) in control and compliance automation or conversely over-reliance on manual processes. The worse kept secret in most organizations is the lack of investment in back-office operations. This includes poorly designed automation that leaves customers frustrated with "self-help" kiosks buried behind layers of web pages that are hard to find. Or customer service bots that direct customers to a cycle of links but do not allow sufficient control of customer accounts or transactions. In the first instance, much of what audit, risk, and compliance deem a risk should be mitigated by technology. In a time of digital transformation and machine learning, much of the internal controls over financial reporting and compliance should be automated and monitored remotely by senior financial executives.

The greatest opportunity to reduce risk and enhance operational efficiency begins with a digital transformation in back-office operations, accounting, and many of the compliance controls that create bureaucracy. The cost of independent public accounting and internal audit can also be reduced significantly with digital automation. Audit sampling and review of controls can be automated in-house and followed up by tests to be arranged to provide evidence.

The *3rd layer of duplicative risk waste* is poorly designed operational workflows. Legacy processes are cobbled together operational workflows that create residual risks over time. When legacy processes are not updated to reflect the current workload or are inefficiently designed, these processes become hidden risks and make organizations less nimble. The three layers of duplicative risk waste are largely hidden from view even though they exist in plain sight. These risks are typically well known but ignored or accepted because management has decided not to focus resources on customer-facing initiatives.

Unfortunately, these risks accumulate over time and eventually lead to significant pain points. The cost of these hidden risks and legacy decisions in back-office operations add up incrementally. The true long-term costs render organizations inflexible and unresponsiveness to changes in business resiliency and competitive nimbleness. A huge opportunity cost!

COGNITION – BLIND SPOTS IN RISK DISCOVERY

Cyber risk is growing exponentially across a spectrum of businesses and government agencies in the largest transfer of wealth by theft in history. The numbers are hard to pin down because losses are not consistently reported publicly. Estimates range from $1–$2 trillion in 2020 to $6 trillion in 2021 globally.[17,18] Cybersecurity Ventures estimates that losses will total $10.5 trillion by 2025 with a 15% CAGR.[19] More alarmingly actual data confirms that cyber theft is impacting the bottom line of financial services firms. The International Monetary Fund (IMF) has estimated that "financial services firms worldwide face potential losses from cyber-attacks ranging from 9% of net income up to half of profits based on actual experience in 2018," according to a blog post authored by Christine Lagarde.[20] The problem has only gotten worse since 2018! To put this figure in perspective insurable losses from natural disaster in 2021 were $105 billion.[21] Cyber risk is a ten times greater threat to economic growth than climate change using the low-end of estimates.

The numbers are hard to imagine with no sign of abating. Cybercrime is a criminal business model that would impress Adam Smith with its economies of scale. A hierarchy of skills in digital theft has evolved on the Dark Web where stolen funds are laundered with cryptocurrency and executed with autonomous bots.[22] The World Wide Web operates on three levels: the "visible web" we all use daily to shop, share on social media, and text with browsers such as Google, Safari, Microsoft Edge, etc.; The *Dark Web* is a separate network with a special browser for anonymous web surfing; and the Deep Web, or "invisible web," is hidden behind company intranet sites, private paywalls, and other restricted sites. The Dark Web is a small part of the *deepweb* that operates on *darknets*, which are accessible only with a *Tor* browser that allows users to surf the dark and visible web anonymously.[23] Tor is a nonprofit volunteer community that maintains updates to private computer networks that allow communications without revealing personal identifying information or user location.

The Tor browser can also be used to surf regular websites like Amazon.com. The Tor tagline, "Tor is the strongest tool for privacy and freedom online. It is free and open source software maintained by the Tor Project and a community of volunteers worldwide." Law enforcement, cybercriminals, research universities, government agencies, and nation states use the Dark Web to store confidential information and, in the case of cybercrime, stolen goods.

Central Bankers have been hesitant to create digital currencies or regulate digital coins within an anti-money laundering regime. The absence of regulatory oversight has led to stratospheric wealth creation for novice investors as well as significant losses, including stolen bitcoins. Cyber-attackers have taken bitcoin mining to new levels. In a recently discovered Log4Shell vulnerability, considered the largest security breach to date, bitcoin mining code is being downloaded into vulnerable systems.[24,25]

On Friday, December 10, 2021, a critical software vulnerability known as Log4Shell was broadly publicized. This vulnerability is widespread, affecting organizations worldwide and putting numerous systems at risk. Log4Shell is a nickname for a vulnerability in a Java software component called Log4j. Log4j is embedded into numerous applications and is used to log activity such as visitors to a website. The vulnerability can be remotely exploited by adversaries to gain unauthorized access to systems. Cyber vulnerability is an example of how hidden risks create blind spots in human behavior using technology. *Cognitive risks* are inherent blind spots in risk discovery. Herbert Simon described these risks as "bounded rationality." Examples of cognitive risk have been discussed earlier; however, these blind spots are sought-after targets by attackers. Before we get into the details of Log4j, and the role human behavior contributed to the vulnerability, let's examine a few basics in cognitive risk.

Human cognition, as a cyber vulnerability, is being exploited with great success. Humans are naturally resilient and possess incredible adaptive abilities, but these same strengths can become a weakness when we fail to recognize limits in our own cognitive load. Cognitive load refers to a tax (*effort*) on the amount of working memory each of us have available for focus.[26] *There are three types of cognitive load: intrinsic cognitive load* is the effort associated with a specific topic; *extraneous cognitive load* refers to the way information or tasks are presented to a learner; *and germane cognitive load* refers to the work put into creating a permanent store of knowledge (a schema), a pattern of thought or behavior that organizes categories of information and the relationships among them. Increased cognitive load reduces situational awareness to risks, and especially cyber risks.

Cognitive load was developed out of studies on problem-solving and then expanded to include a measure of perceived mental effort. Studies have shown that working memory is extremely limited in both capacity and duration. One person's cognitive load is different from others, but, in general, poor organizational work design, overly complex processes, inadequate tools, and other environmental factors can affect workplace productivity more than realized. Organizations have adjusted the workplace for the *ergonomics* of work but missed opportunities to reduce cognitive load in poorly designed workflows. A layperson's interpretation is *disorganization breeds poor performance*. Organizations often blame employees when the issue is deeper but ignored or unidentified because it has become part of the corporate culture.

Employers often equate busyness to productivity.[27] Busyness creates an illusion of productivity, but if an organization is busy doing the wrong things, the work becomes unproductive. Excessive meetings, emails, status reports, projects, and more. What is really moving the needle to achieve organizational goals and objectives? Productivity is the efficient use of time to think about what is working and what needs to change as well as understanding how to enhance customer value, improve operational efficiency, and nurture employee growth. If your organization does not measure productivity, the absence of a metric could be a sign that busyness is valued over productivity, whether it is explicit or implied.

Why is this important? Computer scientists and professional hackers (the good men/women who hack) have found that sophisticated cyber-attackers monitor the tempo of organizational busyness, corporate chatter, and leverage distractions that busy people experience. Cyber bots use algorithms to monitor organizational behavior.[28] The most devastating attacks are hard to detect because they are simple and not recognized as an attack until it is too late. It is only after forensic analysis is conducted does the simplicity of the attack become clear.[29] A human is typically the target, or a simple human error is the cause of a security breach.

Busy people make errors. Cybersecurity professionals focus a lot on the insider threat, dubbed the "Snowden Effect."[30] The Snowden Effect, named for Edward Snowden, a contract security analyst and whistleblower, has become a new bias created by the revelation Snowden stole confidential data and exposed the US government's surveillance program on the American public. This is an availability bias. How many other Edward Snowdens have been exposed since that event?

Few security professionals question the validity of the insider threat because it has become corporate lore among the community, yet cyber threats continue to grow without the discovery of another incident like Edward Snowden's. Research data suggests that human error is one of the leading causes of data breach, including security failures. Why does a single risk event reach mythical proportions that change security behavior without sufficient evidence those actual threats exist in a particular firm? Major risks get amplified in the news grabbing more attention and mindshare than it deserves.[31] What causes this to happen? It's called "social amplification."

Some risk events, assessed as relatively minor by technical experts, can elicit strong public concerns and result in substantial impacts on society and the economy (Kasperson 2012).

> Social amplification is a conceptual framework that seeks systematically to link technical assessments of health and safety impacts with assessments of individual and social risk perceptions and risk-related behaviors. Individuals and social groups can amplify (or in some cases, attenuate) risk as they process information about events, and events can produce secondary ripple effects that may spread far beyond the initial impact and may even affect unrelated technologies or institutions. Events that are highly dreaded, poorly understood, or both have high potential for these second-order effects.

It is human nature to want to prevent a known risk. No one wants to be accused of allowing a clearly recognized risk to occur on their watch. Secondly, if a CISO (chief information security officer) is fired for missing a previously undisclosed risk, the new CISO wants to make sure that mistake never happens again. Organizations overinvest in the last error while ignoring the inherent residual risks that still exist to avoid making the same mistake. The true error is overly focused attention on the last battle and not recognizing how the war has changed. A culture of blame creates risk aversion in many organizations.

Blame is counterproductive albeit the result of a litigious society. Researchers with the National Institute of Health have evaluated culpable control and the psychology of blame.[32,33] According to Professor Brené Brown, "Blame is simply the discharging of discomfort and pain. It has an inverse relationship with accountability." Blame is a short-term remedy. Rather than diffusing a workplace conflict, it can escalate the situation, create bad feelings among colleagues, and undermine working relationships. On an organizational level, blame reduces openness and honesty, because staff members who anticipate blame are more likely to cover up mistakes. If employees see leaders blaming others instead of taking responsibility for their actions, they are more likely to follow suit, which can lead to a "blame culture." What can be learned from mistakes? Instead of blame or worse, typical human error can be a learning opportunity if handled properly. Blame should be reserved until the issue has been resolved and time allows for more circumspection. Blame simply reinforces hiding mistakes and not learning from them.

We have established that traditional risk practice is biased toward internal controls, a focus on the downside of risk. Internal controls are foundational to a risk program but do not provide strategic value to the growth of the organization. In fact, complex compliance programs create risk aversion in organizational behavior and limit one's view of hidden risks.

There are greater risks that threaten organizational performance: Digital transformation, global competition, cybersecurity, and geopolitical risks require a strategic plan that is responsive and not held back by organizational bureaucracy. Targeted automation of prioritized compliance mandates must be balanced with a focus on the science of risk.

Now that we have set the table, let's unpack risk and risk perceptions further. In general, the concepts of risk and risk perceptions are experienced along two parallel tracks (Slovic and Weber 2002): cognition (risk as feelings) and probabilities (risk as analysis). Ideally, the two tracks should work in tandem, one informing the other, when assessing risks. Probabilistic analysis provides rigor in assessing the odds of an event or the impact of outcomes in the likelihood of occurrence; however, cognition is central to making the final decision.

Cognition is a prism for weighing values that are important in balancing risk. Decision-makers using well-grounded analysis must allow for value-based considerations. Factors such as fairness, stakeholders, political considerations, and operating norms are as important as the data and are key to developing persuasive arguments to get others on board. As Slovic argues (1987) "risk mean[s] different things to lay people than it does to scientists." Both perspectives have weight which must be balanced and consistent to ensure trust in judgment.

Far too often the weights are skewed in one direction resulting in judgments, in hindsight, that should have known better. Shapiro (1994) found that executives do not consider the probability parameter as an important dimension of risk and do not tend to calculate the riskiness of choice alternatives in terms of the expected value rule.[34] We also find in social situations people often seem to follow others based on moral and ethical consideration without a careful evaluation of outcomes and probabilities (Tyszka and Zaleskiewicz 2007[35]).

The findings are less a matter of surprise and rather a confirmation of what we already know. If you have ever overheard executives dismiss further analysis as "analysis paralysis," that is the idea, but is it a sound practice? Analysis paralysis is not a problem, per se. Given the inherent challenges in the language and communications of risk, a discipline must be formed to address different perceptions of risk.

This challenge is what Kahneman (*Noise* p. 30) describes as the *illusion of agreement*. The illusion of agreement occurs when a team of executives conducts planning sessions for strategic goals then go their separate ways and make decisions that differ from agreed-upon plans. If you have ever participated in a planning session where everyone is asked to place a color-coded sticky tab under a column of options, you have experienced the illusion of agreement. A color-coded sticky tab is a "risk as feelings" analysis. The process does not allow or encourage alternative discussions when sticky pads decide the outcome.

The "elephant in the room" is the silent discomfort people feel when discussing risks that they do not know how to resolve or to discuss openly. There is often more disagreement (or unresolved confusion) than one may realize when actions run counter to plans. Silence seldom reveals these issues until plans fail or the outcome is less than expected. The *illusion of agreement* is simply another example of cognitive risks that impact performance. Creating a process to raise and address alternative courses of action should help to resolve disagreement.

In other words, decision-makers and their behaviors may run counter to a team's implied agreement on a course of action.[36] The abstract nature of risks is hard to conceptualize even with the advent of visualization tools such as charts and graphs. The lesson here is that most executives make risk decisions based on how they feel without applying appropriate weight to the analysis of a risk. Like any developed skill, practice improves outcomes. A diverse workplace is an environment of psychosocial dynamics where personalities, incentives, and organizational hierarchy are contributing factors to risk perceptions.[37] A diversity of ideas and personal experience should be allowed to flourish to fine-tune decision-making with the values of the firm.

Collectively, these human factors are considerations in developing a robust understanding of enterprise risks. The complexity of human perceptions of risk requires more than a prescriptive, one-size-fits-all risk framework. A cognitive risk framework infuses the human element into enterprise risk by customizing elements from behavioral economics and traditional risk management.[38] CogRisk anticipates the emerging hybrid work environment as a continuation of the wireless work environment that evolved less than 20 years ago. The complexity of risk has also evolved resulting in new challenges in risk perception. Digital risks, cybersecurity, and social media obscure risks in ways that traditional risk practice does not contemplate. This is precisely why the "E" in ERM is no longer applicable.

A recent trend in cybersecurity has involved the quantification of cyber risk. Several firms have become prominent players touting insurance actuarial backgrounds or statistical analysis. "Quantification of cyber risk" is such a generic term that it includes disparate approaches including subjective probabilities and subjectively defined metrics with each lacking real rigor.[39] After conducting a cursory survey of firms, I found a diverse assortment of methodologies. Early entrants in this space provided cyber quantification to assist in cyber insurance risk transfer. These approaches have found their natural limits after insurance firms rushed into the cyber space only to experience huge losses. None of the insurance providers considered their lack of cyber data and suffered from a lack of discipline in underwriting a complex risk that exposed capital to significant losses. As the insurance market peaked in cyber risk and adjusted their exposure limits, cyber risk quant firms have pivoted to advisory services.

The key attributes for cyber quantification have become more generic as well. Examples of key attributes for one firm include: a) cybersecurity resilience, b) frequency, and c) severity. These are classic actuarial "risk triangles" that lack any predicative credibility. These metrics assume that generic or subjectively defined data reflects risk. It may reflect one's perception of risk but is not predictive of actual results. Terms such as "occurrence exceedance probability" (OEP) and "aggregate exceedance probability" (AEP) imply a sense of accuracy but lack insight into the asymmetric nature of a breach, cost of a breach, and cyber threat behavior. No one seems to ask the right questions. What should be modeled, and do we have the data to model those behaviors? Recent attempts to address these questions are presented below.

According to Dan Verton, director of content marketing at ThreatConnect, "Seventy percent of security professionals who took part in a recent ThreatConnect survey said they are receiving medium to high levels of pressure to produce cyber risk quantification data for their business.".

> The growing pace and sophistication of nation state attacks, coupled with an ever-expanding attack surface stemming from continued digital modernization, has focused the attention of business leaders on their ability to accurately quantify and prioritize cyber risks within the context of their individual business.[40]

However, half of those surveyed said they lack confidence in their ability to communicate and report the financial impact of cyber risks, prioritize vulnerabilities and security alerts, and justify their future investments to mitigate those risks. The reason for this is two-fold: 41% of respondents said they do not have a formalized process in place to evaluate and rank cyber risks, and 25% said they do not have a cyber risk quantification technology deployed at their company. Unfortunately, the efforts at many firms will fail, not from a robust effort but instead from the realities of uncoordinated and disparate approaches to quantification. One study demonstrates the problem.

This white paper presents analysis from an Advisen Cyber Loss dataset containing a historical view of cyber events, collected from reliable and publicly verifiable sources. The dataset analyzed in this study comprehends 132,126 cyber events during 2008–2020, affecting 49,496 organizations, with more than 80% of the organizations represented in the dataset residing in the USA. A summary of the findings is provided as follows: (Advisen is a cyber data loss analytics firm.)

> Currently, data collection and databases on losses from cyber events have an unbalanced recording of samples with the strongest emphasis on developing the US centric data collection. However, cyber risk is international in nature affecting both commercial and private industry as well as government agencies across all sectors of the economy. Therefore, we advocate that a concerted effort be made to develop an

adequate measurement and modelling process for cyber-related risks in the domestic landscape, there is a strong need and utility to be gained by collecting such data specifically for Australia.

There are many cyber risk classifications, each designed with specific intent, purpose, and which build on pre-existing laws and policies. Enterprises and market participants should adopt the cyber risk classification that best fits their needs; standardisation within sectors makes sense but standardisation across different sectors may be ineffective.

Over 60% of companies that recorded cyber-related losses have suffered from cyber-attacks more than once in the period 2008-2020. This suggests that governance processes relating to mitigation of such events can significantly be enhanced and that regulation and reporting around best practices as it emerges could help mitigate repeated events of the same nature from reoccurring.

Losses from cyber related events are heavy-tailed. This means that while the majority of losses is typically relatively small (85% of events cause losses <$2 million), there is a chance for extreme losses, e.g., 5% of losses exceed $10 million, while 1.4% of cyber-related losses even exceed $100 million, and 0.17% of events cause losses >$1 billion.

There is no distinct pattern or clear-cut relationship between the frequency of events, the loss severity, and the number of affected records. Contrary to assumptions often made in practice, the reported loss databases don't demonstrate a direct proportional relationship between total loss incurred from a cyber event and attributes from the event such as the number of compromised records (data records breached or stolen), the number of employees in a corporation or the number of units of a company affected. This finding shows that all companies, no matter the volume or size of data record can be susceptible to significant incurred loss from cyber events.

The frequency and severity of the events depend on the business sector and type of cyber threat.

It is clear that even with the increased scrutiny and increased regulatory guidance the rate of cyber-crime has not abated. In fact, the frequency of reported cyber-related events has substantially increased between 2008 and 2016 (4,800 reported events in 2008, 16,800 reported events in 2016). Furthermore, the reporting of such events for modelling purposes could be enhanced as there appears to be a significant delay in the reporting of events that needs to be considered when drawing conclusions on the risks.

The most significant cyber loss event category, by number of events, continues to be Privacy - Unauthorized Contact or Disclosure and Data – Malicious Breach. Data related breaches have become increasingly more common since 2008, while Cyber Extorsion, Phishing, Spoofing and other Social Engineering practices also continue to increase, the pace at which malicious breach related events has occurred has now surpassed these other prominent categories of loss event risk type in recent years.

The heavy tailed nature of cyber loss continues to be present. This is directly observed by the fact that cyber loss are well represented by the expression "one loss causes ruin" adage attributed to heavy tailed loss processes that demonstrate regular variation or power lower severity tail behaviour. As such, in all categories of cyber loss type and in all sectors of the economy it was found that loss severity is often dominated by large individual events. Overall, data breaches have caused the most serious financial consequences in the last four years, while the Information sector, Professional Scientific & Technical Services, and Finance & Insurance have suffered most of the financial damage during the sample period 2008–2020.[41]

A whole of industry, government, and regulatory approach is needed to solve both the data challenges which are significant but also to form agreements on a consistent process and methods for quantifying cyber risks. The results from this authoritative study make it plain that it would be unrealistic to invest confidence in an off-the-shelf cyber quantification platform. Anyone can *quantify* cyber risk; however, the predictive value of risk exposure from existing data is no better than an educated guess. The primary use of these tools is to give senior executives a reference point of risk exposure with the expected caveats of error that exist. The risk management process begins with a discussion of what is an acceptable level of risk planning for different scenarios of security breach and what capital reserves to mitigate the problem.

Some firms have developed models based on critical asset compromise and/or the cost of rehabilitation, but these are business continuity exercises, not cyber risk quantification. Ideally, the time and treasure spent on cyber risk quantification is better spent on periodic *forensic health checks* to ensure hidden risks are exposed early. In these situations, other factors may require a reframing of cyber risk to decision-makers who may be influenced by external causal factors such as a recent cyber-attack on a competitor, news reports of increased ransomware, or perceived changes in future economic conditions resulting from a cyber breach.

Factors such as *trust* are harder to prove over the Internet. Physical and social queues in face-to-face contact allow trust and personal relationships to develop over time, but in the digital sphere, people can impersonate a persona to take advantage of trust. Cybersecurity professionals have begun to adopt a popular new risk posture called "zero trust" in response to the lack of trust that now exists at the human–machine intersection.[42]

Zero trust (ZT) is an evolving set of cybersecurity stratagems that move defenses from static, network-based perimeters to focus on users, assets, and resources. A zero trust architecture (ZTA) uses zero trust principles to plan industrial and enterprise infrastructure and workflows. Zero trust assumes there is no implicit trust granted to assets or user accounts based solely on their physical or network location (i.e., local area networks versus the internet) or based on asset ownership (enterprise or personally owned).

An evolution in thought is also evolving along psycho-technical lines in order to address the blurring of the physical and digital sphere (NIST SP) – 800–207).

Zero *Implicit* Trust Architecture (ZTA) is a way of planning a network and workflow design to ensure that authentication, communications, devices, enterprise resources are strictly enforced before allowing access. Zero Trust is conceptual and will require designers of ZTA to determine a level of assurance. However, ZTA is the first approach that hints at elements of behavioral science. Several versions of ZTA are being developed by different solution providers to capture market share in this new trend in cybersecurity.

New approaches to risk management and cybersecurity are needed in response to sophisticated attackers' ability to exploit unintentional legacy vulnerabilities in technology. The latest massive attack is the Log4Shell vulnerability. Log4j is software that records activities in computer systems, such as errors and routine system operations as well as communications between systems and system administrators and other users.[43]

According to Santiago Torres-Arias, Assistant Professor of Electrical and Computer Engineering, Purdue University,

> This kind of code can be used for more than just formatting log messages. Log4j allows third-party servers to submit software code that can perform all kinds of actions on the targeted computer. This opens the door for nefarious activities such as stealing sensitive information, taking control of the targeted system, and slipping malicious content to other users communicating with the affected server.

Glen Pendley, Deputy Chief Technology Officer at Tenable, said

> Everything across heavy industrial equipment, network servers, down to printers, and even your kid's Raspberry Pi is potentially affected by this flaw. Some affected systems may be on-premises while others may be hosted in the cloud, but no matter where they are, the flaw is likely to have an impact.[44]

Log4j is an example of open source software that is used widely in many systems as computer software that is released under a license in which the copyright holder grants users the rights to use, study, change, and distribute the software and its source code to anyone and for any purpose.[45] Open-source software is a prominent example of open collaboration, meaning any capable user is able to participate online in development, making the number of possible contributors indefinite.

The Internet was designed as an open, collaborative project where anyone can contribute and share code, content, and communications freely.

Unfortunately, the protocols and processes for ensuring security and high-quality code is not always stringently enforced.

> While much of this software is written by employees of tech companies whose products rely on open-source code, the developer community is decentralized, often poorly resourced and typically more focused on adding new features than securing existing ones. But amid the urgent push to patch vulnerable devices, open-source security specialists say recent advances will make future catastrophes less likely especially if this work gets a boost from the federal government.[46]

Human error is often at the root of breaches and vulnerabilities in cyberspace as will be demonstrated with two examples in data breach reports. The risk of human error is often underestimated when innovation is valued above security and access to low or zero cost talent is welcomed. We may never know whether this was a deliberate act or just a case of simple human error, but either way Log4j is one of a number of major vulnerabilities that threaten the experiment we call the *Internet*.

The details of error(s) tend to get buried in silence. But news of the vulnerability has spread rapidly. It hasn't taken attackers long to launch millions of attacks since the discovery of the Log4j vulnerability. Log4j has not yet been fully mitigated as of the writing of this chapter, but patches are being applied. The scope of vulnerability in Log4j is massive and may take years to fully address. This is the nature of human factor risks. The vulnerabilities are simple, yet the threats are large, highlighting the asymmetry of cyber risks. Log4j is yet another example of how risks at the human–machine intersection are hidden until major failure occurs. Risk assessments that only focus on known risks will seldom discover vulnerabilities like Log4j. A more comprehensive approach to risk assessment is needed to account for human factors and the inherent uncertainty in behavior.

Risk is a social and analytical experience with influence factors that are not always obvious to decision-makers. Risks in cyberspace are even harder to recognize in cyber risk. An example of a hard to recognize cyber risk, dubbed cognitive hacks, illustrate how skilled attackers target cognition to change behavior in order to get around security controls. Cyber-attackers have become adroit observers of human behavior, by conducting reconnaissance prior to an attack to avoid detection. It would stand to reason that cybersecurity professionals should also incorporate human factor risk analysis into their existing practice, but it has been a challenge getting risk professionals to pay attention.

Risk professionals need a more nuanced understanding of inherent risks as well as an awareness of residual risks. Risks are not one-dimensional. Three-dimensional risks require that cyber-risk methodologies assume threats exist internally and externally in all devices, systems, and networks as well as with the people, partners, and vendors who use and are responsible for security. That approach requires a *zero trust for humans* as well as technology.

No one-size-fits-all approach is optimal, even ZTA. Cyber risk management involves a multilateral risk assessment of networked environments inclusive of all human activity, including attackers. Assuming otherwise is the same mistake taken in subjectively defined risk frameworks. Instead of looking for a *silver bullet* solution, the evidence of attacker success rates is confirmation a silver bullet does not exist.[47] This is like asking for one risk metric to provide assurance for all organizational risks are being addressed.

This is an honest human desire, but a naïve one. Humans desire simple solutions in a complex world, nonetheless simplicity is a complex design problem that takes time to develop. Risks are not finite, nor static, and a large majority of risks are yet to be discovered. The Covid pandemic is an example of how impatience leads to uncertainty instead of a return to normality. Uncertainty still exists whether a person can look around corners or not. Once uncertainty is accepted, only then can the methods of solving it begin in earnest.[48] Unlike risk, uncertainty can't be seen until it is experienced or is acknowledged as a risk. This fallacy in cognition is called an uncertainty bias.

Uncertainty bias is a real phenomenon. Ever wonder why some investors in financial markets complain about uncertainty when one political party is in office yet when a different political party takes over uncertainty miraculously disappears? That is one form of uncertainty bias, there are others. Uncertainty bias is situational. Uncertainty avoidance is how cultures differ on the amount of tolerance they have for unpredictability.[49]

Uncertainty avoidance is one of five key qualities or *dimensions* measured by the researchers who developed the Hofstede model of cultural dimensions to quantify cultural differences across international lines to better understand why some ideas and business practices work better in some countries than in others.[50] According to Geert Hofstede, "The fundamental issue here is how a society deals with the fact that the future can never be known: Should we try to control it or just let it happen?" Uncertainty acceptance is a societal choice. Some countries have experienced push back in the Covid pandemic resulting in excessive death rates while other countries have lived safely through the virus.

The concept of risk is multidimensional and requires an arsenal of tools to fully address the social and analytical aspects of risk management more effectively. Cybersecurity is an excellent example for demonstrating why purely subjective approaches in risk management fail. Two reports of cyber breach data are presented by different technology service providers to find patterns in cyber threat behavior. The goal is to understand how to recognize cognitive risk patterns in the data in order to reframe how hidden risks continue to leave organizations vulnerable to attack.

A summary of sample data sets is presented by different technology service providers. The findings are interesting in both the frequency and magnitude of breach behavior across different industry types. Verizon's 2021 annual Data Breach Investigations Report (DBIR) is exhaustive in scope. 79,635 incidents were analyzed of which 5,258 were confirmed data breaches sampled across 88 countries around the world.

A breakout of 11 industries is included along with specific categories of breach data. A summary of the findings is presented in a battery of graphic forms in Verizon's report; however, brief textual summaries are presented here (Figure 2.1).

(%s are approximations)

Patterns in breach: (5,275 breaches out of 29,206 incidents)

(1) *Social Engineering** (33%), (2) Web application Attacks (22%), (3) System Intrusion (18%), (4) *Miscellaneous Errors** (16%)

*Eighty-nine percent of breaches make up the top four categories. However, 49% of the four breach categories are the result of the manipulation of human behavior or human error. If you add small percentage

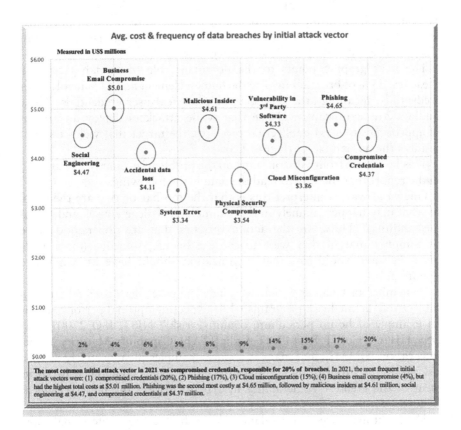

Figure 2.1   Top four attack vectors highlighted.

patterns in breach; *Privilege misuse** (5%), *Lost and Stolen Assets** (2.5%), *Everything else** (1%). Human behavior is the dominate cause of breaches. For clarification, social engineering is the psychological manipulation of people into performing actions or divulging confidential information.[51]

Social engineering is the act of *reconnaissance* before an attack is launched to assess the strengths and weakness of the organization's people, training, processes, and gullibility to attack. I have seen expert social engineers on stage in soundproof booths conduct live demonstrations to prove how effective these attacks are real time. A similar pattern is present in the data on incidents that lead to a breach (Figure 2.2).

(%s are approximations)

Patterns in incidents (29,206 incidents)

(1) Denial of service (48%), (2) Web application attacks (16%), (3) Social Engineering (12%), (4) System Intrusion (11%)

*Eighty-seven percent of incidents make up the top four categories. Approximately, 22% of human error is represented in the top four categories but results in a higher incidence of breach. Categories included are: Social engineering (12%), Lost and stolen assets (5%), Miscellaneous error (3%), Privilege misuse (1.0%), and Everything else (0.7%).

The next graphic points to the dominant role of human factors in breaches. 85% of breaches involve the human element and 61% involve user credentials, meaning attackers were able to steal user credentials. These findings are significant evidence that while attackers deploy an arsenal of approaches to steal intellectual property, the target that yields the best result is the human factor (Figure 2.3).

This last chart from Verizon sums up the problem succinctly. We are told in the report that the way to read the data is the following:

One valid way to interpret this is that the top bar or two are the norm of what may happen, namely in this example "Privilege abuse" and "Data mishandling." Those are the action varieties that are understood to be so common that, if they were to cause a breach, someone (most likely on a website) would say, that organization should have known better (Figure 2.4).

Remember in Chapter 1 that we made the case that "over reliance on subjectively-defined risk programs while expecting optimal performance is an example of homo periculum, cognitive risk." NIST, ISO 27001, PCI DSS, HIPAA, CoBiT, Risk IT, IT Audit (ITAF), Capability Maturity Model Integration (CMMI), and many more are examples of subjectively defined risk programs. None of these frameworks articulate a comprehensive treatment of the greatest vulnerability in cybersecurity – the human element (Figure 2.5).

The point made clear in the data is that cybersecurity professionals, like risk professionals suffer from the same inattentional blindness. Inattentional

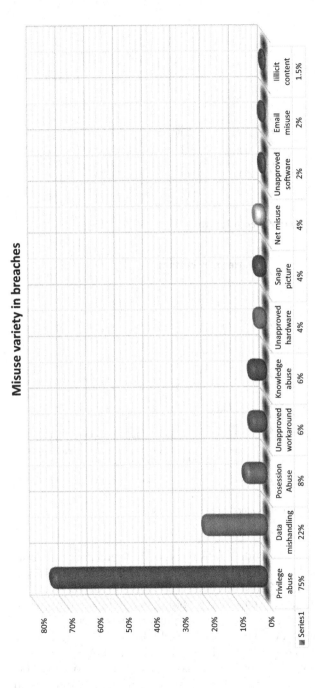

Figure 2.2   Verizon 2021 Report of Human Error.

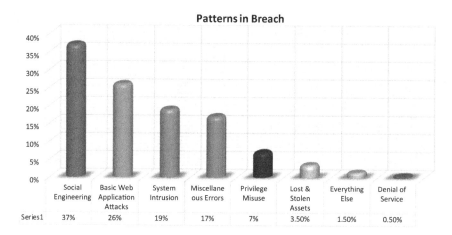

Figure 2.3   Verizon 2021 Report of Breach Patterns.

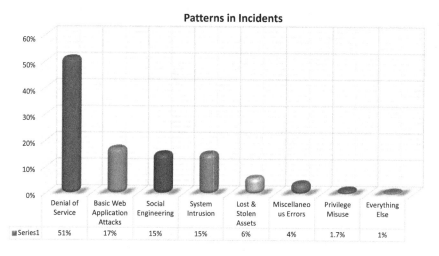

Figure 2.4   Verizon 2021 Report of Incident Patterns.

blindness occurs when an individual fails to perceive an unexpected stimulus in plain sight, purely as a result of a lack of attention rather than any vision defects or deficits. When it becomes impossible to attend to all the stimuli in a given situation, a temporary "blindness" effect can occur, as individuals fail to see unexpected but often salient objects or stimuli.

Would a different report on data breaches yield different findings? A reasonable question you may ask yourself. No two companies present their research data in the same way or use the same semantic descriptions, but the 2021 IBM Cost of a Data Breach Report findings are remarkably similar

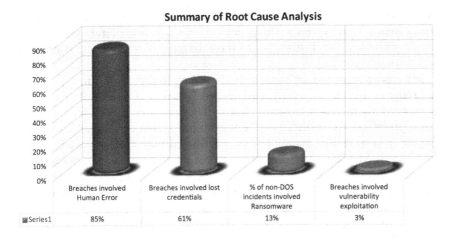

Figure 2.5   Verizon 2021 Report of root cause analysis.

in the categories.[52] It is important to note that IBM is comparing different data than Verizon due to a different customer profile, but the comparative similarities are present.

The IBM graphic displays frequency of incidents relative to cost of attack. The footnote provides additional insight in the role of human factors. 20% of breaches were the result of compromised credentials, similar findings were present in the Verizon report. Phishing represented 17% of breaches, Cloud misconfiguration added another 15%, and compromised business email accounted for 4% of breaches but incurred the greatest costs. The Verizon DBIR report and the IBM Cost of Breach report take different cuts at the data but come to similar conclusions.

The costs of breach and cause resonate with findings in the Verizon report. Human error and cognitive compromise (*business email compromise, social engineering, accidental loss, malicious insider, phishing*) were the leading causes of breach and led to higher cost of breach. A comprehensive analysis and comparison of data breach studies is needed to confirm these observations, but notwithstanding the small samples, there is evidence that attackers are targeting humans and human behavior in contravention of cyber security defenses. Human error (intentional or not) is a significant contributor to data breaches.

More recently the US Government Accountability Office (GAO) published a comprehensive but still incomplete report on the SolarWinds security breach, one of the most extensive attacks by a nation state on government agencies and specifically defense contractors.[53]

Beginning as early as January 2021, a threat actor breached the computing networks at SolarWinds – a Texas-based network management software company. The federal government later confirmed the threat actor to be Russian Foreign Intelligence Service. Since the company's software,

SolarWinds Orion, was widely used in the federal government to monitor network activity and manage network devices on federal systems, this incident allowed the threat actor to several agencies' networks that used the software (Figure 2.6).

Microsoft reported in March 2019 an exploitation or misuse of vulnerabilities used to gain access to several versions of Microsoft Exchange Servers. This included versions that federal agencies hosted and used on their premises. According to a White House statement, based on a high degree of confidence, malicious cyber affiliated with the People's Republic of China's Ministry of State Security conducted operations using these Microsoft Exchange vulnerabilities. In plain language, one or more persons' access credentials to the MS Exchange servers were stolen and used to gain authenticated connections from unauthorized external sources. This implies that human error or some version of a cognitive hack was determined to be the cause of breach (Figure 2.7).

A statement from the GAO provides more clues to the role human error played in the breach.

> The risks to information technology systems supporting the federal government and the nation's critical infrastructure are increasing, including escalating and emerging threats from around the globe, the emergence of new and more destructive attacks, and insider threats from witting and unwitting employees. A second incident involving a "zero-day" vulnerability in the Microsoft Exchange Server had the potential to affect email servers across the federal government and provide malicious threat actors with unauthorized remote access.

Zero-day is a vulnerability in a system or device that may be known or unknown but is not yet patched. An exploit that attacks a zero-day vulnerability is called a zero-day exploit. The SolarWinds attack is "one the most widespread and sophisticated hacking campaigns ever conducted against the federal government and private sector."

More research and attention to human factors is needed as more data point to opportunities in risk, security, and operational workflow design as well as cognitive load factors in cybersecurity and risk management – the human element. Existing cybersecurity and risk management frameworks do not anticipate human factor risks. With that said, the threat of cognitive risks has been evident to researchers for almost 20 years.[54] Researchers at Dartmouth College's Institute for Security Technology Studies, Thayer School of Engineering coined the term cognitive hacking in 2003 in a paper entitled, "Cognitive Hacking." George Cybenko, Annarita Giani, and Paul Thompson published their research before public knowledge of "phishing" or "disinformation" and "misinformation" cyber campaigns now prevalent today.

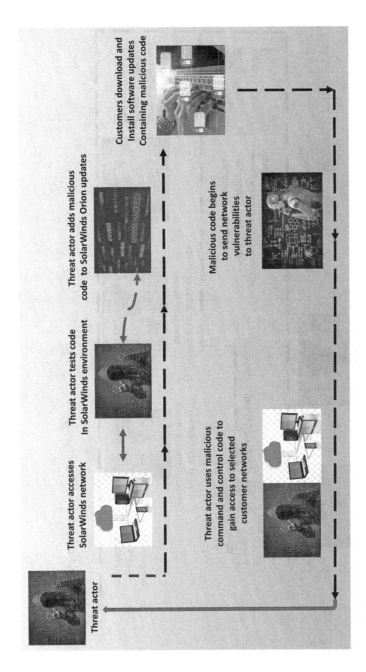

Figure 2.6   SolarWinds threat actor analysis.

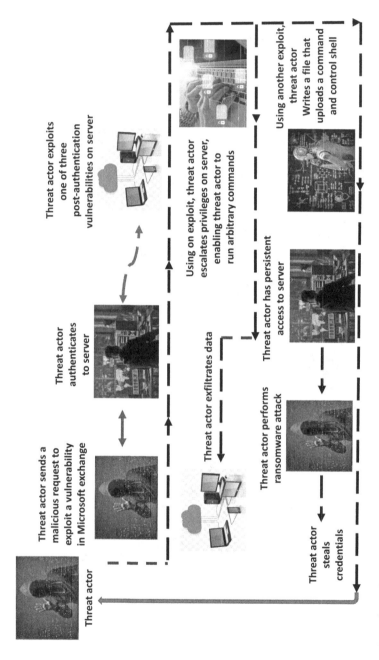

Figure 2.7   SolarWinds analysis of Microsoft Exchange exploit.

A fresh look at cognitive hacking reveals what many in cybersecurity ignored as prescient warnings 20 years ago and play a large role in data breaches and significant loss in intellectual property. *Cognitive hacking refers to a computer or information system attack that relies on changing human users' perceptions and corresponding behaviors in order to be successful* (Cybenko, Giani, and Thompson 2004). Cognitive hacking does not rely on corrupting hardware or software like denial-of-service attacks. Counterintuitively, technology is used to influence perceptions and behavior through misinformation.[55,56]

The risk of cognitive hacking rose in the public eye after it was revealed that Facebook data from Facebook's Open Graph platform was collected by data scientist Aleksandr Kogan and used by Cambridge Analytica to assist the presidential campaigns of Ted Cruz and Donald Trump.[57,58] The story of how Facebook user data was used without user permission in a disinformation campaign by Cambridge Analytica is still unclear. However, a story in Vox, an online magazine, provides some insight (Vox, *Here's how Facebook allowed Cambridge Analytica to get data for 50 million users,* 2018, March 17, 2018).

> Facebook offers a number of technology tools for software developers, and one of the most popular is Facebook Login, which lets people simply log in to a website or app using their Facebook account instead of creating new credentials. People use it because it's easy – usually one or two taps – and eliminates the need for people to remember a bunch of unique username and password combinations. When people use Facebook Login, though, they grant the app's developer a range of information from their Facebook profile – things like their name, location, email, or friends list. This is what happened in 2014, when a Cambridge University professor named Dr. Aleksandr Kogan created an app called "thisisyourdigitallife" that utilized Facebook's login feature. Some 270,000 people used Facebook Login to create accounts and thus opted in to share personal profile data with Kogan.

Back in 2014, though, Facebook also allowed developers to collect some information on the friend networks of people who used Facebook Login. That means that while a single user may have agreed to hand over their data, developers could also access some data about their friends. This was not a secret – Facebook says it was documented in their terms of service – but it has since been updated so that this is no longer possible, at least not at the same level of detail.

Through those 270,000 people who opted in, Kogan was able to get access to data from some 50 million Facebook users, according to the Times. That data trove could have included information about people's locations and interests, and more granular stuff like photos, status updates and check-ins.

Allegedly, Cambridge Analytica received data from Kogan and used it to place targeted misinformation and disinformation ads and content on Facebook and other social media sites to influence the perception and behaviors of millions of US voters. Facebook has since created a misinformation program to monitor suspect content; however, a recent whistleblower has disclosed that Facebook's algorithms help make negative news story viral and is allegedly still a source of broad misinformation on its website.[59,60]

The Dartmouth researchers were focused on detecting when a cognitive hack occurred and determining what legal course of action is possible to prevent these attacks. A *cognitive* attack is much harder to detect because it is only successful if the attack causes change in the user's behavior in the manipulation of the user's perception of reality. The Facebook episode has demonstrated how difficult this is to prove as well as the gaps that exist in legal, security, and regulatory tools to deal with such attacks.

Cognitive hacking campaigns are easily deniable, and attribution is near impossible through the use of proxies and autonomous bots who are able to write campaigns using algorithms.[61] People simply don't believe they have been manipulated nor is there any forensic evidence to confirm the manipulation. There are skeptics, but one need to look no further than the propaganda campaigns put on by the ISIS terrorist group and current conspiracy theories now in full circulation in podcasts, radio shows, and national news networks. The success of the ISIS terrorist group's propaganda campaigns surprised many with slick promotional content on social media that radicalized thousands of normal citizens to join the group from countries around the world.[62,63]

Perception management is not new. Cold war propaganda campaigns have simply been refurbished in video and social media content to give the appearance of truth. Marketing has used perception management for decades to sell everything from soap to cars, but this is a different campaign to deceive for profit, to damage democratic principles, and diminish faith in institutions. Cognitive hacking is part of a deliberate information war carried on by domestic and foreign adversaries.

A definition of semantic attacks closely related to our discussion of cognitive hacking has been described by Schneier,[64] who attributes the earliest conceptualization of computer system attacks as physical, syntactic, and semantic to Martin Libicki, who describes semantic attacks in terms of misinformation being inserted into interactions among intelligent agents on the Internet.[65]

Schneier, by contrast, characterizes semantic attacks as "... attacks that target the way we, as humans, assign meaning to content." He (Schneier 2000)[66] goes on to note, "Semantic attacks directly target the human/computer interface, the most insecure interface on the Internet." Denning's discussion of information warfare overlaps our concept of cognitive hacking.[67] Denning describes information warfare as a struggle over an information resource by an offensive and a defensive player. The resource has an exchange and an operational value. The value of the resource to each player can differ depending on factors related to each player's circumstances. The outcomes of offensive information warfare are: increased availability of the resource to the offense, decreased availability to the defense, and decreased integrity of the resource.

Cognitive hacking defies the norms of trust on the Internet and challenges the legal community to rethink the application of the law (Cybenko, Giani, and Thomson 2002)[68].

> Criminal prosecution and civil lawsuits may help combat cognitive hacking, but this will be possible only in compliance with free speech protection. Laws already exist that can fight disinformation without violating fundamental rights. But cognitive hacking introduces new characteristics requiring revised legal doctrines. Ultimately, confronting cognitive hacking will require integrating legal and technological anti-hacking tools.

Chapter 3 will explore why we need to rethink risk governance and the predominate model of hierarchical governance. A matrix of governance models will be introduced as we examine how science, and a better understanding of human behavior and judgment, is needed in order to mitigate failure and enhance performance. Scaling the human element is a new concept that involves a reframing of human resource management.

The current generation of talent entering the workforce today is more diverse, educated, and skilled than any generation before it. This new cohort is more technologically skilled than its predecessors which is a doubled-edged sword. Technology has opened the flood gates of access to technology that allows today's young adults to create small company stores, become social medial "influencers," and subsidize or replace traditional 9 to 5 jobs with digital platforms where they are the boss. A governance model based on digital platforms will be introduced along with Board 3.0, an emergent model of governance aligned with a new class of corporate owners – private equity investors.

Risks look very different to today's workforce who started their careers in the throes of a global pandemic and have easily pivoted to technology platforms they are well suited to navigate. By the same token, this generation has not learned nor made the mistakes of the Baby Boomers.

NOTES

1. https://www.psychologytoday.com/files/attachments/92349/genderdifferenc esintheperceivedrisk.pdf.

2. Nick Allum (2005), Perceptions of risk in cyberspace, *Trust and Crime in Information Societies*, n. pag. Print.
3. https://www.researchgate.net/publication/255660637_Consumer_Perceptions_of_Online_Shopping.
4. https://www.verizon.com/business/resources/reports/dbir/2021/masters-guide/summary-of-findings/.
5. N. Allum (2005), "Perceptions of Risk In Cyberspace." Trust and Crime in Information Societies, ...
6. https://www.ncbi.nlm.nih.gov/pmc/articles/PMC4679162/.
7. E. Loftus (1993), The reality of repressed memories, *American Psychologist*, 48, 518-537
8. E.F. Loftus (2005), Planting misinformation in the human mind: A 30-year investigation of the malleability of memory.
9. https://en.wikipedia.org/wiki/Availability_heuristic.
10. S. L. Clifasefi, M. Garry and E. Loftus (2007), Setting the record (or video camera) straight on memory: The video camera model of memory and other memory myths, in: Dell Sala S, ed., *Tall Tales about the Mind and Brain: Separating Fact from Fiction*, Oxford (GB): Oxford University Press, 60–75.
11. M. L. Howe and L. M. Knott (2015), The fallibility of memory in judicial processes: Lessons from the past and their modern consequences, *Memory*, 23(5), 1–24.
12. https://us.aicpa.org/content/dam/aicpa/research/standards/auditattest/downloadabledocuments/au-00350.pdf.
13. https://pcaobus.org/News/Events/Documents/10052005_SAGMeeting/Reasonable_Assurance.pdf.
14. https://www.statista.com/statistics-glossary/definition/328/confidence_level/.
15. https://www.synopsys.com/blogs/software-security/the-risk-of-too-much-risk-management/.
16. https://www.researchgate.net/publication/344887952_2020_Study_of_Advancements_in_Enterprise_Risk_and_Governance_pdfGCA.
17. https://ir.mcafee.com/node/6771/pdf.
18. https://cybersecurityventures.com/hackerpocalypse-cybercrime-report-2016/.
19. https://financesonline.com/cybercrime-statistics/.
20. https://blogs.imf.org/2018/06/22/estimating-cyber-risk-for-the-financial-sector/.
21. https://www.theactuary.com/news/2021/12/14/insured-losses-natural-disasters-hit-105bn.
22. https://en.wikipedia.org/wiki/Dark_web.
23. https://www.torproject.org/.
24. https://venturebeat.com/2021/12/12/microsoft-log4j-exploits-extend-past-crypto-mining-to-outright-theft/.
25. https://uit.stanford.edu/news/log4shell-vulnerability-what-you-need-know.
26. https://en.wikipedia.org/wiki/Cognitive_load.
27. https://carsontate.com/busyness-vs-being-productive/.
28. https://www.sentinelone.com/blog/the-most-devastating-cyber-attacks-on-banks/.
29. https://www.upguard.com/blog/biggest-data-breaches.

30. https://en.wikipedia.org/wiki/Snowden_effect.
31. https://journals.sagepub.com/doi/full/10.1177/0096340212444871.
32. https://pubmed.ncbi.nlm.nih.gov/10900996/.
33. https://www.forbes.com/sites/annashields/2020/09/09/from-blame-to-empa-thy-lessons-for-leaders-to-diffuse-conflict/?sh=577f4f92f5af.
34. https://www.researchgate.net/publication/6616847_When_Does_Information_about_Probability_Count_in_Choices_Under_Risk.
35. T. Zaleskiewicz and T. Tyszka (2012), The strength of emotions in moral judgment and decision-making under risk, *Polish Psychological Bulletin*, 43(2), 132–144.
36. https://www.psychologytoday.com/us/blog/after-service/201705/the-science-behind-why-people-follow-the-crowd.
37. https://en.wikipedia.org/wiki/Psychosocial.
38. https://www.corporatecomplianceinsights.com/cognitive-risk-framework-cybersecurity/.
39. https://www.kovrr.com/resource/what-is-cyber-risk-quantification-crq.
40. https://www.techrepublic.com/article/what-is-cyber-risk-quantification-and-why-is-it-important/.
41. Pavel V. Shevchenko, Jiwook Jang, Matteo Malavasi, Gareth Peters, Georgy Sofronov, and Stefan Trueck (June 1, 2021), Quantification of cyber risk – Risk categories and business sectors. Available at SSRN: https://ssrn.com/abstract=3858608 or http://dx.doi.org/10.2139/ssrn.3858608.
42. https://www.nist.gov/publications/zero-trust-architecture.
43. https://news.yahoo.com/log4j-cybersecurity-expert-explains-latest-131226342.html?guccounter=1&guce_referrer=aHR0cHM6Ly9kWN rZHVja2dvLmNvbS88&guce_referrer_sig=AQAAAHxOma8GCGqDpTQ 3ezY9ALU9_fh9gHhBvQ9nBFjL3hTb05n4TY54y4T_8A965UW3Nh8Qz3d ph1YGB5JSCIKTg_2H0W3zwOcTERaNLc_IC7etIj5IQud57nHD0M33Pm 7KkgUgvEY1G-v14lvy55Piz7cpzWuyz6ok68JXJss7Vf5u.
44. https://cisomag.eccouncil.org/log4j-explained/.
45. https://en.wikipedia.org/wiki/Open-source_software.
46. https://thedailycable.co/01/06/politics/360695/lesson-from-log4j-open-source-software-improvements-need-help-from-feds/.
47. https://medium.com/secjuice/busting-cyber-myths-theres-a-silver-bullet-b12056b62bf0.
48. https://www.scientificamerican.com/article/the-certainty-bias/.
49. S. McCornack and J. Ortiz (2017), *Choices & Connections: An Introduction to Communication*, (2nd ed.), Bedford/St. Martin's. ISBN 9781319043520.
50. https://en.wikipedia.org/wiki/Uncertainty_avoidance#cite_note-HofstedeInsights-2.
51. https://en.wikipedia.org/wiki/Social_engineering_(security).
52. https://www.ibm.com/security/data-breach.
53. https://www.gao.gov/assets/gao-22-104746.pdf.
54. https://doc.lagout.org/Others/Cognitive%20Hacking.pdf.
55. https://www.facebook.com/combating-misinfo.
56. https://en.wikipedia.org/wiki/Facebook%E2%80%93Cambridge_Analytica_data_scandal.

57. https://www.vox.com/2018/3/17/17134072/facebook-cambridge-analytica
-trump-explained-user-data.
58. https://en.wikipedia.org/wiki/Facebook%E2%80%93Cambridge_Analytica
_data_scandal.
59. https://www.facebook.com/combating-misinfo.
60. https://www.cnn.com/2021/10/04/tech/facebook-whistleblower-frances-hau-
gen-what-we-know/index.html.
61. https://www.analyticsinsight.net/can-ai-write-article-complete-image-yes
-says-openais-gpt-3/.
62. https://finance.yahoo.com/news/disturbing-reasons-isis-marketing-effective
-000000482.html.
63. https://www.american.edu/spa/news/extremist-marketing-10122016.cfm.
64. B. Schneier (2000), Semantic attacks: The third wave of network attacks,
Crypto-gram Newsletter October 15, 2000. http://www.counterpane.com/
crypto-gram-0010.html.
65. M. Libicki (1994), The mesh and the net: Speculations on armed conflict in an
age of free silicon, National Defense University McNair Paper 28. http://www
.ndu.edu/ndu/inss/macnair/mcnair28/m028cont.html.
66. B. Schneier (2000), A self-study course in block-cipher cryptanalysis,
Cryptologia, 24, 18–34.
67. D. Denning (1999), The limits of formal security models. National Computer
Systems Security Award Acceptance Speech.
68. G.V. Cybenko, A. Giani, and P. Thompson (2002), Cognitive hacking: A battle for the mind, *Computer*, 35, 50–56.

Chapter 3

A matrix of risk governance
– organizational behavior

The global economy has shifted in profound ways. The financial markets in the US have experienced the longest period of positive expansion in history through January 2022.[1] If markets climb a wall of worry, there has been plenty to worry about as we enter a third wave of Covid. Even so key economic indicators tell a different story to date. American job growth has surged with 149 million employed and millions of job openings. Wages increased but not as fast as inflation and unemployment at 3.9%, is the lowest level in decades.[2] Not all countries have fared as well as the US through the Covid-19 pandemic but given the challenges the economy has overachieved mainly due to innovations in technology, hybrid work from home, and huge profits.

China handled the pandemic better than most countries but is now experiencing restructuring brought on by Xi Jinping's massive infrastructure investment at home and abroad through its *Belt and Road Initiative*.[3,4] Countries eager for capital to finance infrastructure projects saw China as an alternative to the International Monetary Fund (IMF) and the World Bank's stringent requirements. China has financed major projects globally with many of the least financially sound countries in the world. Supply chain challenges and disruption from the Covid pandemic have prompted some of China's debtors to request a restructuring of debt. China's global manufacturing prowess and ownership of precious minerals needed by the world are key elements for sustaining global growth putting pressure on other nations to compete and cooperate with China on geopolitical spheres. How will organizations navigate such complexity and respond to new challenges at home and abroad?

Global disruption has been a corner stone of change in market leadership for millennia, but the pace of change has found a new gear. Change has also created a transition in leadership in financial markets that often reflect the larger economy in different countries. In 1980, the top ten companies in the Standard & Poors 500 (S&P) included two technology companies, IBM and AT&T, seven oil companies, and General Electric. The US economy was driven by petroleum-producing firms, change in corporate technology, and telecommunication giants.[5]

DOI: 10.1201/9781003189657-3

Today, in contrast, the S&P 500 is much more diverse by sectors.[6] The largest sectors are *Information Technology* (27.48%), widely disperse across 13 subsectors. *Healthcare* is second (14.58%), *Communications Services* is third (10.9%), *Consumer Discretionary* is fourth (11.18%), *Financials* is fifth (9.89%), *Industrials* is sixth (9.80%), and *Energy* is dead last in eleventh place (2.53%). The change in economic diversity has strengthened the economy and made it more resilient and robust. What has changed little is governance structures. Hierarchical governance models made perfect sense when large organizations dominated economy stability. There is growing evidence that new governance models are needed to account for technological innovation and demands by activist investors.

Private equity and venture capital have played a huge role in the transformation and financial underpinnings of economic growth. Technology has garnered most of the media's attention, but private equity has contributed the most to transformative change in the US economy.[7] Citizens Bank has called this shift a "mega-trend" and explains why the shift is raising the bar in corporate America.[8]

> This is a trend that has helped to boost company valuations to record highs. But this trend also has implications for the business environment. Private-equity (PE) backed companies, now a significant portion of the market, have access to capital and operating expertise. This combination has pushed many industries to be more competitive and sophisticated. The practices PE-backed companies adopt are becoming the norm. To keep up, middle-market managers and owners have to take an aggressive approach to upgrading their own practices or consider ways to tap into private capital.

The move away from publicly held stock toward private equity ownership has been growing for decades. While the number of public companies dropped by half in the 1990s, private equity firms quadrupled during the same timeframe. The number of PE-owned firms exceeded publicly owned firms for the first between 2012 and 2013. The shift from publicly owned stocks to privately owned companies was also driven by the technology industry's desire to control its own destiny and avoid the cost of regulation and initial public offerings (IPOs). Tech firms chose not to go public and instead grew their firms with private funding driven by an appetite from institutional investors seeking higher returns than the stock market delivered. Valuations grew in the incubation stage fueled by serial funding allowing institutional investors to get pre-IPO pricing as valuations surged.

Trends in Silicon Valley, such as Google's unusual auction-style offering and Facebook's failed IPO contributed to a mega-trend in private equity capital funding.[9] Success in technology capital raising campaigns grew investor appetite. Return-seeking asset managers, institutional investors, and high net-worth investors sought out less costly ways to invest in the next

Amazon, Facebook, Uber, and more. Private equity firms grew rich feeding demand for new offerings and contributed operating experience while nurturing young tech entrepreneurs on key drivers of growth. Private equity created an environment that allowed early-stage companies to grow until their fledgling "Unicorns" warranted the high valuations their investors sought.[10] A new stage of growth is now emerging as private equity owners, seeking continued growth, and must also manage the risk of ownership of a portfolio of companies. How should PE-backed CEOs be managed across a diversified portfolio while mitigating the complexities of regulation and risk governance and remain competitive in the long term? PE firms have begun to look to academia and platform models to leverage a combination of technology and effective risk governance models to answer those questions.

As the mega-trend expands, new governance models will be needed to respond in a fast-paced digital economy against sophisticated corporate activists and other private-equity owners. A review of two emerging governance models will be introduced as well as a literature review on the weakness in existing governance models. What is clear is governance must change to evolve in a contemporary economy with advanced risk practice that requires smarter and leaner approaches to governance. The first of the two more recent governance models is the "platform governance" model. Afterwards, a review of *Board 3.0* will provide context for the literature review that follows. Finally, a "matrix of risk governance models" will be presented as an alternative to "one-size-fits-all" models to reflect diverse industry types and risk profiles.

The paper's authors propose that many of the largest most successful businesses operate as "platforms" across multiple industries.[11] Platform companies have disrupted industries in retail, hotels, and taxis and will undoubtedly move to disrupt other industries as well. Fenwick, McCahery, and Vermeulen (2018)[12] propose that the current regulatory framework promotes an unhealthy "attitude" that is failing platform companies. An alternative platform governance is presented that "leverages current and near-term digital technologies that create more community forms of governance," "build an open and accessible platform culture," and "facilitates the creation, curation, and consumption of meaningful content."

These "transaction facilitators" are distinguished from traditional business models by their *organization for innovation* approach which has ushered in a "Platform Age" in business. The argument presented is two-fold. On the one hand, "top-down" hierarchical organizational structures no longer apply in a digital economy that is flatter and innovation driven. Secondarily, top-down governance is narrowly focused on delivering shareholder value while disregarding all other considerations and stakeholders. The side effects of these hierarchical governances are the tendency to become entrenched, inefficient, and too focused on the short-term which creates an overly risk-averse corporate culture. Firms of this type fail to innovate and risk becoming "industry dinosaurs" resulting in disruption, and worse extinction. Furthermore, the rise of platforms is disrupting existing hierarchical business models and traditional understandings of corporate governance.

Firms today must engage with the Internet, cloud services, and mobile technologies with a new wave of advanced technologies in robotics, blockchain, and machine learning. Survival depends on innovating in shorter business development cycles at speeds that exceed traditional governance cadence. What has emerged is a diverse set of platforms which now dominate traditional industries – social platforms (Twitter, Facebook, LinkedIn), exchange platforms (Amazon, Airbnb, Uber), content platforms (Instagram, YouTube, Medium, Netflix), software platforms (Apple iOS, Google Android), and blockchain platforms (Bitcoin, Ethereum, EOS).

A smaller cohort is also represented by emerging platform players in Risk Tech, InsurTech, Cyber, Cloud, and CRM platforms (GRC, RiskTech, InsurTech, Salesforce, Amazon). To be fair, this sector of the tech industry represents 10% or less of total US GDP in 2020. Compared to financial services; the largest sectors by industry type at 22.3%, followed by insurance, real estate, rental, and leasing business, in the same time frame, the comparison between "platform" companies and traditional firms is a little like seeing only white swans while assuming no "black swans" exist.[13,14] The early success of platform companies must be evaluated over decades. What the companies have in common is they were able to create massive scale by leverage surging stock price to grow and make acquisitions.

Platform-style organizations seek stakeholder input through user engagement and feedback by providing "creator's" tools on the platform. That is an attribute more companies could lean on and benefit from. Platform companies reward *content contributors* who create marketing "buzz" while benefiting from advertising revenues. The process as used by platform-style organizations is called "collaborative consumption," the shared use of a good or service by a group, is transformative in understanding "ownership and consumption."

For example, Apple developers create apps for the App Store, musicians contribute content on iTunes, etc. The Apple Ecosystem is an example of a digital ecosystem ("Walled Garden") that has propelled Apple to become the first multi-trillion-dollar company by market valuation.[15]

An argument that has been echoed by opponents of hierarchical organizational structures is that the *shareholder primacy view* has led to "a myopic focus on maximizing shareholder value feeds

an unhealthy short-term focus on firm share price and market valuations that obscures issues of

innovation." Shareholder value maximization has produced counterproductive emphasis on financial reporting, quarterly results, and a preference toward existing products and services ignoring innovative new ideas. Initiatives in shareholder primacy have also marginalized employees through mass layoffs, cost-cutting, and restructuring while awarding executives huge stock-based options. The paper largely ignores the governance issues experienced by Google, Uber, and Facebook among a few of the "platform companies" that have suffered through their own growing pains in attempts to find footing as their firms have grown substantially.

Finally, the chapter proposes regulatory remedies based on regulatory reform in Europe and Asian countries despite the fact that these remedies are currently the duties of the directors of the corporation in the US.

"A recognition that a long-term focus needs to be added to the 'corporate governance equation' has resulted in the adoption of so-called "stewardship codes" across multiple jurisdictions."

The US has fiduciary guidance, but one may argue that directors must improve how they balance shareholder returns with stakeholders such as employees and the community at large.[16] Whether or not the new model is widely adopted, directors always owe fiduciary duties to the shareholders.

> Most notably, they owe duty of loyalty and duty of care. Board directors have a Duty of loyalty is created to address conflicts of interest. It requires a director to be loyal to the company and always act in its best interest.[17]

Directors owe this duty in virtue of their status as agents of the shareholders. Duty of care requires directors to act on an informed basis upon consideration of relevant information reasonably available to them.[18] If a director fulfills these fiduciary duties, she can benefit from the protections afforded by the business judgment rule – that is, she will be shielded from personal liability for decisions that she makes in her capacity as a member of the board.

In the shareholder-centric model, in which shareholders' interests take primacy, it is easy to reconcile the role of board members as agents of shareholders with the duty of loyalty that they owe to the company. That is because the ultimate objective of a company is only to maximize returns for the shareholders. But under the stakeholder-centric view, a director must be concerned with not just returns to shareholders, but also a range of other factors that impact other stakeholders, such as consumers and employees. The stakeholder-centric model broadens the basis for the business judgment rule. Directors are not solely motivated by maximizing shareholder returns but are required to account for a range of stakeholder interests to ensure long-term and sustainable profitability.

A final recommendation in "platform governance" is proposed based on three strategies:

- Leveraging new technologies to create "community-driven" organizations
- Building an open and accessible platform culture
- Facilitating "meaningful" platform content

The final recommendations don't appear to be a significant departure from current corporate governance with the exception of the third strategy. The idea of platform business models is a compelling one given the growth tech companies have experienced. Governance is more than a business model and must include structures that help ensure sustainable operations and competitive innovation throughout an organization's life.

Google's founders, Larry Page and Sergey Brin, brought in Eric Schmidt as CEO to bring structure ("parental supervision") to the start-up and allow the founders to focus on innovation.[19] Uber, Facebook, Twitter, and other "platform organizations" experienced difficult transitions from bootstrapping start-ups to corporate titans. The analogy that the success of platform companies has been hampered by regulatory constraint rings hollow as these firms near trillion-dollar valuations. Platform companies have the same struggles as all other companies, but the struggle involves reconciling competing views in human behavior.

The common denominator in all organizations is human judgment and the execution of processes that ensure cohesive risk-taking and risk management. Transitioning, to an alternative board model, Board 3.0, takes a very different approach. Board 3.0 rises out of a mega-trend in private equity ownership. Private equity investors have accumulated a portfolio of two or more companies and now need to move toward a sustainable growth trajectory while ensuring resilience to activist investors who demand quick returns.

Researchers Ronald J. Gilson and Jeffrey N. Gordan from the Center for Law and Economic Studies Columbia University School of Law contributed to the formation of Board 3.0, an article published in The Business Lawyer, Vol. 74, Spring 2019 is presented as a new board model as an option for public company boards.[20] *The goal is to develop a model of "thickly informed, well-resourced, and highly motivated" directors who could credibly monitor managerial strategy and operational skill in cases where this would be particularly valuable* (Gilson and Gordon 2019).

> Unlike the present board model of thinly informed, under-resourced, and boundedly motivated directors, Board 3.0 directors could credibly defend management against shareholder activist incursions, where appropriate, with institutional investor owners. Similarly, such directors could find a place in extremely complex enterprise, such as finance, where the costs of business failure are profound. One inspiration for Board 3.0 is found in private equity, in which the high-powered incentives of the PE sponsor have produced a different mode of board and director engagement that seems associated with high value creation.

The case is a compelling one. The current governance structure has been in place for 40 years and replaced its predecessor structure which failed as noted earlier in corporate fraud cases. The existing board model is considered a "monitoring board" and notes that the current model is made up of part-time independent directors and reliant on information provided by management and measured by stock price performance. The current model which serves as a monitor and adviser to management has proven to be insufficient in holding management accountable as evidenced by failure in Enron, Tyco, etc. The monitoring board is version 2.0 of governance models. As organizational size and complexity grew, organizations made the switch to the monitoring board model characterized by a smaller board made of active leaders from other companies who are compensated for their time but act as part-time overseers that provide guidance.

The earlier model 1.0 was considered an "advisory board" and consisted of up to 30 directors "in which the directors were part of the CEO's team: other corporate officers ("insiders"), trusted confidants of the CEO personally, and "affiliated" directors, commonly linked to the company's outside law firm, its bank, or its investment bank." Board 1.0 was the traditional model of the public company board; it certainly was dominant in the 1950s and 1960s. The model came under attack for its inability to constrain managerial malfeasance in three particular respects. First, the bankruptcy of Penn Central, a bonafide blue chip until it collapsed, showed that the Board 1.0 model could produce a board that was simply unaware of the business challenges at the firm (Gilson and Gordon 2019).

Second, the spread of the conglomerate merger, which produced unwieldly businesses that were beyond the managers' capacity adequately to manage, showed that directors were unable to constrain managerial appetites for bigger empires. Directors seemed unaware that in many cases the "economic logic" consisted principally in the manufacture of "earnings" through the manipulation of accounting conventions.

Third, the so-called "questionable payments" scandal of the 1970s, in which many firms were found (or preemptively confessed) to illegal campaign contributions in the US and bribes paid abroad, showed that Board 1.0 directors could not be counted upon to constrain or even know about management's illegal behavior – that was not their job. Coincidentally, the three board models spanned the same timelines as the rise of the COSO integrated internal controls framework and ERM model.

The researchers noted the challenges of scaling the board model as organizational and business complexity grows and outpaces the cognitive boundaries of most board directors. Increasing the board becomes untenable as board size expands and increasing director time and compensation creates the appearance of independence expected of directors. Therefore, a new model is needed in response to the sophistication of today's organizational dynamics.

Thus, the firm's stock price performance, year-to-year and in comparison to peers, has become the key metric for Board 2.0 directors, not only because it corresponds to some idea of shareholder welfare but because it provides a thinly informed director the most reliable measure of management's success performance year-to-year and in comparison to peers. The asymmetry of information between the board, management, and the markets demands new approaches to prepare directors with the tools to make a justifiable defense when the stock price does not reflect the value that has yet been recognized by activist investors and other stakeholders (Gilson and Gordon 2019). The board is time constrained and does not have the time to conduct deep analysis on the plans and operations of the company and lacks enough information to perform its monitoring duties: the board is "under-resourced" for this purpose. Board 2.0 directors are "thinly informed." Part-time directors receive only management's view of short- and long-term performance or rely on external sources from market analysts and short-term market sentiment. Another factor considered limiting director performance in Board 2.0 is that directors are "boundedly motivated."

Directors receive compensation in stock and cash, but the amounts are not enough to reward outstanding performance nor incentivized to do more perfunctory duties. Distinguished and accomplished directors tend to be risk averse near the end of their careers and are not seeking high-risk-oriented board assignments. In summary, board behavior has typically been "reactive rather than proactive; directors are information- and time-constrained and have bounded motivation in the intensity of their engagement and the risk-taking they will support."

Board 3.0 is modeled after private equity portfolio company governance models referred to as the PE PortCo Board model. The primary focus of the PE PortCo Board model is to allow private equity owners to defend against activist investors by withholding strategic plans and intellectual property confidential until an opportune time in the market. Secondarily, the PE PortCo model allows PE owners to leverage state-of-the-art financial engineering to drive additional performance while maintaining tighter control with a smaller board size inclusive of financially incentivized insiders on the board.

The makeup of the PortCo board would consist of no more than six directors, one or two "deal-makers" who shape the economic analysis of deals, one to two "operators" from the PE firm, one "outside director" with specific industry expertise, and the CEO. The operator engages with the CEO as frequently as weekly depending on deal activity and the operator drives board discussions. The CEO's performance is determined by the board. One board member would become the lead director basically ensuring complete control over the PE firm's direction and leadership.

Private equity has been driven by executing financial engineering practices for decades to capture "excess free cash" flows in leveraged buyouts. Another method involved the take-over of slow-footed conglomerates to sell off less productive subsidiaries to pay down debt from the LBO and retain any surplus. A third strategy involved borrowing to execute the LBO and using the tax code to shield income from taxes by writing off the expense of the deal over several years. The downside of these deals caused massive disruption in lost jobs, economic pain, and resulted in industry malaise as CEOs focused more on strategies to defend activist investors than growing the business. Over time, the low-lying opportunities have been captured and require PE owners to seek longer-term strategies to maintain "alpha" in their deals. Alpha is the capture of excess returns over market returns and riskless government bonds.

A few highly influential founders and visionary CEOs have conceived hybrid models of version 2.0 with dual-class shares that separate voting from non-voting owners where founders keep control of the firms that minimize external activism. Finally, the researchers propose a hybrid governance model in Board 3.0 that retains elements of Board 2.0 and the full spectrum of resources in Board 3.0. A dual model is proposed whereby the "portfolio of companies" (PortCos) would retain their current 2.0 board governance model while the PE owner would adopt Board 3.0.

The 2.0 board model would be substantially downgraded to focus primarily on compliance-focused committees or ad hoc committees, as needed, while Board 3.0 provide support via a "Strategic Review Committee" and active engagement with management of the portfolio firms. The profile of directors on Board 3.0 would be mid-career professionals, compensated primarily with long-term shareholdings, but term-limited with a firm in the portfolio. There are a number of opportunities and drawbacks to Board 3.0.

The opportunity side of Board 3.0 is that it allows PE owners ultimate control and autonomy in driving a successful business model across each of the PortCos. Centralizing services and administrative support may create synergies that would not be present if each firm maintained redundant support staff and infrastructure. Board 3.0 ensures that communications are consistent and coordinated across diverse firms.

It is not clear however that there is a large enough pool of financially independent mid-career executives who would except a stock-only compensation package based on deal execution or commit to limited contractual terms. Secondly, the designers of Board 3.0 assumes that opportunities in financial engineering are inexhaustible nor subject to regulatory intervention. And thirdly the model would be costly to operate and put strains on a centrally operated "deal office." Board 3.0 looks a lot like a *matrix-reporting* governance model where decision-making is centralized except for operational and compliance-related duties.

The platform governance model and Board 3.0 are interesting models to consider but are so narrowly defined they would not be broadly applicable across other diverse industry types. The benefits and drawbacks of each will require more analysis and experience testing these models in real time. A matrix of governance models will be introduced after a review of the current state in board governance and organizational performance to evaluate additional alternative models for consideration.

ENTERPRISE RISK GOVERNANCE IN REVIEW

Studies of board governance are extensive, yet existing research offers limited insights into the operations of the audit committee (Turley and Zaman 2007).[21] Existing research on board governance and audit committees focus on anecdotal attributes of the board such as board size, composition, and dual role of the CEO as chairman. Board performance is generally viewed in hindsight based on measures of financial performance, shareholder value, and the ability to acquire debt at lower rates as implied factors that demonstrate good governance. Good risk management may be implied by these measures but is seldom evaluated in empirical studies of board governance.

Researchers found that insurance company's board risk committees were positively correlated with higher financial strength ratings and performance but only after the financial crisis of 2008. Prior to that period of time, there was little to no correlation in performance between insurance companies and their board risk committee activities (Ames, Hines, and Sankara 2018).[22] Research on audit committees has conceptualized addressing agency risks with little empirical evidence to support correlations with enhanced financial performance. To a certain extent, these studies have inevitably relied on relatively crude proxies, for example, the number and duration of meetings as indicators of how "active" an audit committee is (see, for example, Abbott et al. 2004; Bedard et al. 2004; Krishnan 2005).[23,24,25]

A separate study set out to investigate the relationship between attributes of corporate governance and performance of companies listed on the Ghanaian Stock Exchange (Kyereboah-Coleman, Adjasi and Abor 2006–2007).[26] The study of corporate governance and firm performance of Ghanaian listed companies between 1998 and 2003 consisted primarily of a regression analysis to determine correlations between variables such as board size, debt financing, external directors, and other factors with corporate performance. Much of the analysis is mixed or inconclusive.

> Though it has been argued (Fama & Jensen 1983, Baysinger and Butler 1985, Baysinger & Hoskinsson, 1990, Baums 1994) that the effectiveness of a board depends on the optimal mix of inside and outside directions, there is little theory on the determinants of an optimal board composition (Hermalin & Weisbach 2002).[27,28,29,30]

The study also revealed a likely optimal board size range where mean ROA levels ranging from board size 8 to 11 are higher than overall mean ROA for the sample. This signals a range of optimum board size (8–11) feasible for good firm performance. A majority of the firms in the study also had a board structure that follows a two-tier structure [separate executive and non-executive boards]. Significantly, firm performance (using ROA or size) is found to be better in firms with the two-tier board structure (Kyereboah-Coleman, Adjasi, and Abor 2006 – 2007).[31]

Although the analysis in this study found an "optimal" board size for good corporate performance, researchers did not include exogenous factors such as candidate selection bias, economic business cycles, and tempo of regulatory change, or include an empirical analysis of risk processes used by the board(s) to achieve "good" corporate performance. Corporate governance involves responding to a range of internal factors as well as external stakeholders who bring influence on board performance. The limitations of this study demonstrate that a correlation of variables alone does not prove causation of performance.

Additional research is needed to better define predictive measures of enhanced corporate governance and risk performance. These topics exceed the scope of this study; however, limited empirical research on board risk committees and the risk function presents an opportunity for further advancements in board governance and enterprise-wide risk management.

ENTERPRISE-WIDE RISK MANAGEMENT

Modern corporations face a myriad of risks across disparate fields of business and complex financial arrangements as well as expectations from external stakeholders to increase value. Legal constructs require corporations to be under the supervision of the board of directors. Corporate directors are generally not required to have any particular skills or expertise other than being a "natural person" (Ramirez and Simkins 2008).[32]

In the wake of repetitive corporate financial fraud, Sarbanes–Oxley of 2002 required "independent auditors" of public companies must report to an audit committee which generally must include, at least one "financial expert." Nevertheless, the audit committee alone cannot anticipate or respond to all of the risks facing a contemporary organization. "It seems axiomatic that today the public corporation too often fails to identify and manage the risks [it] faces" (Ramirez and Simkins 2008) historically leading to a lack of confidence in corporate risk management functions.

The emergence of enterprise-wide risk management

In one critical study of corporate governance and enterprise-wide risk management, researchers from the Loyola University Chicago, School of Law

(Ramirez and Simkins 2008) lay out the barriers to effective board governance and specifically address systemic failings in the current legal framework that fail to facilitate effective enterprise-wide risk management.

Early evidence of risk management dates to around 2000 B.C. from documents of commodities futures trading in India. Ancient records from Greek and Roman markets as well as Japanese trading merchants drafted forward contracts promising future delivery of goods as far back as 1600 A.D. (Ramirez and Simkins 2008). By the turn of the century, more sophisticated financial instruments necessitated advanced mathematics to address growth in options markets, contracts, and other derivatives. The fields of finance and economics have contributed to a deep and rigorous practice of risk quantification in financial markets.

Enterprise-wide risk management did not emerge until the 1990s and has continued to grow in importance albeit without widespread adoption. Enterprise risk management continues to be practiced in silos and fragmented across different organizations. COSO (committee of sponsoring organizations) is widely credited with defining ERM. COSO ERM is intentionally broad with a foundation built on internal controls over financial reporting and strategic risks.

Other organizations, such as the Casualty Actuarial Society (CAS), offer a narrow definition of enterprise-wide risk management that encompass processes that lead to increases in stakeholder value creation. These two divergent views represent a lack of consensus on ERM as well as the fact that there is no "one-size-fits-all" approach that uniformly addresses risk profiles across industry type or operating models. Neither of these definitions of ERM has materially advanced risk practice.

The attributes of good ERM practice have created friction with advancements in corporate governance. At the same time that ERM is deemed strategic, financial risk professionals still struggle with defining the right data for predictive risk intelligence. ERM implementations are varied, and no consensus exists on the proper structure of the risk function or role of a Chief Risk Officer. Board directors express increased support for ERM yet fail to respond in a timely manner. Results show 20% of firms suffered significant loss from a failure to manage risks and 56% of firms had a near-miss in the previous year of the study (Ramirez and Simkins 2008). Misaligned risk activities in high-frequency, low-impact risk distract from uncertainty management in residual risks.

The literature is clear on the aspirational goals of good ERM practice; nevertheless, there is little evidence that board governance has uniformly adopted proactive risk best practice, particularly before adverse events arise. Examples abound of poor board governance prior to the 2002 Sarbanes–Oxley Act and after that serve as stark reminder that enterprise-wide risk management and strong board governance represent opportunities for enhanced performance. Successive failures in board governance beg the question, "what is the appropriate means of managing the risks inherent in a business environment on a comprehensive basis?" (Ramirez and Simkins 2008).

Evidence from studies and surveys indicates that, to date, only about 10% of major companies claim to have implemented many aspects of ERM, while almost all the others claim that they plan to do so in the future (Tonello 2007).[33] In order to understand why ERM has not lived up to its promise, we must examine the structural and cultural impediments to effective corporate governance and enterprise-wide risk management.

Structural impediments to advancements in corporate governance and enterprise-wide risk management

A Loyola University of Chicago Law study found that Sarbanes–Oxley (SOX) is fundamentally flawed and has failed to reform corporate governance and empower risk management (Ramirez and Simkins 2008).[34] The study goes further describing how state corporate governance law and regulation largely fails to take modern financial science on board. Boards are given the autonomy to choose to operate with or without an ERM program or enterprise risk expertise.

SOX regulation was designed to address only the audit function and legal compliance, consequently failing to address risk management. SOX is a compliance mandate of internal controls over financial reporting disclosures and does not address or require a fulsome disclosure of all key risks that threaten the firm. Sarbanes–Oxley fails to contemplate behaviors that lead to fraud beyond internal control weakness such as withholding critical risk data from the board.

An exhaustive review of corporate financial statements finds wide disparity in the disclosure of risks and processes for managing risks at the enterprise level. Boiler plate legal disclosures, common in financial statements, fail to fully inform stakeholders of a spectrum of risks facing the firm. In a recent public statement from SEC commissioner, Allison Herren Lee (January 2020) stated,

> investors are overwhelmingly telling us, through comment letters and petitions for rulemaking, that they need consistent, reliable, and comparable disclosures of the risks and opportunities related to sustainability measures, particularly climate risk.
>
> Investors have been clear that this information is material to their decision-making process, and a growing body of research confirms that. And MD&A is uniquely suited to disclosures related to climate risk; it provides a lens through which investors can assess the perspective of the stewards of their investment capital on this complex and critical issue.

It is also clear that the broad, principles-based "materiality" standard has not produced sufficient disclosure to ensure that investors are
getting the information they need—that is, disclosures that are consistent, reliable, and comparable. What's more, the agency's routine disclosure review process could be used to improve disclosure under the
materiality standard, but in recent years there's been minimal comment
on climate disclosure.

In organizations with no risk committees or CRO office, the CEO becomes
the risk manager by default as a result of the broad powers that accrue to
the office of the executive. This is the natural result of broad public ownership combined with the CEO's power over board selections and the very
minimal duties of board members under the law to supervise CEOs. Thus,
under current corporate governance practices, the CEO is usually a risk
silo (Ramirez and Simkins 2008). Board governance has routinely failed
to detect and prevent fraud formulated and executed by powerful CEOs as
evidence of proof of the ineffectiveness of SOX regulation.

The conclusion of the study? Corporate governance is flawed by virtue of
gaps in Sarbanes–Oxley, corporate law, and regulatory financial disclosure
that mandate compliance with accounting standards without equal weight-
ing of risk management requirements and accountability at the board level.
Sarbanes–Oxley provides internal audit and the board audit committee
independence but fails to make risk management independent inclusive
of disclosure of material risks beyond weakness in internal controls over
financial reporting. Information processing of key risks is cited as an opportunity to improve board governance in more than one study. Similar findings were noted in a second study by researchers examining the financial
crisis of 2008 (Pirson and Turnbull 2011).[35]

In a study (Pirson and Turnbull 2011) of the causes of the financial crisis of 2008, researchers noted that "hierarchical structures – as reflected
in unitary boards – do not function well in dynamic and complex environments, partly because they are inflexible and do not support information processing as well as, for example, network structures."[36] Network
governance is interfirm coordination that is characterized by organic or
informal social system, in contrast to bureaucratic structures within firms
and formal relationships between them. The study goes further to examine
the root cause of inefficiencies in hierarchical structure through a focus on
information processing at the board level defined as "systematic information processing problems."

The research in the (Pirson and Turnbull 2011) study identified two reasons boards failed to manage risks in the 2008 mortgage financial crisis:
(1) board members did not have access to relevant information on the risks
incurred because they had no control over information supply; and (2) board
members were unable to process the available risk-related information and
lacked incentives or power to influence managerial decision-making.

The paper found a systemic misfit between the information processing needs and the information processing capabilities in risk-related decision-making at the board level during the crisis. Fligstein and Goldstein (2010)[37]observe that

> in 2007, the US market for prime and sub-prime mortgages became highly concentrated with 25 firms being responsible for 90 per cent of the combined prime and sub-prime market. All 25 firms operated as centrally controlled hierarchies with a unitary board.

The study provided several examples where risk information within a firm was intentional withheld from the board by management. In one example, risk reports of violations exceeding the firm's risk appetite [mortgage securities] were withheld by the firm. In another example, disagreements between the CEO and the chairman of the board about risk-taking were not shared with the board. The argument being that senior executives have great power to filter information from the boards about their activity and risk-taking that could be instrumental to oversight. Boards do not have the power to compel risk information if they do not know it exists.

In a novel approach, a study (Pirson and Turnbull 2011) noted behavioral science findings juxtaposing the supply of information with the ability of boards to absorb the complexity of the information presented to them.

> Nevertheless, real-life time constraints would decrease the transmission rates even further, as humans are limited in their ability to transmit and receive information of any type (Williamson 1975; Williamson 1979). Furthermore, there are few incentives for communicating risks in command and control hierarchies.

The researchers conclude that there are structural problems in information processing between the board governance process and oversight of management. The information problems are described as: (1) insufficient information access; (2) insufficient information supply; (3) information overload increases the risk of relevant information not being processed; and (4) information bias and group dynamics distort rational information processing.

The remedies to these and other structural challenges to improving board governance and efficacious risk management practice are similar – empowered independent risk committees and enhanced risk information. Legal structures allow accumulation of power and decision-making at the executive level creating friction in risk information transmission between the board and senior executives. As noted earlier, boards are social constructs based on trust and information sharing. Boards operate efficiently during normal business conditions; however, during periods of financial crisis or significant uncertainty, the social constructs on the board may become fragile and dysfunctional.

"Good" risk management is often cited by researchers, scholars, and risk professionals as a process that improves decision-making. Risk management assists the organization to achieve its goals and objectives by providing relevant information in a timely manner. When information flows are disrupted or disintermediated between the risk advisor(s) and decision-makers, the process of good risk governance is circumvented.

The conclusion reached by researchers with different perspectives identified similar conclusions – corporate board governance needs an update to address the agency management problem. Human behavior and decision-making under uncertainty are the key elements of good governance and risk management, but are humans up to the task? How does an organization define state of the art in influence management? Building an organization with a culture of competitive excellence requires constant fine-tuning and open-mindedness.

We have covered a spectrum of externalities that contribute to poor board governance, but we have not yet explored the scale of the human side of the equation. If board governance is reduced to managing risks and selecting profitable risk-taking strategies, there would still be a host of human issues to deal with. Employees, span of control, safety, security and privacy, regulation, and much more.

Why are human factors an important element in organizational governance? Whenever discussions turn to how employees are treated, compensation, benefits, and performance metrics have become the standard toolkit. What people really want is to do meaningful work. To participate in the success of a firm and get rewarded for achieving success. Organizational performance is about scaling talent. An understanding of a few basic hurdles to performance is a new way of looking at human resources. What are the human factors that hinder performance? What channels of communication are working and how can they be improved? Why are people silent when bad behavior hurts performance? The core of good board governance is really about how effective people are at working together to achieve a collective goal. Is it constructive or destructive? The biggest companies have been started in garages and home basements without a board or committees.

The structures such as board governance, committees, and regulations are designed to enforce the right human behaviors. These constructs are crude remedies especially when the process is about reducing control. Naturally, there is pushback and tension, but the unanswered question is how do groups of leaders form a consensus on important decisions? Communications that influence how decisions are made drive organizational behavior. How is feedback integrated? Who gets to decide? How are choices framed? What are the value propositions used in the decision-making process? What is the analysis of the consequences of alternative choices and what are the limiting factors? And finally, what are the constraints in skills, resources, tools, and capabilities needed to achieve stated results?

Hierarchical structures impose layers of supervision between senior executives and line workers responsible for achieving objectives in strategic plans. Middle management plays an important role in interpreting strategic plan directives to line operations, but these hand-offs are vulnerable to failure. A great deal of interpretation takes place between executive direction and execution in operations. An analysis of organizational behavior is critical but provides only one dimension of a three-dimensional picture of human factor risks.

The two board models reviewed are diametrically opposed on the surface, but both are attempts at solving the same problem. The platform model is open-ended and feeds on user experiences. Board 3.0 model is closed-ended and strategy-driven in execution. Those are the superficial attributes. The real difference is who's in control? Google's founders, Sergey Brin and Larry Page, are polar opposites of both models. Brin and Page have stepped away and turned over the company to Sundar Pichai to run the firm. No one hardly mentions Brin and Page when talking about Google, an almost $2 trillion firm. Nurturing talent, Clarity in vision, giving up control, and managing the innovation process may be the positive side of human governance that unifies board risk governance.

Amazon's founder, Jeff Bezos has done the same. Another multi-trillion-dollar business. Maybe the answer to board governance is not expecting perfection in execution but excellence in solving problems that lead to even greater performance. Bezos' idea of building an online bookstore to compete with Barnes & Nobel seem like a quaint idea at the start. Bezos' idea to build a huge cloud business from access data storage capacity seems serendipitous, but he turned that business over to trusted lieutenants who had to learn how to succeed.

Good governance may come in many forms, but the most successful ones may be hiding in plain sight, if only we looked a little closer. Many examples exist consisting of simple, clear strategies that scale, aided by technology and an environment of competitive excellence where a pool of talent is homegrown and evolves over time. If you think back to the early days of partnerships in financial services, each partner's performance contributed to or was deducted from the final results each year. Partners managed their own risks in the interest of their own reputational damage. Winning happens with a team of diverse talent. Good governance is less about doing one thing right and more about a way of behaving that influences the qualities and attributes that lead to high-performing teams. Designing good governance takes the same effort as developing a winning product that pays dividends over time. It's hard to do but the benefits are worth the effort.

Blackstone's Stephen Schwarzman has epitomized the principles of good governance aspirational goals in ESG. There has been confusion about how a focus on ESG leads to better performance. The results from Blackstone demonstrated what these behaviors look like.[38] The behaviors are principles-based and value-based: (1) "We invest in companies and property to make them stronger," (2) "We build strong stronger communities and drive economic growth." (3) "We provide teachers, nurses, firefighters and other pensioners with greater financial security." The is not about being "woke," it is about doing good business and being rewarded by scaling people. Scaling people creates sustainable processes that has made Blackstone one of the largest most profitable portfolio managers in the world.

Blackstone and BlackRock saw the opportunities to use the public markets to scale their business models and have far exceeded banks and many of the largest asset managers in the process. Blackstone and BlackRock invested in platforms that created scale to grow assets and manage costs. BlackRock, now a $10 trillion asset manager, is the largest in the world. BlackRock's Larry Fink is also a firm believer in ESG principles and the history of these two men has paved the way for proper governance that few firms have emulated.[39]

> During Fink's tenure, he had lost $100 million as head of First Boston. That experience was the motivation to develop what he and the others considered to be excellent risk management and fiduciary practices. Initially, Fink sought funding (for initial operating capital) from Pete Peterson of The Blackstone Group who believed in Fink's vision of a firm devoted to risk management. Peterson called it Blackstone Financial Management. In exchange for a 50 percent stake in the bond business, initially Blackstone gave Fink and his team a $5 million credit line. Within months, the business had turned profitable, and by 1989 the group's assets had quadrupled to $2.7 billion. The percent of the stake owned by Blackstone also fell to 40%, compared to Fink's staff.
>
> By 1992, Blackstone had a stake equating to about 35% of the company, and Stephen A. Schwarzman and Fink were considering selling shares to the public. The firm adopted the name BlackRock in 1992, and by the end of that year, BlackRock was managing $17 billion in assets. At the end of 1994, BlackRock was managing $53 billion. In 1994, Schwarzman and Fink had an internal dispute over methods of compensation and equity.
>
> Fink wanted to share equity with new hires, to lure talent from banks, unlike Schwarzman, who did not want to further lower Blackstone's stake. They agreed to part ways, and Schwarzman sold BlackRock, a decision he later called a "heroic mistake." In June 1994, Blackstone sold a mortgage-securities unit with $23 billion in assets to PNC Bank Corp. for $240 million. The unit had traded mortgages and other fixed-income assets, and during the sales process the unit changed its name from Blackstone Financial Management to BlackRock Financial Management. Schwarzman remained with Blackstone, while Fink went on to become chairman and CEO of BlackRock Inc.

Both men had a vision for good risk management and fiduciary duties. Human behavior is the key to growing strong business.

The lesson is simple, but the discipline is hard to maintain. A clear vision, good principles, strong ethics, and a belief in people. BlackRock has 18 Directors on its board.[40] Sixteen are independent including seven women and six non-US or dual-citizens. Three of the 16 independent directors self-identify as racially/ethnically diverse, one African American, one Hispanic/ Latin American, and one Middle Easter/North African.[41] Blackstone does not break out its board diversity but has 13 directors of which four are executives of the firm including Stephen Schwarzman, three are women, with five directors on the Audit Committee. BlackRock with $10 trillion in assets under management and Blackstone with $731 billion have very different boards, but it is easy to see which one has far exceeded the other.

Now that we have examined what good and bad governance looks like, no one should assume that following someone else's version of a corporate board will lead to success. So, if no one-fits-all board governance approach works, what other options are there?

MATRIX OF BOARD GOVERNANCE MODELS

There are between three and eight dominant board types that have evolved in different countries and cultural influence. Generally speaking, board models have changed incrementally with foundational principles by country and historical legal precedent. What is available either examines why boards fail or lists examples of "good" practice. There is little evidence of empirical metrics and examples of how boards contribute to organizational performance. The challenge is illustrated in a literature review in healthcare governance.[42,43]

> An examination of literature across the social sciences to assess the evidence for effective board working leads to the identification of three issues surrounding the construction and development of boards. One, the is no evidence or consensus about an "ideal" board form. Two, the evidence about board working suggests that there are some key principles but also that local circumstances are really important in steering the focus and behaviors of effective boards. And three, there is an emerging proposition that boards, including in healthcare, need to embody a culture of high trust across the executive and non-executive divide, together with robust challenge, and a tight grip on the business of delivering high quality [patient care] in a financially sustainable way (high trust – high challenge – high engagement).

Here is yet another industry that finds the same navigational challenges in board governance – human behavior. What follows are examples of board governance that exist today but are not sufficient to account for the fast-paced, high-stakes business models in a technology-enabled work environment. An explanation of a matrix of organizational governance will follow after the types of boards.

There are several common types of boards each having distinguishing characteristics.[44]

Collective

The collective is a group of people with a shared focus or purpose. They make decisions collectively and each individual represents themselves and their own interests. Common in nonprofits.

Governing boards

The board leads the organization using authority to direct and control provided by the owners and the legal act of formation. They set initial direction and have the full authority to act in the owners' best interests. Governing boards function at arm's length from the operational organization. They focus on the big picture, future-oriented and act as a single entity. Common in traditional corporate legal structures.

Working boards

The board leads the organization but also does double duty as the staff. These are common in very small organizations and community-based organizations that do not have the resources to hire employees. Working boards often get caught up in project management and set aside the governing function.

Advisory boards

The board serves to provide insight and perspective to any decision-maker including boards. An advisory board typically does not have authority of its own but works to educate some person or body. Common in cybersecurity educational firms that advise and direct messaging to grow the member base and promote learning.

Managing boards/executive boards

A group of people who actually manage the operations as a collective group (instead of a single CEO). They are not the same as a governing board but may work under one. They make the day-to-day decisions of what gets done and the long-term decisions about how to organize operations to achieve the organization's purpose. These boards are typically inside large organizations responsible for oversight and led by a Chief Administrative Officer, Chief Risk/Audit/IT/Compliance Officer, etc.

Carver board governance model

As noted in the section on nonprofit models, the Carver model works for nonprofit and for-profit organizations. The Carver model places its focus on the "ends" of the organization's purpose. This means the organization actively works toward what it needs to achieve or what it needs to do to put itself out of business. Within defined limits, the board gives the CEO the bulk of the responsibility for using the means to get to the ends.

Cortex board governance model

The cortex model is a model that focuses on the value that the organization brings to the community. The board defines the standards, expectations, and performance outcomes according to the aspiration of the organization. Clarifying and setting outcomes to achieve success become the primary duties of the board under this model.

Consensus board governance model

The consensus, or process, model is a form of the cooperative model that nonprofit organizations use. It gives all board members an equal vote, equal responsibility, and equal liability. The consensus model is appropriate for corporations without major shareholders.

Competency board governance model

A corporate board that is interested in developing the knowledge and skills of the board members will benefit from the competency model, a model that focuses on communication, trust, and relationships to improve overall board performance. The organization's bylaws do the work of outlining practices and strategies.

The **Anglo-American model**: These boards typically have eight to 12 members elected by shareholders. In the US, the chairman is often also the company's CEO, and the other members are often outside (i.e., non-executive) directors. In the UK, the CEO rarely pulls double duty as the chair.

The mission of the one-tiered board is to maximize shareholder profits. But this approach to corporate governance has some drawbacks. Thomas Clarke, the director of the University of Technology Sydney's Centre for Corporate Governance, writes that this board model allows CEOs to amass incredible wealth and power and gives them an overwhelming amount of influence in stakeholder relations. This system is firmly in place in the UK, the US, Australia, and Canada. Boards in former British colonies and common-law countries like India and Malaysia often have some variation of the Anglo-American model. Variations of this model are also present in China.[45]

The German model: The defining characteristic of the German model is that boards are two-tiered, meaning executives and non-executives are separated into a management board and a supervisory board, respectively. "Shareholders appoint members of the supervisory board (other than employee members), while the supervisory board appoints the members of the management board," writes the World Bank.[46] This also means the boards are larger than the average one-tier board – the average board in Germany has 17 directors (on both tiers combined), though other countries with the two-tier model have smaller boards.

German corporate governance, which is based on the principle of codetermination, allows for labor representation on both board tiers – an element largely absent from one-tier boards. The size of these boards is also ideal for implementing inclusion policies like gender quotas and can improve the representation of minority stakeholders.

In Europe, companies in most countries can choose between one- and two-tier boards, as often dictated by law. In France, for example, companies can choose between the two, and within the one-tier option, they can choose whether to combine the roles of chairman and CEO or keep them separate. Peugeot has a two-tier board, while Christian Dior's board has one tier. Most Scandinavian countries, meanwhile, can choose between the Nordic model and the German model.

The Nordic model: The Nordic model, like the German model, has a high degree of separation between the board of directors and executive management. In fact, most boards are entirely composed of non-executive directors. Unlike the German model, the boards are typically small. Sweden's boards have an average of 6.5 directors, according to the World Bank. These boards also boast a high number of women, and employees have the right of representation.

Another distinction in the Nordic model is that the general meeting, an event where shareholders exercise voting rights, is the highest decision-making body of the company "and the main forum for the shareholders to exercise their ownership rights."[47] The chain of command begins with the general meeting, goes through the board, and ends with executive management.

This model is localized in Denmark, Sweden, Norway, and Finland.

The Japanese model: If the Anglo-American model is represented by a triangle, the Japanese model is a hexagon representing outside shareholders, the government, management, independent directors, the bank, and something uniquely Japanese called *keiretsu*. The term can be defined as "conglomerate."[48]

"Keiretsu exist as a network of industries, with one- and two-way agreements to favor each other in business deals and share in shouldering temporary burdens that would otherwise cause instability for the group." Also uniquely Japanese is the place of the bank or financial institution and the government.

One last point before the final section on a Matrix of Board Governance. Germany has an interesting two-tier board structure versus one tier in the US. The University of Pennsylvania Carey Law School and Goethe University presented a seminar paper comparing the two models. "The Anglo-American model of a one-tier board structure is largely a reflection of the neo-liberal norms of shareholder primacy and free market capitalism. The German two-tier model is a reflection of stakeholder primacy."

Both countries are recognized economic powerhouses, and each country has achieved success following very different tracks. Germany is also home to more entrepreneurial specialty manufacturing shops whereas the US has used capital markets to grow and finance conglomerates. The US one-tier board incorporates managerial and supervisory responsibilities into one unified board of directors. Other executives in management may also report to various committees on the board but not serve as executive directors.

US boards operate under two mandates: "The mandate to advise and the mandate to oversee." Six general responsibilities are outlined that fall under the two core mandates. (i) recruit, supervise, retain, evaluate, and compensate the managers, (ii) provide direction for the corporation, (iii) establish a policy-based governance system, (iv) govern the organization and the relationship with the CEO, (v) uphold the fiduciary duty to protect the organization's assets and member's investment, and (vi) the monitor and control function.

US directors operate under two fiduciary principles that have evolved over decades of legal precedent (Block and Gerstner 2016): (1) duty of care and (2) business judgment rule. A duty of care requires directors to act in good faith with the care of a prudent person and in a manner the director reasonably believes is in the best interest of the organization. The business judgment rule presumes that if business decisions made by the board are made by disinterested, independent directors, with informed due care and with a good faith belief that the decision will serve the best interest of the corporation, the courts will not second guess a decision made by the board.

The Delaware court is used as a proxy for other state court precedent. The courts do not measure, weigh, or quantify directors' judgments. They do not even decide if they are reasonable in this context. Due care in the decision-making context is process due care only.[49] Directors in Delaware are protected from liability for unwise or poor decision-making but may be held liable for breach of duty of care when directors fail to perform their duties responsibly, in good faith, and in a reasonably prudent manner.

Delaware statute authorizes shareholders to adopt provisions in certificates of incorporation that eliminate or limit personal liability of a director to the corporation or its stockholders for breach of fiduciary duty as a director. Sarbanes–Oxley is considered, by some legal scholars, to encroach upon state's law by adding new supervisory duties to directors and providing more substance.

Conversely, German law is based on a wide range of statutory regulation and the non-statutory German Corporate Governance Code (GCGC). Some statutes allow certain company forms to adopt a voluntary two-tier board structure governed by the corporations' articles of incorporation. A European limited liability company (*Societas Europaea, SE*) may also choose its own board structure governed by Council Regulation on the SE, the German Implementation Act allowing for certain deviations. Other statutes such as the German Stock Corporation Act make a two-tier system for limited companies mandatory. Germany also incorporates state supervision of certain industries (banking or insurance) under codetermination laws.

Under Germany's mandatory two-tier system, executive directors on the management board select the company's objective and take the necessary steps to achieve them. Directors on a non-executive supervisory board monitor the decisions of the executive board on behalf of other parties. Members on the management board are appointed and dismissed for cause by the supervisory board. There are no requirements for a specific number of board members (management or employees) and varies according to company size, codetermination rules, and statutes in the articles, but the average in 2012 was 5.6 members.

The management board represents the company in legal matters and provides strategic direction for the company. Shareholders appoint members of the supervisory board during the annual meeting. The size of the supervisory board is determined by one or more of the following criteria: state codetermination laws, amount of share capital, size of the workforce, and by election of company employees, up to one third and one half of supervisory directors. Additionally, certain shareholders may be granted the right to directly appoint one third of shareholding representing members of the board as well as the right to remove the member(s).

Supervisory board member qualifications include the expertise of the member, limits on the amount of parallel supervisory board mandates, and a prohibition of a simultaneous seat on the management board. The supervisory board can represent a diverse set of stakeholders including shareholders, employees, labor unions, the company's group holdings, business partners, creditors, and state representatives. The structure of a two-tier board system is an "open book" process where the supervisory board has access to inspect the books, review the annual report, issue, and oversee the work of external auditor, analyze the information provided by the management board, reporting to the general meeting, and exercise control over the decisions of the management board.

The supervisory board has extraordinary powers of influence on the management board. Although not able to interfere in the running of the company, the supervisory board has influence over the extension of credits to members of the board, an ability to change the metrics of measures that impact the assets and earnings of the firm, extensive networking among all stakeholders, and the extension of incentives through renumeration.

The annual meeting of shareholders is also used as a lever of influence and control of the management board through resolutions regarding key company decisions and appointments of members on the supervisory board or auditor. Both countries' board models evolved over centuries of cultural norms and historical precedence adopted by the US from United Kingdom trust law and a framework of Roman laws in governance by Germany. Both separate supervision and management and provide protection of shareholders and stakeholders which have become sacrosanct in board governance in most countries.

Each country has adopted and evolved board governance to meet their specific needs and cultural acceptance. A good exercise would include a comparison of each country's governance models and create an arbitrary scoring system to grade the pros and cons of each. That exercise is the beyond the scope of this book, but the stark difference in board governance between the US model and the German model is instructive of the spectrum of approaches and motivation for enhancing board governance.

Let's now turn to the human side of the story to better understand the root cause of board performance and why human nature is the greatest risk to organizational success.

NOTES

1. https://www.cnn.com/2020/03/11/investing/bear-market-stocks-recession/index.html.
2. https://www.cnn.com/business/economic-growth-indicators.
3. https://www.forbes.com/sites/miltonezrati/2021/10/15/chinas-debt-problems-are-a-serious-matter-for-americans-too/?sh=588bab4643ea.
4. https://www.cfr.org/backgrounder/chinas-massive-belt-and-road-initiative.
5. https://public.tableau.com/app/profile/john.vangavree/viz/Top10SPCompanies1980-2020/SPTop10.
6. https://advisor.visualcapitalist.com/sp-500-sectors-and-industries/.
7. https://www.costar.com/article/835867220/ownership-balance-shifts-to-private-equity.
8. https://www.citizensbank.com/corporate-finance/insights/shift-from-public-equity-to-private-equity.aspx.

9. https://www.cnet.com/news/google-files-for-unusual-2-7-billion-ipo/.
10. https://www.techadvisor.com/feature/small-business/what-is-tech-unicorn -3788654/.
11. https://papers.ssrn.com/sol3/papers.cfm?abstract_id=3232663.
12. M. Fenwick, J.A. McCahery, and E.P.M. Vermeulen (2018), The end of 'corporate' governance: Hello 'platform' governance (August 16, 2018), Lex Research Topics in Corporate Law & Economics Working Paper No. 2018-5, European Corporate Governance Institute (ECGI) – Law Working Paper No. 430/2018, Available at SSRN: https://ssrn.com/abstract=3232663 or http://dx .doi.org/10.2139/ssrn.3232663.
13. https://www.statista.com/statistics/1239480/united-states-leading-states-by -tech-contribution-to-gross-product/.
14. https://www.statista.com/statistics/248004/percentage-added-to-the-us-gdp -by-industry/.
15. https://en.wikipedia.org/wiki/Apple_ecosystem.
16. https://news.law.fordham.edu/jcfl/2020/10/27/fiduciary-duties-in-a-stake- holder-model-of-corporate-governance/.
17. M. Marcus and J. Sipes (2020), *Directors and Officers: Key Considerations for Continued Response to COVID-19*, Baker Donelson (July 14, 2020), https://www.bakerdonelson.com/directors-and-officers-key-considerations -for-continued-response-to-covid-19.
18. G. Bradshaw, *Duty of Care and Duty of Loyalty Owed by Directors in Delaware*, Bradshaw Law (Grouphttps://bradshawlawgroup.com/duty-of -care-and-duty-of-loyalty-owed-by-directors-in-delaware/).
19. https://www.theverge.com/2019/12/4/20994361/google-alphabet-larry-page -sergey-brin-sundar-pichai-co-founders-ceo-timeline.
20. https://millstein.law.columbia.edu/sites/default/files/content/docs/Jeff %20Gordon%20-%20Gilson-Gordon%20Board%203.0%20SSRN%20w %20abstract.pdf.
21. S. Turley and M. Zaman (2007), *Audit Committee Effectiveness: Informal Processes and Behavioural Effects*. Available at SSRN: https://ssrn.com/ abstract=1069911 or http://dx.doi.org/10.2139/ssrn.1069911.
22. D. Ames, C.S. Hines, and J. Sankara (2018), Board risk committees: Insurer financial strength ratings and performance, *Journal of Accounting and Public Policy*, 37, 130–145.
23. A. Abbott (2004), *Methods of Discovery: Heuristics for the Social Sciences*, New York: Norton.
24. J. Bedard, S. M. Chtourou, and L. Courteau (2004), The effect of audit com- mittee expertise, *Auditing: A Journal of Practice & Theory*, 23(2), 13–35.
25. J. Krishnan (2005), Audit committee quality and internal control: An empiri- cal analysis, *The Accounting Review*, 80, 649–675. https://doi.org/10.2308/ accr.2005.80.2.649.
26. A. Kyereboah-Coleman (2007), The impact of capital structure on the perfor- mance of microfinance institutions, *The Journal of Risk Finance*, 8, 56–71.
27. E. F. Fama and M. C. Jensen (1983), Separation of ownership and control, *Journal of Law and Economics*, 26, 301–325. http://dx.doi.org/10.1086 /467037.
28. B. D. Baysinger and H. N. Butler (1985), Corporate governance and the board of directors: Performance effects of changes in board composition, *Journal of Law, Economics, & Organization*, 1, 101–124.

29. B. Baysinger and R. E. Hoskisson (1990), The composition of boards of directors and strategic control: Effects on corporate strategy, *Academy of Management Review*, 15, 72–87.
30. William M. Baum (1994), *Understanding Behaviorism: Science, Behavior, and Culture*, United Kingdom: HarperCollins College Publishers.
31. A. Kyereboah-Coleman, C.K. Delali Adjasi, and J.Y. Abor (2007), Corporate governance and firm performance: Evidence from Ghanaian listed companies, *Corporate Ownership and Control*, 4, n. pag.
32. B.J. Simkins and S.A. Ramirez (2008), Enterprise-wide risk management and corporate governance (March 1, 2008), *Loyola University Chicago Law Journal*, 39, Available at SSRN: https://ssrn.com/abstract=1657036.
33. M. Tonello (2007), Reputation risk: A corporate governance perspective (December 10, 2007). The Conference Board Research Report No. R-1412-07-WG, Available at SSRN: https://ssrn.com/abstract=1077894 or http://dx.doi.org/10.2139/ssrn.1077894.
34. Simkins and Ramirez, Enterprise-wide risk management and corporate governance.
35. M. Pirson and S. Turnbull (2011), Toward a more humanistic governance model: Network governance structures, *Journal of Business Ethics*, 99(1), 101–114.
36. https://en.wikipedia.org/wiki/Network_governance#:~:text=Network%20governance%20is%20%22interfirm%20coordination,are%20defined%20in%20this%20context.%22.
37. N. Fligstein and A. Goldstein. "The Anatomy of the Mortgage Securitization Crisis." (2010).
38. https://www.blackstone.com/wp-content/uploads/sites/2/2020/09/BX_ESG-Brochure_.pdf.
39. https://en.wikipedia.org/wiki/BlackRock.
40. https://ir.blackrock.com/governance/board-of-directors/Board-Diversity-at-BlackRock/.
41. https://www.blackstone.com/the-firm/our-people/.
42. N. Chambers (2012), Healthcare board governance, *Journal of Health Organization and Management*, 26(1), 6–14.
43. https://www.researchgate.net/profile/Naomi-Chambers/publication/224822808_Healthcare_board_governance/links/59ca8d774585155 6e97e29f5/Healthcare-board-governance.pdf.
44. https://policygovernanceconsulting.com/about-governance-and-board-work/different-types-of-boards.
45. https://www.diligent.com/insights/corporate-governance/different-approaches-to-governance-from-around-the-world/.
46. http://documents.worldbank.org/curated/en/750681468001781687/pdf/97118-WP-PUBLIC-Box391470B-CG-Practices-in-EU-Guide-PUBLIC.pdf.
47. https://www.sns.se/wp-content/uploads/2016/07/the_nordic_corporate_governance_model_1.pdf.
48. http://www.smithsonianmag.com/innovation/how-eight-conglomerates-dominate-japanese-industry-180960356/.
49. Brehm v Eisner 746 A.2d at 259 (Del 2000).

Chapter 4

Incorporating human risk factors into organizational performance

"Human Factors"

> Managing risk through human factors can take many forms; managing
> the risks associated with equipment that is not designed with the user
> in mind; managing the risk that an operator or maintainer will perform
> in a way that was not anticipated; managing the risk that changes made
> to the organization at the micro- or macro-level will impact on the per-
> formance of individuals or the organization as a whole.[1]

This description of human risk factors is a segment of the abstract from a
book titled *Human Factors in the Chemical and Process Industries* (Elsevier
2016, pp. 73–91), where the author, R. Chaife, goes on to provide example
after example of hidden risks that are ignored in all organizations, in part,
due to a current orientation in risk management to focus on controls and
not the factors that inhibit human performance. We blame people instead
of examining how a workflow or process limits optimal performance in
corporate performance. Human risk factors have begun to gain the attention of industry executives who understand the key to better performance
in healthcare,[2,3,4] engineering,[5,6,7] shipping, aeronautics, automotive manufacturing, and more.

The history of human risk factors dates back to 1487, when Leonardo
DaVinci began research in the area of anthropometrics. The Vitruvian Man,
one of his most famous drawings, can be described as one of the earliest
sources presenting guidelines for anthropometry.[8] Anthropometrics is the
study of the human body and its movements, especially in terms of its measurements, but ergonomics is the scientific discipline that involves designing
products and environments to match the individuals who use them.

Human factor is recognized for its focus on safety but has expanded and
will continue to grow as more research is spread to other industries.[9] A
human factors framework includes the following elements: technical systems, people systems, internal (cognitive load) factors, and thinking (deci-
sion-making/support) factors, which convert to actions (influence) factors
and produce outcome reliability.

DOI: 10.1201/9781003189657-4

While it may seem logical that human factors would apply to workers in manufacturing, aeronautics, and other industries who work with heavy equipment, in reality many organizations have missed an opportunity to design or redesign work to optimize performance in the office, on the battle field, and in mom and pop shops by reimagining the work environment to reduce human error. We have already reviewed the cybersecurity data to demonstrate how busy cybersecurity professionals and worker errors result in significant and costly data losses and productivity.

A culture of blame has become a pandemic where errors are considered personal failures in judgment and work proficiency.[10] There is an implicit and often explicit expectation that workers follow a myriad of compliance policies and procedures and perform their work flawlessly at all times. But people are not machines and machines break down sometimes as well. The term hybrid work is bantered around as if someone discovered a new way of working. The reality is hybrid work has been the norm since the dawn of technology.

My definition of hybrid work is human–machine (after evolving from human–animal work) interactions with digital simply a new iteration of manual and digital work types. The transition of scribes of books who hand-copied transcripts, to typewriters, copy machines, and to laptop computers, disconnected from the office, is the same hybrid work with different tools. Errors occurred in every segment of this evolving work model, but the pace of change and the velocity of complexity has outpaced our attention to adapt properly. People fear change more than they anticipate the potential benefits. This innate risk aversion obscures the accumulation of hidden risks until something or someone breaks. The so-called digital transformation will fail to meet expectations if we do not fully contemplate how to effectively integrate the human element into an ever-evolving workplace or remote work.

Whether we care to admit it or not, we are all bounded, and those limitations are situational when the pressure is on, and time is shortened to get the work done in the midst of rapid change. Nonetheless, the expectation is to get more done with less. This expectation is suboptimal and will lead to poor performance, not from inaptness, but from natural human limitations over time. Yet, the tendency in most organizations is to pile on more; policies, procedures, consolidate teams, and shortened time frames for completion in the short-sighted need for expedience. An alternative is to design the organization for speed if that is what is valued. The same for accuracy, or patient care, etc. This requires a new way of thinking about productivity and performance.

The leading cause of cyber-risks and operational failure is work complexity. Organizational restructuring has always been considered a given in modern times, but the reasons are taken for granted. Change in the business environment, new methods of operation, buyouts, a different direction, and more often not, a change in leadership. Change is inevitable but planning for it often resembles a fire drill. Restructuring the organization is disruptive and damages productivity.

The metrics for synergistic change are primarily financial in the short run, but what is damaged is productivity, execution, and sustainable growth. Organizational redesign is about people who help drive it. If organizational goals are short-term, such as, streamlining a firm to be resold quickly is the objective, an investment in people may not produce quick returns, but if positioning an organization for sustainable growth is the objective, the process of paying attention to the human element is critical. The following case study is a prime example of what happens when management ignores the human element.

CASE STUDY – YAHOO AND MARISSA MAYER

The Yahoo story was complex and troubled long before Marissa Mayer joined the firm. A brief diversion to the beginning will shed light on how tragic the Yahoo story turned out to be given its amazing start. Two Stanford graduate students, Jerry Yang and David Filo, developed the biggest search engine before the Google founders graduated Stanford University.[11] Yahoo enjoyed a $125 billion valuation and was considered the leader in technology in several categories, such as cloud storage, beyond its core platform, Internet search. The company became a one-stop shop for online surfing for entertainment, news, travel, chat, and community groups. Yahoo's community of developers created content on the site and pioneered online advertising among many other accomplishments that are now commonplace across Silicon Valley social media companies.

Yahoo! also pioneered the "coder culture" of work all day and night creating new ideas in a laid-back, "no shoes and shorts" freestyle atmosphere. Yahoo's fortunes rose with many of the "dot.com" *Unicorns* of its time and crashed and burned with them as well in 2000. To make matters worse, Yahoo's founders were offered to buy Larry Page and Sergey Brin's code for a new search engine for $1,000,000 and turned it down and instead referred them to Sequoia Capital. The rest is history.

Losing out on Google was the first of many missteps that started the Yahoo decline. The rumors and true stories of other missed opportunities to buy Google, Facebook, sell to Microsoft for $47 billion, and a poor track record of monetizing or over-paying for acquisitions all contributed the legend of why the company failed but do not explain what was happening inside with the people running the firm and why so many mishaps occurred. The Yahoo story is tragic, but the DNA of the company runs deep in Silicon Valley startups that followed, including Alibaba, the Chinese Internet giant formed by Jack Ma. Although Yahoo's management team is blamed for these failures, the board was present during every one of these opportunities or not present as an adviser. It is not clear how these failures were missed by the board, but industry observers and media pundits placed a lot of the blame on dysfunctional board behavior throughout Yahoo's tumultuous rise and fall including during Marissa Mayer's tenure.

YAHOO! BOARD

The revolving door in the CEO office of Yahoo is hard to follow. Scott Thompson was Yahoo's fourth CEO over five years. Before Thompson, Carol Bartz held the job from 2009 until she was fired in a public fashion. Bartz had taken over in late 2008 from company co-founder Jerry Yang, who had returned to Yahoo in 2007 to replace Terry Semel. Allegedly, Daniel Loeb, founder of hedge fund Third Point, LLC, a major shareholder, and activist investor, orchestrated the firings for cause and recommended changes on the board.[12,13] The inner workings of the board became public in dramatic fashion with the termination of Carol Bartz, the third largest outside shareholder.[14]
(In letter that became public from Loeb to the *Yahoo!* board)

> While the decision to hire her alone is grounds for questioning the Board's competence, its willingness to turn a blind eye to these serious problems and inexplicably remain supportive of Ms. Bartz notwithstanding the negative impact she was having on the company is even more troubling. As recently as June 23, 2011, at the company's annual meeting, Chairman Bostock reportedly stated that the board remained "very supportive of Carol and this management team" and that they were "confident that Yahoo [was] headed in the right direction." These comments demonstrate that this board lacks the courage to urgently make the difficult decisions required by the situation today.

When Marissa Mayer was appointed president and CEO in July 2012, she was the fourth in four years and the eighth in 18 years which says a lot about the governance of Yahoo long before Ms. Mayer took over. Industry observers and Yahoo employees were abuzz at the announcement of Ms. Mayer's ascension to the top of the industry and becoming the youngest female executive to do so. More importantly, Yahoo's employees were hopeful for stability at the firm, especially the engineers and product managers who felt a kindred spirit would bring more focus to these areas of the business.[15] The early tenure of Ms. Mayer seemed to confirm the hopefulness of employees. Productivity took off again and the firm was given awards for new products and recognition that the new CEO was making progress to turn the company around or at least get its footing again.
    Prior to leaving, Yahoo's co-founder, Jerry Yang, had engineered a coup by making a 40% investment in Jack Ma's Alibaba which Marissa Mayer

inherited. The $1.3 billion investment grew to $7.1 billion when Alibaba repurchased half of the investment. The remaining Yahoo stake in Alibaba rose in value to $26.5 billion providing Yahoo and Ms. Mayer with an unexpected windfall to invest in strategic initiatives. Simultaneously, the value of Yahoo's assets was losing or had lost value which set up a confrontation with activist investors and a new set of hedge funds with representation on the board. The conflict between Marissa Mayer and the two hedge funds, Starboard Value and SpringOwl Asset Management, was a classic one. Where should strategic investments be made in the business and which parts of the nonperforming business to cut?

The board argued for cuts in staff to reduce costs while Marissa made the case to retain talent as the board debated strategy. Tensions between the board and management spilled out in media reports and reverberated in the firm as the fear of cuts grew louder. Instead of making cuts immediately, the CEO started a new performance evaluation program similar to one Jack Welch of General Electric made famous where the bottom performers were cut from the firm and the top performers were rewarded. Unfortunately, middle managers circumvented the program by retaining "friendlies" who would ensure that performance rewards went to close cohorts resulting in top talent leaving the firm. After a series of layoffs started, the impact on employees of the firms was chilling and did not inspire trust or loyalty and led to an exit by many who had hoped for a return to better days.

By 2016, Yahoo had lost ground to Google, Facebook, and a bevy of tech startups, many founded by former Yahoo alums. Yahoo's board had become fodder for ridicule in the *New York Times* and other national publications as one strategic plan after another was floated as "strategic options," then abruptly changed.[16] This is how Yahoo was portrayed in a *New York Times* article in January 2016.

It's hard to believe, but after all these years, the Yahoo board is still a contender for America's worst corporate board.

The announcement last week that the board is officially exploring "strategic alternatives" — code for a sale — and hiring advisers is confirmation that it is still stumbling, refusing to take a stand as its chief executive, Marissa Mayer, flounders.

Yahoo's decision is something of an about-face from only a few months ago. Then, the board had decided that a spin-off of Alibaba stock was too risky. The issue was tax — the I.R.S. had stopped approving these transactions — and although its law firm was willing to bless the transaction, the Yahoo board decided not to go forward. Instead, the company said that "market perceptions" dictated that it do another transaction. The board would spin off Yahoo itself and, for good measure, said it would consider "alternatives."

At the time, the announcement of this "reverse spin" was seen as a sop to the market and a way to buy time, perhaps up to a year, for

Ms. Mayer to enact yet another turnaround plan. One hedge fund, SpringOwl Asset Management, argued in a 99-slide deck that to sell Yahoo now would be to do so on the cheap before the full value of a platform that has almost a billion users could be exploited. But only a few months later, the board has again shifted course, this time initiating a full-fledged process to sell the company. An independent committee of the board has been formed, and lawyers and three investment banks — Goldman Sachs, JPMorgan Chase and PJT Partners — have been hired. Even the hiring of three banks shows the bloat at Yahoo as it searches for someone to lead it somewhere.

The company says that this is only one option, but independent committees have a life of their own. The train has started, and it will probably stop at a sale. Moreover, it is nearly impossible to run a turnaround plan when you are actively exploring a sale and are contacting bidders. The board knows this, and so the talk of a sale being "only an alternative" is cheap. It is exactly what a weak board would do at this time — throw its hands up, despite the possible value of waiting.

As you may recall in the proposal for Board 3.0, the model was designed to respond to the kind of disruptive activist behavior in board governance that contributed to Yahoo's demise and board dysfunction. Activist investors, as opposed to leverage buyout (LBO) operators, found arbitrage opportunities in the regulatory system itself. Activist investors buy small stakes in companies – typically 5–10% of their stock – and then use their position as a minor shareholder to pressure the companies to make changes. In many situations, such as at Microsoft and Yahoo, activists have won board seats, while at others they have forced their targets to buy rivals, sell business lines, and change how they allocate capital. Between 2009 and 2015, more than 40% of the 500 largest US-listed companies were subject to activist scrutiny, with 15% facing such investors in a public stand-off, according to data provider FactSet.[17]

In a bizarre twist of irony, the SEC approved new rules that will give activist investors a new tool to lever more power overboard governance with less effort.[18,19] In a blog post from the Harvard Law School Forum on Corporate Governance, lawyers from Harvard's Law School opposed the new rule and proposed amendments to it.[20]

On November 17, 2021, the US Securities and Exchange Commission (SEC) adopted new Rule 14a-19 and amendments to existing rules under the Securities Exchange Act of 1934 to require the use of "universal" proxy cards in all nonexempt director election contests at publicly traded companies in the U.S. The new "Universal Proxy Rules" contain only slight modifications from rules the SEC first proposed in October

2016, for which the SEC reopened the public comment period during 2021. The rules will take effect for shareholder meetings after August 31, 2022. We expect a significant increase in proxy contest threats once the Universal Proxy Rules go in effect.

Members of Sidley's Shareholder Activism & Corporate Defense Practice sent a formal comment letter to the SEC regarding the proposed rules — the only letter from a U.S. law firm suggesting material amendments that would protect against the potential for misuse of a mandatory universal proxy system. As we argued previously, the Universal Proxy Rules create the equivalent of "proxy access on steroids." While comparable to the vacated Rule 14a-11, which allowed shareholders holding at least 3% of a company's outstanding shares for three years to put dissident directors on the company's proxy statement, the Universal Proxy Rules confer substantially more significant rights to shareholders without any minimum ownership requirements (i.e., owning only one share for one minute will be sufficient).

Although this was a concern voiced by several Commissioners, the SEC proceeded with the adoption of the Universal Proxy Rules as originally proposed. The new rules will reshape the process by which hostile bidders, activist hedge funds, social and environmental activists, and other dissident shareholders may utilize director elections to influence control and policy at public companies.

A majority of shareholders do not attend annual meetings and instead vote on board members and corporate proposals through a proxy; mutual funds, asset managers, etc. using an electronic proxy voting form or printable pdf to mail in votes. Most of these ballots are ignored by mutual fund owners and the public which allows the proxy to vote on behalf of the shareholders. Proxy votes rely on board recommendations or receive input from proxy advisory firms.[21]

In 2019, solicitation influence at proxy advisory firms became acute enough for the SEC to issue new guidance to curb unethical behavior. In a statement from the Securities and Exchange Commission,

The SEC noted that the definition of the term "solicitation" in its proxy rules is broad and includes a communication to security holders under circumstances reasonably calculated to result in the procurement, withholding or revocation of a proxy. The SEC stated that proxy rules can cover a person even in cases where the person is not seeking the procurement, withholding or revocation of a proxy for itself or is indifferent to the ultimate outcome.

In assessing the applicability of the definition of solicitation to communications from proxy advisory firms, the SEC stated that whether a particular communication is a solicitation often turns on whether the purpose is to influence shareholders' decisions. In a summary provided by

Osler, a Canadian law firm that specializes in financial services and proxy solicitation,

> The SEC observed that proxy advisory firms market their expertise in researching and analyzing matters submitted to a shareholder vote for the purpose of assisting their clients in making voting decisions at shareholder meetings and that many investment advisers retain and pay a fee to proxy advisory firms to provide detailed analyses, including how to vote on shareholder proposals. As a result, the SEC expressed the view that voting advice provided by proxy advisory firms for the purposes of helping clients make proxy voting decisions (as compared to performing merely administrative or ministerial services) should be considered as solicitations subject to the SEC's proxy rules, even if the clients may not follow the advice.

Shareholders are not given the right to propose set of directors but are instead expected to rely on the board's selection or alternatively, a slate of board nominees from an activist investor group. This is how Dan Loeb's Third Point, LLC pocketed $600 million dollars from Yahoo. Dan Loeb's letter to the Yahoo Board of Directors is a textbook activist investor maneuver and feared by almost all CEOs. Here is an excerpt of the letter:[22]

> Third Point LLC ("Third Point") is a registered investment adviser with approximately $8 billion under management. We are writing to inform you that certain investment funds we manage have acquired a 5.1% interest in Yahoo! Inc. (the "Company" or "Yahoo"), bringing our holdings of common stock and currently-exercisable equity options to 65,000,000 of the outstanding shares, and positioning us as the Company's third largest outside shareholder. This letter details our principled demands for sweeping changes in both the Board of Directors (the "Board") and Company leadership, and outlines the hidden value of Yahoo, which has been severely damaged – but not irreparably – by poor management and governance (dated September 8, 2011).

On July 22, 2013, Reuters and CNBC News reported that Yahoo had repurchased 40 million shares from Third Point, LLC from a reported $610 million pre-tax profit on the deal while retaining 20 million shares, or less than 2% of Yahoo stock. Loeb and two other board directors resigned from the Yahoo board after completing the transaction which further demonstrates how a minority investor can agitate and disrupt for profit as an activist investor extracting value without contributing meaningful value in time or resources to ensure a firm is positioned for growth.

The fallout from the new SEC ruling will become clearer in the fall of 2022 if the effective date is not extended or modified. What is clear from this case is that poor management and mismanagement by the board of directors is a sign of weakness that has been and will continue to be exploited by savvy investors on Wall Street and opportunistic innovators who create technology in competitive markets. The costs of poor governance can also be counted in terms of lost productivity, lost innovation, lost talent, market share, and an opportunity to grow a competitive company. The US market needs competitors in technology and social media to counter the problems now seen in global markets where Google, Facebook, and others are being sued by European regulatory bodies for anticompetitive behavior. And social media has become a dominant source of misinformation and disinformation in public and private life.

There are plenty of media pundits and market observers who have an opinion about the failure of Yahoo, Marissa Mayer, and the board of directors, but let's take a more nuanced look at how leadership in management and the board over the entirety of Yahoo contributed to failure. A cognitive map is used to recap and navigate the events that lead to failure in human judgment in the cases and stories presented. Each cognitive map will summarize the judgments, behaviors, and actions that contributed to failure in each case study.

COGNITIVE MAP: DECISION-MAKING, GOVERNANCE, AND LEADERSHIP

The Yahoo saga is important from a historical perspective because the lessons learned from the failure of Yahoo have made today's generation of Big Tech firms more resilient and capable of defending themselves from a similar fate even as activists continue to influence CEO outcomes broadly as demonstrated by the Board 3.0 proposal. The question before the markets now is how does an organization prepare for and effectively defend against an invasion of activist investors, competitors, and self-destruction?

This case leaves unanswered questions about whether financial markets benefit from activist investors. Those questions are beyond the scope of this book. Nonetheless, the question is valid and should be studied by law makers with public input. There are several issues associated with these practices that appear to exceed any normal concepts of free capitalism. Why should minority investors in the form of investment advisers be allowed to hold organizations more accountable than majority investors? Why aren't majority shareholders given similar access to select board seats or demand strategic change? Why aren't activist investors required to share their profits with the majority shareholders since they have inside information not provided to majority shareholders? Shouldn't poor board governance be mitigated by all shareholders, not a privileged few, who have no interest in the long-term viability of a target firm? It is not clear whether this is the most efficient way to hold a company accountable for performance, but one thing is clear there is demand from institutional investors who place money with these firms for higher returns.

Let's recap the lessons learned first, then explore mitigation in Section 4.4. Some factors were ignored in the analysis above such as the cyber breach, which was a product of distraction, and other externalities that did not help in the long run at Yahoo but were not the core factors that ultimately led to Yahoo's purchase by Verizon alongside AOL for a bargain basement price of $5 billion and subsequently resold to Apollo for $5 billion in a bizarre but not final episodic story.

Daniel Loeb, an activist investor, is credited with ousting Scott Thompson and Carol Bartz and installing Marissa Mayer after collecting more than $600 million exited the board with two executives he installed during his campaign at Yahoo. Loeb's abrupt exit left doubts among investment analysts about the strategic direction of the firm under Mayer. On the date Loeb exited, Yahoo still had a multibillion-dollar cash cow in Alibaba stock which had not yet gone public, and valuations anticipated for Alibaba were between $70 and $80 billion valuing Yahoo's stake at $18 billion. Loeb's early exit left a billion-dollar windfall on the table instead of staying and mentoring Melissa Mayer's strategy.[23]

Why did Loeb leave the Yahoo board early? Loeb was reported to have lobbied Yahoo to sell half of its stake in Alibaba which turned out to be a terrible decision given the value of the remaining stock had increased by 80% at the time of Loeb's departure.[24] Yahoo's business had stalled, and its revenues were in decline which left the Alibaba stock as the greatest asset remaining. Loeb had no experience running an Internet business and did not know how to turn the company around but saw value in Alibaba but grossly underestimated its true worth. Loeb's advocacy for Marissa Mayer, an executive at Google, must have appeared to be a logical candidate even though she had never had the responsibility for running an entire company let along one as complex as Yahoo.

Marissa credited Daniel Loeb for seeing the value in Yahoo on his exit from the firm, and undoubtedly for bringing her on board to run the firm, but, in hindsight, this was the start of Marissa's problems. Loeb's exit signaled to the markets that Yahoo's value had peaked but the stock rose based on Alibaba's earnings. Eleven directors have left Yahoo's board by the time of Loeb's departure draining Yahoo of leadership at the helm right when Marissa needed steady hands to help right the ship.

According to media reports,

> A former Yahoo executive, speaking on the condition of anonymity, said that Loeb's departure was not unexpected. "Yahoo could have gone two ways after Scott Thompson: a media company under Ross Levinsohn or tech company under Marissa Mayer." Yahoo currently

generates most of its revenues on the media and advertising side. It has steadily lost ground to other tech giants like Google in the search and email market. But Loeb pushed hard for Mayer because the stock market typically values tech companies at a higher price-to-earnings ratio than media companies. "Ross would have been the slow steady choice, the long term choice," said this executive. "For Yahoo, Marissa was the riskier move."

Viewed through this lens, Loeb's departure looks like a quick flip. He is selling the majority of his stake in Yahoo and leaving the board along with the two men he nominated, Michael Wolf and Harry Wilson. "Loeb leaves a lot richer. Yahoo has a great new CEO," the executive noted. "But it's not clear that, in the long term, it can really compete with the new breed of tech companies."[25] In a brief report from *Reuters* (dated July 22, 2013), headlined "Dumped," everyone benefited except shareholders.

> The only ones missing out are regular shareholders.[26] Their stock has been shunted to the back of the buyback line. Nor are there any obvious candidates on the board to take on Loeb's role either as a restraint on Mayer's ambitions or as an advocate for proper capital allocations.
>
> That's important because it's still not clear Yahoo can turn its Internet business around without lots of dealmaking and spending – last week the company trimmed its 2013 sales outlook, for example. Without proper oversight, that could destroy some of the very value Loeb has just cashed in on.

Marissa had been set adrift without a life raft. This is should not be considered a sentimental excuse for Marissa Mayer. She left the firm in excess of $200 million dollars richer, notwithstanding that the employees and shareholders never fully recovered the value of Yahoo's worth. Therein lies the challenge with activist investing and short-termism now pervasive in financial markets. Is it possible to reform corporate governance when the drivers of board governance and senior executive strategy are personal survival in defense of opportunistic financial engineers who employ financial and legal arbitrage to extract value and create disruption?

But what happened after Loeb's departure? What role did the new activist investors play in Marissa's loss of control of Yahoo's strategic execution? Eric Jackson, writing in Forbes, gives us a clue about the start of contacts from a new set of activists.[27]

> A couple of days ago [March 9, 2015], Starboard Value wrote a new letter to Yahoo with their continued requests for how the company should increase value in the company. Katie Benner (who I really like as a keen tech observer) of Bloomberg View said that she didn't find the

letter "creative." She says their suggestions are mostly about financial engineering rather than on increasing advertising at the company. If Starboard chooses to fight a proxy contest against Yahoo later this year, it's likely that Yahoo will use this kind of argument to rebut Starboard in the eyes of their biggest institutional holders and ISS. Yahoo will say – as Benner did – Starboard is a Wall Street firm and therefore is both short-term oriented and ignorant when it comes to the world of technology. Prior Yahoo management teams have used this same type of argument against both Dan Loeb in 2012 and Carl Icahn in 2008 during their respective proxy contests.

Starboard Value followed the exact same script used by Daniel Loeb by sending a letter to the Yahoo Board on March 9, 2015. The summary of the letter was published in a newswire, Starboard Value

> states that the tax-free spin-off of Yahoo's Alibaba stake is a good first step, but not nough to solve Yahoo's current valuation discrepancy [and] continues to believe that there are other opportunities within the company's control to create significant value for Yahoo shareholders believes that implementing the following recommended steps can unlock $11.1 billion of shareholder value, or approximately $11.70 per share:
> * Right-sizing the company's bloated cost structure
> * Exploring opportunities to monetize Yahoo's intellectual property and real estate assets
> * Separating Yahoo! Japan stake in a tax-efficient manner
> * Returning $3.5–$4.0 billion of excess cash to shareholders through share repurchases

Marissa Mayer and Yahoo's board attempted to ignore Starboard Value and SpringOwl Asset Management to no avail. Once again, Yahoo's board failed to prepare Marissa Mayer for what would come next. Under the threat of a proxy fight from SpringOwl Asset Management and Starboard Value, Yahoo's board acquiesces to their demand [February 19, 2016] setting up a complete disruption of Mayer's strategic plans and commitments made to employees.[28]

> Yahoo Inc, under pressure from impatient investors, took steps on Friday to handle the possible sale of parts of the struggling Internet company. Yahoo shares jumped after the company announced its board has formed a committee of independent directors to explore strategic alternatives. This signaled Yahoo is open to selling its core business including search, mail, and news sites, rather than spin it off as previously planned. Yahoo advisers started working on the sale process on

Friday, people familiar with the matter said. The step followed more than three years of effort by CEO Marissa Mayer to turn around Yahoo, focusing on mobile apps and trying to boost advertising revenue.

Despite her efforts, revenue has dipped since she took the helm in July 2012. Yahoo shares rose 2.26 percent to $30.09 in midday trading. The announcement came as activist investors appeared to be preparing for a possible proxy fight for control of the board. Starboard, which owns about 0.75 percent of Yahoo, has been pushing for changes since 2014, asking it to separate its Asian assets and sell the core business. On Wednesday, Bloomberg reported that Starboard was taking initial steps toward a potential proxy fight. "*It seems pretty clear that the only reason this is happening even is because of the threat of the proxy fight*," Pivotal Research analyst Brian Wieser said.

Yahoo said the newly formed committee and its advisers are working on a process for reaching out to and engaging with potentially interested strategic and financial parties. Earlier this month, Yahoo dealt with interested parties individually, without running a formal auction process, according to people familiar with the matter. Yahoo announced this month it was considering strategic alternatives for its core Internet business, after shelving previous plans to spin off its stake in ecommerce giant Alibaba Group Holding Ltd. "Separating our Alibaba stake from Yahoo's operating business is essential to maximizing value for our shareholders," Mayer said on Friday.

Starboard was not immediately available for comment. "I think a proxy fight would be the right thing to do," said investor SpringOwl Asset Management's Managing Director Eric Jackson. Yahoo's board is concerned about the risk of losing a possible proxy contest, he said. The committee has engaged Goldman Sachs & Co Inc, J.P. Morgan and PJT Partners Inc as financial advisers, and Cravath, Swaine & Moore LLP as legal adviser. Verizon Communications Inc is among the companies seen as a potential buyer of Yahoo's core business.

On April 27, 2016, Yahoo announced the addition of four new directors to the board in a deal with Starboard Value LP to avert a proxy battle.[29]

A truce with its most vocal activist investor helps Yahoo clear the way for the auction of its core businesses, which is underway. Yahoo said Starboard Chief Executive Jeffrey Smith and three independent directors associated with him will join the board immediately. Yahoo's four new directors were on Starboard's slate that the hedge fund proposed last month to overthrow Yahoo's entire board. The two sides spoke frequently about ways to avoid putting the fate of the board in the hands of shareholders, according to people involved with the negotiations, but it was not until recently that a deal came into focus.

The public and vitriolic battle for control of Yahoo and its strategic direction took a tremendous toll on employees and the new CEO, Marissa Mayer, in a literal baptism by fire as the two activist firms called for her resignation, termination of 9,000 of the 12,000 jobs at the firm, replacement of the entire board of directors, and sale *Yahoo!* Japan. The deal that was finally struck ended some of these tensions, but now the board members were insiders. It is important to note that Starboard and SpringOwl owned only 0.75% of the outstanding shares!

The battle had been won, temporarily, but the war was just beginning.

> [Eric Jackson, managing director of SpringOwl Asset Management], said he believes his plan will unlock billions of dollars of value in Yahoo (YHOO), ultimately taking the stock price from $35 to $113, helped by Yahoo's stakes in Alibaba and Yahoo Japan. He's not alone in his pitchfork and torch routine. Activist shareholder Starboard Value, which holds a significantly larger stake in Yahoo, got the company to reverse its previous plan to sell off its lucrative Alibaba stake. And Canyon Capital Advisors sent a letter to Yahoo's board on Friday urging the board to find a buyer for Yahoo's core Internet business.

However, schadenfreude has consequences for the victims and the victors. One online site described the Verizon deal to purchase Yahoo as "poetic justice," but Eric Jackson's comments summed up a sentiment that describes how Marissa Mayer probably felt as well. "Subdued." Verizon had its own challenges with Yahoo.[30] It is not clear if Verizon's board asked these questions before spending $10 billion on two failed Internet companies, but market watchers were asking the right questions.

> Will Yahoo's billion monthly users and content such as sports and finance be enough to make Verizon a contender in a digital advertising cage fight with Google and Facebook? "If Verizon starts to build an alternative, will advertisers flock?"
>
> "Will the advertisers want and support an alternative to Facebook and Google?" asked Steve Beck, managing partner of competitive strategy firm cg42. "It's a tough road but it would not surprise me that advertisers would love for an alternative if nothing else but to … keep pricing in check." The $4.83 billion deal, announced Monday and to be finalized in the first quarter of 2017 pending shareholder and regulatory approval, puts Verizon solidly in the No. 3 position behind Google and Facebook among sellers of digital ads, Pivotal Research analyst Brian Wieser said in a note.

In the end, Verizon gave up on Yahoo five years after its purchase as well and sold the firm to Apollo Global Management in a deal worth half what Verizon paid for Yahoo and AOL.

DECODING THE FAILURE AT YAHOO AND BOARD GOVERNANCE

Yahoo is an interesting case study for many reasons. Its founders, Jerry Yang and David Filo, were brilliant young innovators who invited free spirits to join them in the creation of a new universe on a platform called the Internet that had no boundaries. They were literally "masters of a digital universe" of their own creation. Money was no object as it poured in from digital ads and online sales that I am sure seemed endless. Unfortunately, the founders did not understand the strange world of capital formation that is fluid and raises capital to achieve its best returns. The *masters of the universe in finance* possess a voracious appetite for risk and can sense weak and timid boards by sifting through financial statements and analyzing strategic plans. The speed at which activists move gives them an advantage; therefore, boards must be proactive in order to respond and defend the firm in a timely manner.

Given that it is hard to call Yahoo a complete failure. Yahoo fundamentally changed how the Internet is used in eCommerce. Yahoo planted seeds of innovation that are still germinating new ideas, products, services, and companies on the Internet. It is not uncommon for an early pioneer to stumble, but Yahoo still persists, as endless possibilities, when the right mix of strategy, leadership, and creativity is mustered for the "next new thing." Apollo Global Management may be able to bring in fresh blood to reimage Yahoo in the emerging meta-verse or a bridge between eCommerce and corporate infrastructure. Yahoo and its board did fail its employees. Employees were the biggest losers in the entire saga of the firm. It may be hard to imagine but the final story of Yahoo may not yet be written.

One of the lessons that Yahoo taught the world is how to free the intellectual energy and creativity of employees, by providing them the right tools and environment, and allowing them to create more than could ever be imagined by a strategic plan from board members alone. This lesson is not only ignored by most firms, but also intentionally managed out of existence. Hierarchical firms are designed to concentrate decision-making and strategic planning at the top of the firm. Yahoo proved that this approach is inherently risk averse and leads to stagnation, not innovation, especially now in a digital economy. Management's fear of losing control is a self-reinforcing phenomenon that provides the opportunity for outsiders to see what management cannot see in their myopic vision of self-protection.

The second lesson from Yahoo is they proved that today's technology provides organizations with the functional capability to reinvent themselves from the whole cloth. Yahoo created billions of dollars from digital zeros and ones! The progeny of Yahoo is Google, Facebook, Twitter, and more which have replicated the same formula of wealth creation out of nothing but digital code. Out of all the news articles and naysayers who focused on what Yahoo lost, none have recognized how Yahoo and its seed has created a formula for success for a new generation of companies that now dominate wealth creation – multi-trillion-dollar firms. The cost of doing business on the Internet compared to building a factory is miniscule. Yahoo's board did not create its wealth, its employees did.

The cognitive risk failures by the board, activist investors, and the markets were a singular assumption the value of Yahoo resided only in the Alibaba stock. Alibaba was a bonus. They all missed the point. The disruption created by activist investors on the board saw employees purely as an expense on the financial statements but missed the value employees created in revenue from new products. Yahoo needed guidance, not destruction to grow. Alibaba followed the same formula for success as Yahoo, Amazon, Google, and others have. Each has used technology to reduce or eliminate fractions in business by removing the middleman and closing the gap between the manufacturers of goods and customers in ways that reduce costs. They all missed the upside potential that Yahoo created. This lesson is still largely ignored for short-term gains by activist investors. Third Point left billions on the table when it left early. The short-sightedness of activist investors is that they can only see what is visible on the balance sheet and financial statements when the real value is how to leverage the talent that created the wealth in the first place.

Yahoo's failure is defined by someone else's expectation of what it could have been, but the firm was, if nothing else, a fountain of new ideas of the possibilities of an Internet company and we see its offspring has achieved the value short-sighted investors missed. If there is a failure, it certainly starts with the board of directors who failed to shield Jerry and David from the vulnerabilities inherent in not being schooled in the discipline of corporate America and Wall Street. The early investors and board members appear to have been naïve about what they owned and its future direction, but they had the resources to get help, talent, and direction from their institutional investors and other seasoned executives.

Clay Christensen is credited with coining the term "innovator's dilemma"; defined as when new technologies cause great firms to fail. Christensen documents "how disruptive innovation creates new and unexpected competitors that rise up and overtake markets." The innovator's dilemma comes from a paradox created by success. The decision-making process and the allocation of resources that led to success can be limiting factors when innovators fear losing what they have created and stop innovating. When companies create disruptive technology, boards become comfortable and narrowly focused on protecting what they have and miss new opportunities hiding in plain sight. Customers are one point of contact but often don't know what they want until they see it. Organizations cannot rely on the limited vision of customers while ensuring customer needs are exceeded. In Yahoo's case, there were no competitors from which to judge success or failure. Yahoo started as an endless stream of conscious innovation because of the freedom its founders provided coders who made money doing what they loved and experimenting with new ideas.

Yahoo's board needed to protect and defend the firm against activist investors who saw an undisciplined, cash-rich firm with no clue what they were up against. By the time the board realized they were in trouble, they had no defenses in place to counter the moves made by Third Point, LLC, Starboard, and SpringOwl. Legal remedies were available in poison pills, staggered boards, shark repellant, green mail, and more, but none of that happened.[31] Why didn't the board respond more aggressively? The answer may have been as simple as a lack of experience or a fear of admitting they needed help. The answer may be more complicated. But what is clear is the board lacked an understanding of fiduciary and prudent duty of care.

By the time Marissa Mayer joined Yahoo, the company's fate had been sealed and a blueprint had been provided by Third Point, LLC for the next corporate raider. The lessons learned demonstrate why strong boards are critical for protecting the firm from itself and the leaders of the organization. A third lesson is that boards need to give leadership space to execute by providing cover while the strategy is being tested in the marketplace. Activist investors are a real threat to the stability of a firm and must be dealt with firmly but more importantly with clarity of vision that is above reproach. How can this be done consistently?

To build a resilient board in this environment is to adopt an activist investor mindset as a first line of defense. Boards that are overly focused on compliance will become the next Yahoo failure story. Most firms are reluctant to invest or fail to do so properly in compliance and risk mitigation. Compliance is important, but boards must make a choice on reasonable investments in regulatory compliance that mitigate the risks of regulatory intervention. There are plenty of cost–benefit methods to reduce compliance to reasonable levels to create space for a concentrated focus on opportunistic strategic objectives.

Not mentioned in the case study was the discovery of a massive cyber breach that contributed to the devaluation value of Yahoo prior to being bought by Verizon. Yahoo's breach was the largest of its kind at that time. The breach was just another example of the dysfunction by the board and management caused by distraction fighting activist investors. If you will remember the activists publicly called for massive cuts in staffing and the CEO. Cyber threat actors understand that distracted firms and their employees are more vulnerable than firms that are vigilant and have well-developed defensives. If employees are surfing the web looking for jobs, they are more susceptible to click on an infected link from stealthy cyber criminals seeking ways around security. Yet another reason board governance behavior is critical to organizational sustainability.

If outside activist investors are able to propose strategic ideas in a corporate raid, there is no reason insiders on the board should not be able to do the same with the proper perspective. Automation is one of the most efficient ways to reduce the escalating costs of compliance. However, investments in automation must be made to enhance employee performance. More on how to make this mindset switch in the latter chapters.

Boards who adopt an activist investor mindset take risk-informed decisions on asset allocation to increase stock price. What this means in practical terms is investments to reduce costs, increase efficiencies in operations, and strategic partners who can help grow business. Secondarily, this means investments in upscaling skills in employees and the tools they need to create revenue and reduce friction between products, services, and customers.

In other words, the best defense is a risk-informed offensive strategy that does not rest on its laurels and anticipates incremental successes instead of *creative destruction.*[32] According to Schumpeter, the "gale of creative destruction" describes the "process of industrial mutation that continuously revolutionizes the economic structure from within, incessantly destroying the old one, incessantly creating a new one."

In Marxian economic theory, the concept refers more broadly to the linked processes of the accumulation and annihilation of wealth under capitalism. Karl Marx was a critic of capitalism. "Marx's critique of [a] political economy or critique of economy is a critique that questions the very object of the economy, and hence rejects the axioms, institutions and social categories, abstractions as well as the entire paradigm of what is usually referred to as 'the economy.'" Marx views the economy as a zero-sum gain where wealth simply changes hands such as in an activist campaign. The old *robber baron* or *Robin Hood* analogy. My view is a more optimistic one, and the Yahoo story partly confirms its possibility under the right stewardship.

What is the value in wealth destruction? I view Marx's observation as a critique of the forces of cognitive risks at play – as opposed to a prescription of wealth creation out of wealth destruction. I propose an alternative view of *wealth capture* contrary to creative destruction. Wealth capture is the investment of profits and access capital for sustainable growth. The methods to realize wealth capture will be presented in subsequent chapters as a new way of thinking of positive alternates to governance rather than the negative, risk-averse mindset that has dominated corporate governance and fueled debates in taxation and employee compensation. Wealth capture assumes that change and obsolescence are sunk costs that must be anticipated in preparation for reinvestment for growth.

In summary, human factors in organization performance are the source of success or failure. Decision-making, judgment, ideas, and innovation are human factors that a board can leverage to skill up people, processes, and performance within organizations. Hierarchical structures may work well as systems of controls, but boards and management must understand the opportunity costs of micromanagement, overly controlled and rigid structures that lead to failure. Lastly, a failure to ignore the latent potential and value of employees may be costly to organizational success. Trust is a very small price to achieve huge organizational success when combined with the right organizational behaviors that are self-reinforcing.

NOTES

1. R. Scaife (2016), Chapter 6 – Human factors in risk management, in: Janette Edmonds, ed., *Human Factors in the Chemical and Process Industries*, Elsevier, 73–91, ISBN 9780128038062. https://doi.org/10.1016/B978-0-12 -803806-2.00006-6.
2. http://www.knowledge.scot.nhs.uk/hfe/systems-thinking/seips.aspx.
3. https://www.weahsn.net/wp-content/uploads/Human-Factors-How-to -Guide-v1.2.pdf.
4. https://improvementacademy.org/our-expertise/effective-investigations.html.
5. https://www.imia.com/wp-content/uploads/2013/05/wgp-800-Human -Factors-in.pdf.
6. X. Xie and D. Guo (2018), Human factors risk assessment and management: Process safety in engineering, *Process Safety and Environmental Protection*, 113, 467–482, ISSN 0957-5820. https://doi.org/10.1016/j.psep.2017.11.018.
7. https://www.abs-group.com/What-We-Do/Safety-Risk-and-Compliance/ Safety-Management/Human-Factors-Engineering/.
8. https://www.aircraftsystemstech.com/2017/07/history-of-human-factors .html.
9. https://safestart.com/the-human-factors-framework/.
10. https://www.researchgate.net/publication/12418323_Culpable_Control_and _the_Psychology_of_Blame.
11. https://www.fastcompany.com/40544277/the-glory-that-was-yahoo.
12. https://money.cnn.com/2012/05/13/technology/yahoo-ceo-out/index.htm.
13. https://www.sfgate.com/news/article/Key-players-in-Yahoo-s-CEO-succes- sion-3555871.php.
14. https://latimesblogs.latimes.com/technology/2011/09/carol-bartz-calls -yahoo-board-doofuses-major-investor-calls-for-changes.html.
15. https://www.forbes.com/sites/roddwagner/2016/03/08/the-seven-lessons-of -marissa-mayers-loss-of-command-at-yahoo/?sh=5c6f2c3121dc.
16. https://www.nytimes.com/2016/02/23/business/dealbook/yahoos-decision -to-explore-a-sale-exposes-a-weak-board.html?_r=0.
17. https://www.ft.com/content/e81857c2-3162-11e6-bda0-04585c31b153.
18. https://www.marketwatch.com/story/sec-to-vote-on-rule-giving-activist -investors-more-power-in-board-elections-11637164892.
19. https://www.sec.gov/news/press-release/2021-235.
20. https://corpgov.law.harvard.edu/2021/11/19/sec-dramatically-changes-the -rules-for-proxy-contests/.
21. https://www.osler.com/en/resources/cross-border/2019/sec-issues-guidance -regarding-activities-of-proxy-advisory-firms.
22. https://www.sec.gov/Archives/edgar/data/1011006/000089914011000474/ a6970038b.htm.
23. https://www.hollywoodreporter.com/news/general-news/daniel-loebs-wild -yahoo-ride-590390/amp/.

24. https://www.firstpost.com/tech/news-analysis/yahoo-investor-dan-loeb-to
-leave-board-610-million-richer-2-3632333.html.
25. https://www.theverge.com/2013/7/22/4545072/yahoo-dan-loeb-leaving
-marissa-mayer-profit-flip-third-point.
26. https://www.breakingviews.com/considered-view/dan-loebs-yahoo-exit
-hurts-investors-twice-over/.
27. https://www.forbes.com/sites/ericjackson/2015/03/11/yahoo-management
-doesnt-deserve-the-benefit-of-the-doubt/?sh=70d5e3951783.
28. https://finance.yahoo.com/news/yahoo-board-forms-committee-explore
-strategic-alternatives-131355062--finance.html.
29. https://finance.yahoo.com/news/yahoo-adds-four-starboard-nominees-board
-131316546--sector.html.
30. https://www.mercurynews.com/2016/07/25/4-83-billion-yahoo-purchase
-gives-verizon-extended-reach/.
31. https://www.biryuklaw.com/hostile-takeover-defenses/.
32. https://en.wikipedia.org/wiki/Creative_destruction.

Chapter 5

How emotions mislead decision-makers

CHOICE THEORY

My first introduction to a national recession began in 1987 as a young financial advisor with a new defunct venture capital firm. After graduating from college with a short stint in graduate school, I watched as other graduates who had joined Wall Street firms were making money and living a life I envied. In order to get a license to sell securities, you must be sponsored by a brokerage firm and pass a series of exams to sell specific types of securities on a state-by-state basis. This was the time of the Wolf of Wall Street, Michael Milken of Drexel Burnham Lambert, The Junk Bond King, and the beginning of the Savings and Loan crisis.

Between 1980 and 1982, the US economy experienced a deep recession caused by disinflationary monetary policies by the Federal Reserve Bank. Ronald Reagan, as president, had just launched steep cuts in domestic spending leading to a revolt in the Republican Party.[1] Eventually, monetary policy was loosened through tax cuts and military spending to bolster a weak US economy. The economic recession was precipitated by the Iranian Revolution of 1979 which sparked oil prices to increase sharply sparking inflation.

The Federal Reserve Chairman, Paul Volker, used very tight monetary policy to dampen the inflationary flames which weakened the recovery in 1981 and 1982. Congress had deregulated the Savings and Loan industry and failed to provide sufficient oversight. Risk-taking by S&Ls and high inflation ultimately led to the Savings and Loan crisis in the early 1980s. Banks and Savings and Loan Associations began to fail at such high rates that the US government had to create two new federal agencies, the Federal Home Loan Bank Board and the Federal Savings and Loan Insurance Corporation. Ronald Reagan signed the Economic Recovery Act in 1981 which led to speculative real estate loans, investments in casinos, fast food franchises, ski resorts, and junk bonds.

However, by 1982 economic stimulus policies and military spending started an economic recovery that would accelerate into 1987. The 1987 financial crisis earned its name on October 19, Black Monday.[2] My career

DOI: 10.1201/9781003189657-5

in financial services had only recently started with fear and dread of financial ruin. People were in two camps, some investors who took my call expected the crash, which was dramatic and swift, to be short-lived and a buying opportunity. Others who had lost homes from over-speculation or lost a fortune from margin calls were more tragic with committing suicide. There were rumors of stockbrokers being attacked by their clients in their office. Needless to say, there was fear and panic on the street. The Dow Jones dropped almost 23% in one day, a loss that remains the single largest stock market decline in history, and the sharpest decline since the Great Depression at that time.[3]

What is remarkable looking back is the surprise and the behavior of market participants on Black Monday. Veterans on Wall Street panicked and were caught off guard by the speed of the decline and how events in one part of the world lead to losses globally. The financial markets were still paper based at that time. When I had a stock trade, I had to write a ticket and hand it to a clerk who entered the order into a back-office system to be executed on whatever exchange the security traded. When the market closed because of the crash, traders had no idea which trades were good or bad and it took weeks to sort through transactions. Stock certificates were still being printed and those certificates were transported by bike carriers to banks for processing, so the idea of interconnectedness was not digital like it is today. One wonders what systemic risks lie hidden in the digital maze of today's financial markets, banks, and businesses through the Internet of Things (IoT).

Not unlike modern-day systemic events, the 1987 crash started as a cascading event. Global stock markets were nervous the week prior to Black Monday. By Monday, markets in Asia began to fall hard. New Zealand's stock market dropped 60% and the race to sell grew rapidly. "There is so much psychological togetherness that seems to have worked both on the upside and on the downside," Andrew Grove, chief executive of technology company Intel Corp., said in an interview. "It's a little like a theater where someone yells 'Fire!'" (Glaberson 1987)[4]. "It felt really scary," said Thomas Thrall, a senior professional at the Federal Reserve Bank of Chicago, who was then a trader at the Chicago Mercantile Exchange. "People started to understand the interconnectedness of markets around the globe." For the first time, investors could watch on live television as a financial crisis spread market to market – in much the same way viruses move through human populations and computer networks.

"You learn how interrelated we all are and how small we are," said Donald Marron, chairman of Paine Webber, at the time a prominent investment firm. "Nowhere is that exemplified more than people staying up all night to watch the Japanese market to get a feeling for what might happen in the next session of the New York market" (Cowen 1987).[5] What events led to the sudden and dramatic crash?

The US stock markets had been on a speculative run after the 1980s recessing and recovery. By 1987, US looked more attractive relative to foreign markets prompting international investors to enter US stocks driving up prices even further. At the same time, US investment firms began selling complex financial arrangements, called "portfolio insurance," involving the use of leverage through the purchase of stock options and other derivatives that allowed investors to control more securities on margin or small investments. The fear of losing money and taking risk by taking out a home mortgage, buying on margin, and leveraging up returns was being done by novices and professionals alike.

Once it hit Wall Street in the US, it then swept east to Tokyo and then later to London. "There was a panic going on, everybody had to liquidate" (Steve Miller, market maker). "I saw two grown men crying, they had lost everything" (Al Sherbin, market maker). Millions tried to clear their portfolios and get cash from banks. It was a matter of minimizing losses, not making a profit. At the end of "Black Monday," over 500 billion dollars evaporated, and it all happened in a single day.[6]

Market regulators noticed structural flaws in the clearance and settlement of stocks, options, and futures markets, creating the potential for negative trading account balances, and possible forced liquidations.

At that time, the process of clearing and settling trades between investment house was mostly manual and took up to one week, not the three days today. The volume of trading and the speed of the decline overwhelmed investment houses who were unable to respond in a timely manner. The floor of the New York Stock Exchange has floor brokers and market makers all who move billions in paper stocks around by hand.

Market makers were particularly vulnerable because they are responsible for financing security trades to maintain an orderly market until the trades settle. The system was simply overloaded. In the days before October 19, the US stock markets dropped 30% on Wednesday, October 14. Traders and novice investors had to go with their guts about the sentiment of the markets and their risk exposures. There were also externalities in the economy that may have contributed to ratcheting fears. "This was also a busy time for mergers and acquisitions, which many blamed for job losses. Members of Congress in the powerful House Ways and Means Committee proposed legislation to make leveraged buyouts no longer tax deductible, which would likely have killed the deals," says Scott Nations, president of NationsShares and author of *A History of the United States in Five Crashes*.

The straw that may have broken the camel's back was that bond yields for 30-year US Treasury bond had just risen to 10%. Earlier that week, then-Treasury Secretary James Baker had remarked that the US should devalue the dollar to counter a record trade deficit, and Iran attacked a US-flagged oil tanker in the Persian Gulf. "We thought we were finally at war with Iran," Nations says. "So, if you are worried about the stock market because of what it had done the week before, and now you think we're also at war with Iran, what do you do? You sell."[7]

The largest global financial collapse on a percentage basis was triggered by emotions. The fear of a loss is greater than the possible additional gains in the markets. Investors who held on to their investments ended up recovering much of their losses and some made gains by the end of 1987. Financial booms and busts have repeated these cycles in the Dutch Tulip Bubble of 1637,[8] the start of the Great Depression in 1929 following the Black Thursday market crash, and more recently, the Great Recession of 2008.[9]

What have we learned by these repeated errors in judgment and excesses in speculative (risk-seeking) behavior? Are we now in a period of excessive risk-taking and speculative (risk-seeking) excess that may lead to an inevitable economic collapse? Today's stock expansion is the longest, broadest in history, and prior to each financial collapse, the sentiment is "this is different," we have learned how to handle risks. But have we? Each time has been different, but the reasons appear to rhyme with past historical economic peaks.

Speculative housing, easy financial terms, rising inflation, complex financial instruments, cryptocurrencies, NFTs (nonfungible tokens), and other digital financial currency with little to no regulatory or financial backstops. The risk of another financial calamity seems primed if given the right circumstances such as a Russian invasion in Ukraine and North Korean missile launches in the Pacific Ocean. The trigger is pulled, and emotions are running high! Markets have shown signs of weakness and cryptocurrencies have retreated by 50% from their high mark. We will know the answer in weeks or by the time of the publication of this book. The stock market is driven by "fear and greed" and is an excellent proxy for exploring how emotions lead us astray when assessing risks. The reasons have been well documented by Dan Kahneman, Amos Tversky, Dan Ariely, Nassim Nicholas Taleb, and many other researchers. Dan Ariely's book *Predictably Irrational* and Nassim Taleb's *The Black Swan* give us clues as to why we fail to learn the lessons that are as repetitive and predictable as the tide. As stated earlier, I call these risks, cognitive risks, the inability to recognize the errors in our own judgment.

What *are* these hidden forces that shape our decisions (Ariely 2009)[10,11] Marketers like to promote FOMO, the fear of missing out; however, in 1987 and in many other systemic, financial, and economic events, FOGO, the fear of getting out, is greater than FOMO. Financial analysts or "Quants" are students of risk and rational thinkers but become as emotional as a novice investor during severe financial collapse.

Economists formed a rational market theory (RMT) that has been assumed correct for 40 years or more and is still embedded in predictions of market performance. The RMT model posits that the markets are always right. Keep in mind, economists also believed in *homo economicus*, a portrayal of humans as agents who are consistently rational and narrowly self-interested, and who pursue their subjectively defined ends optimally. That theory has been debunked, but as we see, the remnants of rational choice theory still persist, even with empirical evidence to the contrary.

We all share one thing in common, an object of ignorance of the future. However, it is innately human to want to know the future and control it as best we can. Without uncertainty however there is no opportunity for outsized gains, still the only thing that is certain is uncertainty, and more than we know. Nassim Nicholas Taleb describes the problem succinctly, "Black Swan logic makes *what you don't know* far more relevant than what you do know (prologue xxiii)." Uncertainty (black swans) often occurs simply by not expecting the event to happen or ignoring the signs leading up to an event. In that sense, preparation, and planning for an eventuality, may prevent or mitigate the impact. The cognitive risk is assuming confidence in an outcome that is either overestimated or underestimated. (WYSIATI) *What you see is all there is* the fallacy of assuming black swans don't exist.

The inherent inability to distinguish between uncertainty and risk is compounded by *noise* in the environment. What is noise? In today's contemporary society we are bombarded by "expert" opinions, advertisements, news events, misinformation, and disinformation. Few people have the time or take the time to fact-check fake news from real news and simply choose to accept as fact what they agree with and ignore information that does not comport with what they do not believe. I could hear the moans as I wrote the last sentence. Most of the time common sense is sufficient or will suffice for everyday matters which is an unconscious and automatic response. If someone tells you the sun is shining, you can quickly decide if they are correct. However, when people were warned of a Category 5 hurricane named Katrina, many assumed they could ride it out because they had done so in previous storms.

These same conflicting emotions are not confined to the probable impacts of hurricane damage they also apply to business decisions. Senior executives can unwittingly lull themselves into a false sense of security because of a win streak in successful dealmaking then get wiped out by overconfidence underestimating novel risks. This phenomenon can be illustrated in risk management by the current practice of developing a risk tolerance level. One example is value-at-risk metrics.[12] Value-at-risk limits are bounds placed on risk-taking. For example, a bank may invest a certain amount of its capital to get higher returns. The firm will set a limit on the risks it decides to take on a given day which is the value a firm has decided can be put at risk of loss in an adverse risk event. The idea is that given a certain standard deviation of trading days, gains and losses, a range can be determined with some level of confidence. However, those bounds may be breached adversely when a trader's discipline is violated as was the case in JPMorgan's "Whale Trade."

LONDON "WHALE" TRADER

In 2012, JPMorgan lost $6.2 billion dollars on a trading strategy by a trader based in London who became known as the "London Whale" for his outsized trades.[13] JPMorgan netted more than $21 billion the same year but the loss slightly dented Jamie Dimon's suit of armor Dimon had earned by thriving through the 2008 Great Recession economic collapse as compared to other large banks. According to Bloomberg news,

> the bank (JPMorgan) admitted violating securities laws and agreed to pay fines of more than $1 billion, a U.S. Senate subcommittee wrote a scathing report and the bank's chief executive, Jamie Dimon, took a pay cut. The London Whale case drew a bigger reaction than other missteps by banks since the 2008 financial crisis, partly because of Dimon's previous rock-star status.

The loss also questioned the ability of banks to assess and manage risks as well as whether regulators failed to spot the risk early enough to prevent such a big loss. Bruno Iksil, the Chief Investment Officer (aka, the *Whale*), nor any senior executives were criminally charged; however, the head of risk management was fired (Figure 5.1).

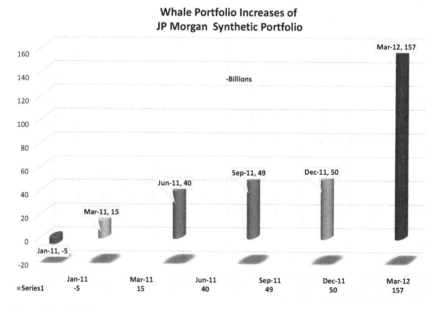

Figure 5.1   J.P. Morgan change in synthetic portfolio.

Morgan experienced its first quarterly loss on Dimon's watch, faced $7.2 billion in legal fees, paid a $150 million settlement in investor lawsuits, and a $100 million dollar fine from the Commodities Futures Trading Commission on what was supposed to be a routine hedging strategy against market and credit risk of a portfolio of safe investments.

As a result, the $6.2 billion trading loss resulted in almost $14 billion or more in expenses when considering lost time by executives, including Dimon's addressing the damage, severance pay, and expenses to prevent future errors. So, what happened?

Bruno Iksil was tasked with investing $350 billion of the bank's federally insured customer deposits. In safe, short-term investments. Traders use hedging strategies to protect their trades from loss by minimizing risk while attempting to make returns on customer deposits. Banks can make hundreds of millions on the difference between what they pay customers in interest on these deposits and what banks can earn trading on idle cash. All banks have internal controls that assist in guarding against losses such as value-at-risk limits, limits on the use of complex derivative securities (which are largely illiquid contractual agreements payable on a future date), as well as risk officer responsible for overseeing market and credit risk limits on sizable trades. In addition to these controls, the Federal Reserve requires bank examiners to monitor these trades and evaluate risks, in some cases, sitting on the trading desks of banks supervised by the Reserve. How did one of the premier banks and the Federal Reserve missed the growing risk brewing on the JPMorgan trading desk? Noise may be one of the reasons to be explained next.

It was reported at the time of the discovery of mounting losses that Jamie Dimon dismissed the losses as nothing more than "a tempest in a teapot," but as the tempest grew larger Dimon become more circumspect and acknowledged the errors, calling the trades "flawed, complex, poorly reviewed, poorly executed and poorly monitored." The Senate report, however, depicted not the work of a rogue trader but a broader systemic failure: Risk limits, for instance, were breached more than 300 times before the bank switched to a more lenient risk-evaluation formula – one that underestimated risk by half because of a spreadsheet error. The report by the Fed's inspector general also supported the view that deeper issues were involved here, as it showed failures in prioritization, loss of institutional knowledge through turnover, and poor coordination among agencies. To critics of Wall Street, the real lesson of the London Whale is that megabanks such as JPMorgan are not only too big to fail – they may also be too big to manage and too big to regulate.

Dimon's delayed response added to losses as hedge fund traders sensed vulnerability in JPMorgan's derivative strategy causing more pain until they decided to relent after making millions on the bank's trading errors. The case is a study in human behavior that is not accounted for in traditional risk programs. A copy of the US Senate, "Permanent Committee on Investigations," Committee on Homeland Security and Governmental Affairs report by Carl Levin, Chairman and John McCain, Ranking Minority Member made clear the accountability. The report, JPMorgan "Chase Whale Trades: A Case History of Derivatives Risk and Abuses" was published on March 15, 2013, in conjunction with an investigation of JPMorgan Chase bank.[14]

The opening statement of the report,

> JPMorgan Chase & Company is the largest financial holding company in the United States, with $2.4 trillion in assets. It is also the largest derivatives dealer in the world and the largest single participant in world credit derivatives markets. Its principal bank subsidiary, JPMorgan Chase Bank is the largest U.S. bank. JPMorgan Chase has consistently portrayed itself as an expert in risk management with a "fortress balance sheet" that ensures taxpayers have nothing to fear from its banking activities, including its extensive dealing in derivatives. But in early 2012, the bank's Chief Investment Office (CIO), which is charged with managing $350 billion in excess deposits, placed a massive bet on a complex set of synthetic credit derivatives that, in 2012, lost at least $6.2 billion.

The report sums up the human risk failures quite nicely,

> [the loss and lack of intervention] demonstrates how inadequate derivative valuation practices enabled traders to hide substantial losses for months at a time; lax hedging practices obscured whether derivatives were being used to offset risk or take risk; risk limit breaches were routinely disregarded; risk evaluation models were manipulated to downplay risk; inadequate regulatory oversight was too easily dodged or stonewalled; and derivative trading and financial results were misrepresented to investors, regulators, policymakers, and the taxpaying public who, when banks lose big, may be required to finance multi-billion-dollar bailouts.

In other words, the cover-up by many parties within the firm and failure by regulators to intervene contributed to the magnitude of the loss. It is customary for traders to "cut their losses" when a trade goes badly on a given day or over a period of time. However, a classic mistake in trading is to attempt to trade out of a loss which can lead to massive losses when the market recognizes the error and trades against the firm which is allegedly what happened to the Whale trade.

The only tools available to Congressional overseers are to expose the failures, suggest corrective regulatory actions to the problem, shame management, and impose penalties which in most cases are barely punitive given the balance sheets of large banks. But few of these actions have been effective at changing behavior over long periods of time.

The JPMorgan Chase whale trades provide another warning signal about the ongoing need to tighten oversight of banks' derivative trading activities, including through better valuation techniques, more effective hedging documentation, stronger enforcement of risk limits, more accurate risk models, and improved regulatory oversight. The derivatives overhaul required by the Dodd-Frank Wall Street Reform and Consumer Protection Act is intended to provide the regulatory tools needed to tackle those problems and reduce derivatives-related risk, including through the Merkley-Levin provisions that seek to implement the Volcker Rule's prohibition on high risk proprietary trading by federally insured banks, even if portrayed by banks as hedging activity designed to lower risk.

Incremental regulatory creep is not an effective tool as suggested by the aforementioned guidance. The failures are human failures, and the only way to address human failure is to penalize organizational behavior when wholesale systemic failure occurs. The board of directors is ultimately responsible for addressing organizational behavior, but when that fails and a "slap on the wrist" is the response what then can be done?

Barring the removal of the CEO and CFO, the penalties should not further damage shareholder value. Shareholders delegate responsibility of fiduciary oversight to the board and their removal is up to [them] for remediation. The regulatory response should target specific risk-taking behaviors, risk training of regulatory overseers, and investments in analytical tools funded by the firm that gives regulators insights into the risk behaviors at the firm. The threat of real-time regulatory oversight through technology might be sufficient to prevent future failures like JPMorgan, Wells Fargo, Bear Stearns, Long-Term Capital, Lehman Brothers, Freddie Mac, Fannie Mae, etc.

Innovations in financial engineering in complex securities trading have long since exceeded the capacity of regulation and regulatory bodies to keep pace or even fully grasp risk exposures to capital. This is why the remedy is to require firms that fail to manage complex risks should be required to make investments to facilitate better risk decision support tools for the firm's risk staff and regulatory bodies to correct the problems without creating even more bureaucracy by adding compliance and policies that fail at addressing the real problem, the inability monitor changes in risk real time. These investments will have a long-term effect on risk management in high-risk industries such as finance but also raise the bar for risk professionals dealing with synthesizing disparate risks across complex operations where exposures can grow quickly. Doing so before being required by regulation as opposed to in the middle of a crisis would allow firms to leverage the investments broadly.

A technology solution would serve a dual purpose: On the one hand, risk departments would be able to monitor and adjust risk exposures in real-time with limits; on the other hand, regulators will be able to monitor changes in risk exposure and convene management for corrective action but not intervene preemptively. While this may sound like micromanaging, too often changes in risk-taking behavior are buried in silos allowing senior officers to obscure risk until failure occurs. Back-office operations in many organizations are often the last place major capital expenditures are made to update transparency and efficiency. Spreadsheets, manual processing, and the speed of change in risk exposure can easily be missed or hidden while the markets move against a firm. Escalation procedures are often not followed because of the fear of taking a loss but should be exposed early through technology not dependent on the person responsible for the error.

It is actually not surprising that Jamie Dimon would have been left in the dark either because of a fear to deliver bad news to a demanding boss or the difficulty firms have in collecting the data to piece together complex risks in a timely manner. The worse kept secret in some of the best run firms is a lack of sufficient investment to understand operational risks in world-class back-office operations and true insight into the bowels of the firm. Like many demanding bosses, problems in the back office will not rise to the level of the CEO. Operational risks accumulate over time and the noise represented by errors becomes accepted as minor risks that are immaterial. Examples of the operational noise that contributed to the failure will become more obvious as the case unfolds. The failure to disclose risks and the inability to communicate risk issues without the fear of judgment is one of the biggest cognitive risk issues that never get uncovered. Why? Risk is the elephant in the room everyone wants to avoid. Discussions of risk are often framed in the negative; therefore, the opportunity to find value in risk is missed because of silence.

In part, the confusion is found in the comparisons made between audit findings and risks at the audit committee level. While risks are known and verifiable, auditors do not provide a quantified measure for the probability of risk occurrence or a distribution of possible outcomes. A lack of scientific rigor is missing in public and private accounting due to a lack of accounting standards which provide only reasonable assurance. Senior executives want and expect more rigor. A lack of statistical context is pervasive in enterprise risk including cybersecurity because auditors, both public and private, often lack risk analysis training to make predictions of risky outcomes. What never happens, at least until a failure occurs, is a deep dive into the residual risks that exist in all back offices. The audit noise is never fully understood because errors in manual processes are accepted as a cost of doing business.

The data to evaluate human error is available but seldom used by risk professionals or auditors to provide more context for risks. Noise in audits, and confusion in classifying an audit finding as a risk is part of the problem, but a lack of rigorous training in risk analysis is the core issue.

Professional risk analysts recognize the cognitive dissonance that is pervasive in corporate boardrooms. This phenomenon has been described as *risk as feelings* versus *risk as analysis*. This is part of the failure of not investing in automation or enhancements in back-office operations. Risks as feelings are typically emotional evaluations while risk as analysis are non-emotional based on stochastic data. Risks are also political which causes senior executives to perceive a loss of control over the narrative to the board. Risks are hidden due in part to a lack of quantitative analysis of decision-making that leads to risky events. The board of directors is the last to know or understand the scope of operational risks at large, complex firms due to the challenges in assessing these risks and the asymmetry in information flows between decision-makers in the C-suite and the board of directors. Regulatory oversight also complicates corporate governance when a firm has demonstrated a weakness in controls. The cure is rigorous analysis which helps provide the context for regulators and boards but is often buried or ignored when the data contradicts the narrative used by executives to explain risk. More on this topic later.

The investigation into the Whale trade was exhaustive. The following details the extensive effort it takes to clean up errors on Wall Street: On June 13, 2012, the US Senate Committee on Banking, Housing, and Urban Affairs held a hearing in which JPMorgan Chase's Chief Executive Officer Jamie Dimon testified and answered questions about the whale trades. On June 19, 2012, Mr. Dimon appeared at a second hearing before the US House Committee on Financial Services. In July 2012, the US Senate Permanent Subcommittee on Investigations initiated a bipartisan investigation into the trades. Over the course of the next nine months, the Subcommittee collected nearly 90,000 documents, reviewed, and in some cases transcribed, over 200 recorded telephone conversations and instant messaging exchanges, and conducted over 25 interviews with bank and regulatory agency personnel.

The Subcommittee also received over 25 briefings from the bank and its regulators, including the Office of the Comptroller of the Currency (OCC) and Federal Deposit Insurance Corporation (FDIC), and consulted with government and private sector experts in financial regulation, accounting practices, derivatives trading, and derivatives valuation. The materials reviewed by the Subcommittee included JPMorgan Chase filings with the Securities and Exchange Commission (SEC), documents provided to and by the OCC, JPMorgan Chase board and committee minutes, internal memoranda, correspondence, and emails, chronologies of trading positions, records of risk limit utilizations and breaches, audio recordings and instant messaging exchanges, legal pleadings, and media reports. In addition, JPMorgan Chase briefed the Subcommittee about the findings of an internal investigation conducted by a task force headed by Michael Cavanagh, a senior bank official who is a member of the firm's Executive and Operating Committees. That investigation released its results to the public in a report on January 16, 2013.

Bank representatives also read to the Subcommittee portions of notes taken during interviews conducted by the JPMorgan Chase Task Force of CIO personnel, including traders, who were based in London. In addition to bank materials, the Subcommittee reviewed documents prepared by or sent to or from banking and securities regulators, including bank examination reports, analyses, memoranda, correspondence, emails, OCC Supervisory Letters, and Cease and Desist Orders. Those materials included nonpublic OCC examination materials and reports on the whale trades and on the OCC's own oversight efforts. The Subcommittee also spoke with and received materials from firms that engaged in credit derivative trades with the CIO.[15]

THE FINDINGS OF THE WHALE TRADE LOSS

JPMorgan Chase's Chief Investment Officer used its Synthetic Credit Portfolio (SCP) to trade high-risk derivatives; hid hundreds of millions in losses on his trading books and records; disregarded multiple internal indicators of escalating risk limits; manipulated internal risk models; dodged OCC regulatory oversight; and misinformed investors, regulators, and the public about the nature of its risky derivatives trading. The Subcommittee's investigation also exposed broader, systemic problems relate to the valuation, risk analysis, disclosure, and oversight of synthetic credit derivatives held by US financial institutions.

A failure to raise red flags or escalate risks

Synthetic Credit Collateralized Debt Obligations (CDO) are contractual agreements in noncash assets to obtain exposure to a portfolio of fixed-income assets.[16] CDOs are structured as a package of debt instruments such as mortgages, credit cards, corporate bonds, auto loans, and lines of credit which are then sliced into tranches allowing investors to buy different levels of "risk" within a pool of debt repayments. CDOs are rated by credit rating agencies that assess the creditworthiness of debt instruments. Investors willing to take more risk can buy a tranche of the pool with higher interest payments and higher risk of default, or non-repayment of the loan. The economic collapse of 2008 and the Great Recession that followed placed some of the blame on highly leveraged investments in CDOs and other "toxic" derivative instruments.

The risk of investing in these securities is two-fold. The income stream from interest and principal is not guaranteed and depends on timely repayment by borrowers; secondarily investors are allowed to buy large amounts of these securities using margin, a small percentage of money, say 10%–15%, for example of the full value of the tranche. Even more risky bets can be taken by buying or shorting credit default swaps on CDOs depending on an investor's view of the risk of default. Insurance can also be purchased in the event of default. Needless to say, a combination of illiquidity, complexity, and leverage creates opportunities to credit "alpha," higher market returns than normal or massive losses.[17]

In an article in CFO magazine noted, "a Federal Reserve order found deficiencies in JPMorgan Chase's risk controls, loss modeling, and audit functions, two of the firm's former CFOs were hit with tough criticism by an internal probe Wednesday."

An internal task force report on last year's "London Whale" trading incident lays part of the blame for the risk-management breakdown on two of the financial institution's CFOs. The two were singled out for criticism despite the presence of a chief risk officer for the overall bank and a CRO in the flawed trading business. While JPMorgan's normally conservative CIO was dabbling in synthetic credit derivatives, the CFOs missed opportunities to "meaningfully challenge" a trading strategy that led to $6.2 billion in mark-to-market losses and shaved more than $20 billion off the bank's market value last year, the task force report found. The report, said JPMorgan's former top CFO, Douglas Braunstein, "bears responsibility" for weaknesses in financial controls related to the investment portfolio and could have asked more questions about changes in its value and its increasing exposure to adverse movements in the financial markets.

The other former finance chief criticized in the report was John Wilmot, who headed the CIO's finance function. Wilmot and his team failed to set up robust reporting controls, the report said, "including sufficient circulation of daily trading activity reports, [which] made early detection of problems less likely." While the task force noted that the "primary control failures were risk management failures," the finance organizations headed by Braunstein and Wilmot "could have done more." In the case of the CIO's finance team, the task force stated that in part it took "too narrow [a] view of [its] responsibilities," believing the issues related to the CIO's credit portfolio "were for the risk organization and not finance to flag or address."

Further, employees at all levels of the CIO failed to escalate the issue to senior management of the bank and the board of directors. Braunstein stepped down in October 2012 and is now a vice chairman of JPMorgan. Marianne Lake, the former CFO of the bank's consumer and community banking unit, replaced him. In the CIO unit, former CFO Wilmot, who had "dotted line" reporting to Braunstein, has resigned and is leaving the bank this year. He was replaced by Marie Nourie last May.

JPMorgan CEO Jamie Dimon had a role in the debacle also, the task force found. It said Dimon "could have better tested his reliance on what he was told" about the CIO unit's losses. The report "demonstrates that more should have been done regarding the risks, risk controls and personnel associated with CIO's activities, and Mr. Dimon bears some responsibility for that."[18]

Dimon moved quickly to distance himself from the losses and assign blame. As part of an internal investigation, bank executives were asked to draw up lists of risk managers and other executives who bear responsibility, a source said. JPMorgan attributed the losses in large part to a flaw in the way it tracked and limited risk-taking in the CIO, the source said. Instead of limiting risks for every individual trader as is standard on Wall Street, the bank assigned limits to groups of traders, allowing individuals to take outsized positions.

The design of risk oversight was flawed which allowed aggregation of risk exposures instead of clear insight into each trader's book of business. This is part of the "golden boy" fallacy that occurs with star performers. Even more troubling is the fallout after and the culture of blame.[19] Clearly, several of the "risk" failures should have been caught had more attention been applied to the mounting losses but the true failures were errors in judgment in the CFO office who looked the other way and complicit behaviors by those close to the trading desk who failed to break the silence of growing exposures on the Whales trading desk.

Ina Drew, who ran the Chief Investment Office and was deeply trusted by Dimon, has resigned, and a number of her lieutenants have had their trading terminals revoked, sources said. Dimon testified to Congress last month that "complacency" following years of success at the CIO led him and others to miss signals about the office's money-losing trades. "This synthetic credit portfolio did earn several billion dollars of income in the three or four years before it just lost some of it," Dimon told the Senate Banking Committee on June 13.[20] Dimon's disclosure of how "complacency" in success led him and others to dismiss risk signals that were growing is the cognitive risk of concern. Complacency and silence by subordinates doomed the firm to a spiraling loss that could have been resolved far sooner.

In addition to blaming Drew for the surprise loss, Dimon went on to criticize his chief financial officer, the bank's risk managers and others in the chain of command for failing to alert him to the risk that was accumulating. "I have a right to rely on them," he said.

What changed at JPMorgan Chase?

In 2005, JPMorgan Chase created a separate unit within its Chief Investment Office, which was charged with investing the bank's excess deposits, and named Ina Drew, the bank's CIO. In 2006, the CIO approved a proposal to trade in synthetic credit derivatives, a new trading activity. In 2008, the CIO renamed the credit activity the Synthetic Credit Portfolio.

By 2011 the risk profile of the SCP changed dramatically, from $4 billion to $50 billion, a more than ten-fold increase. Later in 2011, the SCP made a profit of $400 million on a $1 billion credit derivatives trading bet. Banks are required to maintain and reserve capital relative to risk weighted assets (RWA) exposed to market risks therefore because of a gain in early trading, JPMorgan Chase instructed SCP to reduce RWA in line with regulatory requirement. However, instead of reducing the amount of trading in RWA, the CIO launched a trading strategy that gave the appearance of reducing RWA by creating a hedging strategy to offset the trades to satisfy the "spirit" of the regulatory mandate rather than the letter of law leaving the firm exposed. The new trading strategy not only ignored the instructions to reduce RWA, but it also increased it substantially, along with the size of the portfolio and its risk posture as well by eliminating its "hedge" to protect the downside risk.

In the first quarter of 2012, the CIO increased the size of his trading book from $51 billion to $157 billion in a failed attempt to recover from a growing deficit in losses. By the end of March, more than different credit derivatives were traded increasing the risk of the trades by offsetting short- and long-term positions, some rated investment grade, and others non-investment grade. Losses in the portfolio began to grow as rapidly as the trading volume and size increased. By the end of the quarter, over $700 million in losses had accumulated. This type of trading behavior should have triggered concern by the Chief Investment Officer, Ina Drew, and it did, ordering the traders to stop trading immediately.

The size of the trades also drew the attention of the London media and the credit market as well. Normally, in liquid markets a trader would cover the losses by selling to end the bleeding, but trading in largely illiquid holdings makes that prospect harder given the attention and the size of the trades. No one firm could have offset that much debt and why would anyone step in to help? The SCP trading losses grew from $2 billion in June to $6.2 billion by the end of the year.

Market observers noted the root cause of the trading desk losses which aligned with the Subcommittee report:

> The business risks hedged were obscure, however. They were described as the risk of companies around the world going bankrupt. The SCP had, in reality, become a complex set of transactions that seemed not to hedge anything in particular. Risk mitigation had increasingly become secondary to trading for profit over a three-year period in which the SCP had grown tenfold in notional amount. The witnesses confirmed that, regardless of the initial intent, the SCP was a massive risk position designed to make (or lose) large sums of money.

This very fact was in fact a manipulative deception. The CIO was designed to invest excess deposits (*i.e.*, deposited funds that had not been loaned) in safe securities and to enter into hedges that would offset bank risks. This deflected the attention of regulators from the CIO who ascribed a low priority to red flags associated with the CIO that could have attracted inquiry. Based on appearances, there were other areas of the bank that were far more susceptible to dangerous losses.

By early 2012, the SCP had created two separate problems for the CIO. First, it simply started to yield losses rather than profits and the losses were large. Second, the internal risk management calculation of forward-looking risk meant that, under the soon-to-be implemented international Basel 2.5 rules, the SCP would force JPMC to set aside large amounts of capital to offset its risks. This was the result under Basel 2.5's risk weighted capital rules, or "RWA." Instead of winding down the SCP, the CIO and other parts of the bank set out to solve these two problems in extremely dubious ways.

The cumulative market gains or losses were determined by comparing current market prices of the SCP positions with their acquisition costs. This is referred to as "marking to market." Market prices are really the prices to buy and sell that are quoted on the markets. The spread between the two is the "bid/ask" spread. JPMC, and most financial institutions, had commonly used the midpoint between the bid and ask prices to mark their holdings to market.

In January, the CIO traders abandoned that practice and started using prices closer to bid or ask, the boundaries of the bid/ask spread. Uniformly, they picked prices at the border of the bid/ask to spread that lowered the measured losses in the SCP compared with marks based on the midpoint prices. The effect on the understatement of losses was not cumulative. For example, assume a position acquired a 7. If the current midpoint price is 5 and the manipulated price is 6 on day one, the mark would be the difference between 7 and 6 rather than 7 and the midpoint, or 5. The misstatement of cumulative loss is 1. On the next day, if the midpoint price is 4 and the manipulated price is 5, the cumulative loss would be measured at 2 rather than 3, still a cumulative misstatement of 1.

Of course, the cumulative loss would be misstated every day, but never more than the current difference between the midpoint and the highest price within the bid/ask spread. It was a manipulation that did not get substantially worse quantitatively each day but was persistent over a period of months.

As has become familiar in investigations of financial institutions, emails told the story. The CIO traders who applied the marks called them "idiotic" and openly discussed what they were doing. Later in the first quarter, senior bank management defended the marks internally as within GAAP accounting rules, which is of course beside the point. Senator Levin successfully forced the bank witnesses to agree that manipulating mark-to-market practices for the purpose of hiding losses in a portfolio is unacceptable, even if it were in accordance with GAAP, an assumption that he did not agree with.

In bilateral derivatives transactions, margin collateral is often posted based on marks that are to be agreed to by the two counterparties. That was the case with the SCP. The marks used by the CIO traders for SCP precipitated serious disputes with counterparties starting in March. The amounts disputed peaked in mid-April at $690 million. These disputes, which were a clear indication of problems with marks, came to the attention of senior bank officials and the regulators in April, after news accounts had revealed the issues associated with the SCP.

Notwithstanding losses as early as January 2012, the CIO doubled and tripled down on the SCP positions. The SCP grew to $157 billion in notional amount by the end of the first quarter, even though the CIS had told regulators in January that it intended to reduce its size over 2012. The traders were literally out of control. As the SCP got bigger and the indexed credit derivatives market was showing signs of stress, in large part because of CIS's buying spree, the forward-looking measurement of risk associated with SCP deteriorated badly. This set off alarms within JPMC, because risk limits were being exceeded and the RWA Basel 2.5 calculations were requiring more capital to be taken out of circulation.

The primary (but not exclusive) problem for CIO was two variations of Value at Risk, a statistical estimate of how much the bank might lose in SCP in one day of trading based on historic experience. One variation looked at "normal" market conditions and the other looked at "stressed" market conditions. Limits were exceeded for both (as well as for other, less critical metrics).

JPMC addressed the breaches of VaR limits by temporarily increasing the limits, an act that CEO Jamie Dimon approved. This was intended as a stopgap until the VaR mode could be changed. The CIO had been constructing a new VaR model that would lower calculated risk in the SCP. It had not yet been properly tested and there was no system in place to transmit data on new trades automatically. New trades would have to be manually recorded on a spreadsheet and then loaded each night, a cumbersome process fraught with the potential for human error.

Nonetheless, CIO put the new VaR model in place at the end of January. The apparent risk of the SCP dropped by 50% instantaneously, well below limits. Nothing had changed, but the flashing red lights were turned off. And the original risk limits were reinstated, not new more stringent limits appropriate to the new model's built-in lower risk calculations.

It would be reasonable to anticipate that CIO would cut its losses and reduce the SCP in an orderly fashion. But instead, the traders used the new risk headroom to lay on more trades, increasing the SCP notional amount to $157billion by the time the "phones down" order came from management at the end of the first quarter stopping all trading in the SCP. In the interim, the manual data inputs had, predictably, created a corrupted data set that added to the problems of the new model. The old VaR model was reinstated in May, after press reports had made the London Whale trades public and billions had been lost.[21]

COGNITIVE MAP OF THE JPMORGAN CHASE WHALE TRADE

The psychology of this error is simply because it happens over and over again in large financial services firms with traders whose career is made or broken by the profits they contribute to the firm. Bonuses are a large part of compensation packages and performance is measured in profits, and lesser so how risks are managed, per se.[22] Risk-taking is part of a culture that evolves as market dynamics evolve from investment banking and deal-making to trading and back. The following analysis was written in by Andre Spicer, Professor of Organizational Behaviour, Cass Business School, City, University of London for *The Conversation*, an online journal describing the behavioral challenges found in JPMorgan's Whale saga.[23]

> The first thing that struck me about this case is just how complicated the day jobs of the people involved were. They traded in credit default swaps. These are like an insurance policy on an underlying credit risk. Sounds complicated right? Well imagine trying to manage a huge institution full of people doing equally complicated activities.
>
> Oversight is going to be difficult when the task to oversee is so baroque. This creates significant space for traders to hide mistakes and operate off the regulatory and even managerial radar. Research on knowledge workers – those who, like traders, "think for a living" – suggests that the technical complexity of their tasks often creates ambiguity: the right and wrong answers are unclear and difficult to understand. These workers can take advantage of ambiguity to buffer themselves from the prying eyes of would be managers and regulators. This can be good, as it creates autonomy and intellectually challenging work for the professional. But it can be bad insofar as there is a lack of monitoring which can stop potentially disastrous mistakes being made. Such conditions of complexity create the perfect conditions for rogue trading to flourish.
>
> It's a long way down from the heights of JPMorgan.
>
> The next big insight to be found in this document is the fact that it was not just one individual engaged in the London Whale trade, but a

group of people. The losses were quickly identified and there are several emails in which Iskill tells his superiors that the losses are escalating, and he could no longer hide them. But because these things are complex and based on risk, there was hope the loss was recoverable – they just had to wait, and the market would change.

According to the court documents, the more senior manager (Martin-Artajo) noted that he was under pressure from New York (the headquarters) to deliver good results. The more junior (Groute) recognised he certainly had some wriggle room in how he kept track of the results every day (the difference between bid and ask price on which the contracts were valued), and he used it to avoid having to report the losses. By doing this, both of the managers were able to look good to HQ, thereby preserving their own prospects and the prospects of their department.

If the prosecution's version of events is true, why did the group not come clean when it was clear how much money they had lost? Research suggests that as soon as we commit to one minor misdemeanour, we are far more likely to commit to a larger related one. So, for instance, if I say to my colleague I will go for a beer with them during work hours, then I am more likely to go on to drink many more beers (even though I know it is probably a bad idea). This is what we call escalating commitment. In the London Whale case, we see a perfect case of "escalating deception", when small deceptions lead to ever-larger ones.

The final big insight from this report is there was little independent checking. The legal document notes that only one person was charged with independently checking the risk of decisions made by traders in this part of the organisation. And given the lack of capacity, this person did not tend to make independent judgements. Instead, they relied on the expert of advice of the traders. The result is that the very people who were supposedly being monitored were providing expert advice to the person who was supposed to be checking on them.

LESSONS FOR INDUSTRY

Recent examples of traders making huge losses not only offer some important lessons about what can go wrong, but also what financial institutions may need to fix in the future.

First, it is quite clear that the complexity of the products many traders are dealing with created room for highly specialised experts to exploit the widespread ignorance about what they were up to. Dealing with this might mean cutting back on complex products. Where this is not possible, it might mean trying to contain complexity so failures cannot happen on such a grand scale.

Second, organisations must get over the bias towards reporting good news. To do this, financial institutions need to allow and indeed positively encourage employees to give bad news when they see it. The kind of no-fault reporting of safety issues found in the petro-chemical industry is an example of this. What this means is that if you are an employee and see a problem on an oil-rig and you report it, you will not be held at fault. This often liberates the identification of minor problems and an ethos of continued improvement.

Third, it's clear rogue trading builds up over time. To stop this, circuit breakers and clear decision points are useful. These force people to periodically stand back and reflect on whether they are making wise choices. An example here is the treadmill which forces a runner to slow down every 30 minutes, thereby potentially saving them from an injury. It is also important to offer people easy ways out when they realise they have got themselves in too deep.

It's also interesting that Iksil was not charged with wrongdoing. A case was brought against two of his managers (Javier Martin-Artajo and Julien Grout) but later dropped suddenly with little to no explanation.[24] The two were charged with conspiring to falsify books and records of JPMorgan, to commit wire fraud, to make false filings with the Securities and Exchange Commission and to commit securities fraud. Martin-Artajo and Grout live outside of the U.S. and have refused to appear in court, according to court documents, and efforts to secure their appearance, including through extradition, have "been unsuccessful or deemed futile."[25]

Finally, we saw that rogue trading is often missed because there is a lack of independence in oversight. To address this, it is vital that financial institutions build in better risk management roles that can take genuinely independent views. This has certainly already begun to happen in most large institutions. The really big challenge is to make these internal critics into a daily part of the trading floor who are not treated as impediment to doing business. Doing this involves bringing together a risk loving culture of the traders with a more risk averse culture of the compliance team. It may sound impossible, but it is a daily reality in many other sectors like resource exploration, the military, and emergency services.

Jamie Dimon explained it more simply, "we got complacent given our success." I agree with Dimon's observation and don't believe it needs to be overly analyzed. Complacency creates blindness to risks.

Were risks missed because of the $400 million gain? Why weren't losing trades stopped earlier? Value at risk (VaR) are daily risk limits not weekly or monthly. Traders know each day how a trade or trades did by the end of the day or the next at the latest. Fear may be the reason. When mistakes happen, the hardest thing for some senior executives to do is to admit their own faults. Jamie Dimon immediately looked for someone else to blame instead of taking responsibility. Professional coaches are fired when their teams don't perform as expected but this aspect of emulating sports analogies is seldom copied in corporate settings. Second guessing is not the purpose of this case study. The questions that are posed are lessons that can help identify these cognitive risks before they lead to self-imposed black swan events.

Teams take on the personality of the leader, coach, mentor, etc., and are inspired by leaders or feared depending on the emotional reaction to errors big and small. More importantly, instead of a generic statement about culture, the demeanor and tone of the leader defines success or failure. Bosses who make examples out of people tend to hide mistakes or blame others to avoid being blamed. It is also telling that Dimon fired Ina Drew but promoted CFO Douglas Braunstein to vice chairman of JPMorgan Chase who was as responsible as Ms. Drew. In situations like that, the actions and behaviors of who gets blamed and who gets protected signs signals to the rank and file.

I am not suggesting that there were no reasons for the difference treatment. Any decision can be justified by the decider in chief, but the optics of those decisions play a bigger role in reinforcing stereotypes and behavior more so than annual compliance statements of ethical behavior. Risks are part emotions and part analytics. Few can be 100% rational although when it comes to errors in judgment organizations often respond as if 100% rationality is the unspoken standard. Human resource officers easily use a mistake to justify termination or damage a person's career. The emotional tempo of an organization is lost in the heat of a massive failure like the one experienced by JPMorgan Chase.

Is it not fair to ask why Jamie Dimon approved the change in RWA and value-at-risk limits? Why Ina Drew waited so long to stop the bleeding on the trading desk? Ina Drew created the function from scratch. What were the emotional drivers that compelled Iksil, the Whale, to change his behavior so drastically or was his risk-taking exactly the kind of trading Dimon and Drew wanted to grow the business?

I don't know the answers, and I believe Jamie Dimon and Ina Drew may not fully understand why either – that is the nature of cognitive risk. Each of us share the same blindness in risk. It is not possible to fully avoid cognitive risk, but it is possible to develop a discipline to mitigate errors in judgment: decision hygiene.

BEFORE YOU MAKE THAT BIG DECISION – A TEMPLATE FOR DECISION HYGIENE

The concept of decision hygiene was introduced by Dan Kahneman, Dan Lavallo, and Olivier Sibony to avoid bias in strategic decision-making ("Before You Make That Big Decision," *Harvard Business Review* June

2011). Dan Kahneman and Amos Tversky (posthumous awards are not permitted) brought the idea of heuristics and bias to popular culture after winning a Nobel Prize for combining psychology and economics.

It is now common to read and hear commentary about the ills of bias in decision-making yet awareness of errors in judgment has not improved decision-making in business or at the individual level. This article acknowledges that talk alone will not eliminate the impact of bias. This is, to my knowledge, one of the first times someone has provided examples to identify and mitigate this risk. More recently, Kahneman, Cass R. Sunstein, and Olivier Sibony followed up on the idea in a new book, *Noise*.

The premise of noise and the concepts in the article are presented to make decision-makers aware of the costs of noise and bias. Computer scientists have recognized the same errors in their algorithms in machine learning and the effects on predictive outcomes. Interestingly, there is an equation that sums up this problem succinctly: Error = Bias + Variance + Noise. Both Average Error (Bias) and Variability of Error (Noise) lead decision-makers astray.

The idea is that in order to improve the accuracy of decision-making and reduce negative outcomes, you must make efforts to reduce both noise and bias in decision-making whether you are a smart machine or a human. Counterintuitively, both of these errors are hidden from sight or ignored by a failure to re-examine our decisions objectively. The implications of effectively applying decision hygiene are enormous in terms of correcting societal harm and recapture of savings for all organizations interested in sustainable practices with minimal effort. In the design of models of events and outcomes, the use of back-testing is one form of outcomes analysis that involves the comparison of actual outcomes with model forecasts during a sample time period not used in model development at a frequency that matches the model's forecast horizon or performance window.

If computer programmers and designers of algorithmic models see value in establishing discipline in their processes, why shouldn't senior executives and the board do the same? All organizations possess a treasure trove of data that represents decisions or the lack of decisions that produce outcomes that can be evaluated. Historical decision data is a road paved with limitless possibilities for future innovations and examples for identifying organizational fragility and robustness. Robust yet Fragile is an engineering concept developed to model design risk on the Internet.[26]

Organizations are complex networks; a corollary of complex networks is the Internet.

> The search for unifying properties of complex networks is popular, challenging, and important. For modeling approaches that focus on robustness and fragility as unifying concepts, the Internet is an especially attractive case study, mainly because its applications are ubiquitous and pervasive, and widely available expositions exist at every level

of detail. Nevertheless, alternative approaches to modeling the Internet often make extremely different assumptions and derive opposite conclusions about fundamental properties of one and the same system. Fortunately, a detailed understanding of Internet technology combined with a unique ability to measure the network means that these differences can be understood thoroughly and resolved unambiguously.

"A popular case study for complex networks has been the Internet, with a central issue being the extent to which its design and evolution have made it 'Robust Yet Fragile' (RYF), that is, unaffected by random component failures but vulnerable to targeted attacks on its key components. One line of research portrays the Internet as 'scale-free' (SF) with a 'hub-like' core structure that makes the network simultaneously robust to random losses of nodes yet fragile to targeted attacks on the highly connected nodes or 'hubs'.[27,28,29] The resulting error tolerance with attack vulnerability has been proposed as a previously overlooked 'Achilles' heel' of the Internet. The appeal of such a surprising discovery is understandable, because SF methods are quite general and do not depend on any details of Internet technology, economics, or engineering."[30,31]

Organizations are also *robust* through their network of people, systems, customers, and third-party vendors but *fragile* to targeted errors or specific areas of operation. Organizations that have learned to model where they are robust and understand areas of operational fragility will become more sustainable by making strategic investments to build greater robustness and reduce fragility in risk practice and operational efficiency. Just as the researchers noted, the previously overlooked *error tolerance* is the "Achilles' heel" in business as well.

Complex systems risks are prone to hidden error tolerance because of noise in the network. Organizations are seldom aware of error tolerance in their own shop; therefore, most do not conduct risk assessments to evaluate its impact. Decision hygiene is a process of discovery for unrecognized *error tolerance* that leaves an organization fragile to attack by competitors, corporate raiders, or self-inflicted errors of judgment.

According to the report,
a recent McKinsey study of more than 1,000 major business investments showed that when organizations worked at reducing the effect of bias in their decision-making processes, they achieved returns up to seven percentage points higher. ("The Case for Behavioral Strategy," McKinsey Quarterly, March 2010)[32] Reducing bias makes a difference.

Several simple examples of decision hygiene will be presented to demonstrate how easily different methods can be used to uncover bias and enhance decision-making in your strategic plans.

A few caveats before we get started. Decision-makers cannot avoid their own biases however they can learn to identify bias in their own thinking and the actions of their direct reports. It is difficult to avoid bias in ourselves and easier to see it in others. "According to cognitive scientists, there are two modes of thinking, intuitive and reflective (Thaler, Sunstein *Nudge*)." Intuitive thinking deals with emotional responses and happens quickly creating a sense of effortless flow. People often describe the sensation as "being in the flow" in sports or work where accomplishments seem natural without much thought. In contrast, reflective thinking is deliberate requiring us to slow down to learn a new skill and it takes time for the newly acquired skill to become intuitive. These two modes of thinking are constantly active as we go through our day, and we shift from one to the other without noticing.

Intuitive thinkers rely on context and framing to illicit the right memories to form a coherent interpretation of the subject being discussed. That is why story-telling is so compelling to many people when describing an event or a problem that needs to be addressed. The narrative an intuitive thinker forms from the context, emotions, and associations they piece together from the story helps to focus attention on the topic and suppresses alternative stories. The contextual stories we create in our minds are so compelling we can become susceptible to misleading disinformation or misinformation because we *want* to believe them. "An insidious feature of cognitive failure is that we have no way of knowing that it's happening. We almost never catch ourselves in the act of making intuitive errors. Experience doesn't help us recognize them."

Often when confronted with business decisions or recommendations say in the annual budget cycle, the opportunity to practice decision hygiene is presented in the following example. Crude measures such as padding forecasts are imprecise approaches for evaluating the merits of a recommendation for strategic planning. Executive planning will focus on the content presented in the presentations and not the process taken by participants to form the recommendation. The purpose of examining the "process" instead of the "content" is to evaluate the factors that influenced the decision-making process. Decision-makers must ask themselves a set of qualifying questions before asking questions of the team or the respective head of the team.

The first question is, what motivations are implied by the process? Does the proposal benefit the team or the company? Second question is, how well researched are the *risks* and the *benefits*? What weights were applied to each side of the scale and how did the team reach their decision on risks versus benefits? Third question is, was the decision unanimous or were there any disagreements about a course of action proposed or were concerns not fully vetted? Overly optimistic agreement may imply the process was not rigorous enough. Fourth question, is the recommendation based solely on what competitors are doing? Is there a thorough understanding of the full scope of resources needed to achieve the expected results? Fifth question, what data is relied on to help reach their conclusions and does the team have insight into the assumptions in the data used for reaching a conclusion? And finally, how many viable alternatives were presented and how did the team narrow the alternatives to decide on one of more final options? Ideally, these questions can become decision gates for the team to address proactively as they go through their process for choosing the best proposal.

The questions are designed to encourage the team to reveal any latent bias upfront and deal with them without consciously being aware of decision hygiene. Different versions of these questions can be supplemented in a template and the team can be challenged to come up with their own qualifying questions. A final way to test the process is to propose that one-quarter to one-third of the resources may be taken away. Is it still possible to achieve similar outcomes if that eventuality came about? What changes would be needed to achieve success in that scenario?

Our inability to sense when or how we make cognitive mistakes is a key reason we trust our intuition without second guessing. It is challenging to fix these errors when we do not believe there is a problem. This phenomenon has been consistently demonstrated by researchers' inability to make progress helping others address bias in the workplace or to encourage change to counter the impacts of bias in society broadly. This is why knowing, or being told by someone you have a bias, is not enough to encourage change. Suggestions of bias may be taken as a personal insult and cause a decision-maker to become resistant to change.

No one likes being called biased, whether it's true or not. So how is it possible to use this knowledge to make progress toward a less biased organization and improve decision-making? The definition of bias actually has multiple meanings: (a) "an attitude that always favors one way of feeling or acting especially without considering any other possibilities," (b) "bias (prejudice) against someone who is different or preferential bias in favor of someone or an idea," (c) "a statistical sampling or testing error caused by systematically favoring some outcomes over others." There are many examples of diverse bias but the version that I am referring to is the third version of bias in *statistical sampling or testing error* in judgments. Researchers have demonstrated that both bias and noise are pervasive in all organizations where subjective decision-making is relied on. Studies and statistical sampling have shown that bias and noise lead to less optimal outcomes but the persistent behaviors that create bias (average error) and noise (variability of error) are largely hidden because we are not aware we make these cognitive mistakes. So how do we correct these mistakes if we are not aware these errors exist? We will discuss two simple approaches: *constructive dissent* and *decision audits*. But this can't be done alone!

CONSTRUCTIVE DISSENT

A team approach is needed. Organizations that form agreement to reduce bias and work on methods that mitigate bias in decision-making can make remarkable progress. Given that we are unable to see our own biases, we need the help of others. One method that has been used for many years in business and in diplomatic circles is the concept of "constructive dissent." Traditionally, being a good team member means you *don't rock the boat.* Loyalty and consensus are values most executives agree with. It takes courage to push against the tide when you go it alone. Nonetheless, groupthink can lead organizations astray if constructive dissent is not a part of the critical thinking process. "All the first-rate decision-makers I've observed had a very simple rule," says Peter Drucker: "If you have quick consensus on an important matter, don't make the decision. Acclamation means nobody has done the homework."[33]

How does constructive dissent work? In a blog on the Harvard Law School website a discussion on the "right kind of conflict and constructive dissent is instructive." In the 1970s, psychologist Irving Janis used the term "groupthink" to describe the common tendency for group members to withhold their true views for fear of being excluded or antagonizing others. In real-life conflict scenarios, groupthink can lead negotiating teams and other groups to overlook critical information and ignore looming crises.

The best leaders avoid groupthink by surrounding themselves with people with diverse views, styles, and perspectives, Lesley University president and conflict management expert Jeff Weiss told NPR's *Marketplace*. This diversity of opinion helps leaders view a problem from all angles, a benefit that Trump appears to appreciate.

The key to effective group decision-making is *constructive dissent* – disagreements that respectfully and productively challenge others' viewpoints, according to Harvard Business School professor Francesca Gino. We often wrap up negotiations too quickly and leave value on the table because we fear to disagree with others, she says. By contrast, when we feel free to disagree with others, we foster a more rigorous decision-making or negotiation process.

At the same time, diversity of opinion can foster unconstructive and damaging real-life conflict scenarios. In their research, University of Virginia professor Kristin Behfar and her colleagues found that when negotiating teams disagree on substantive issues, such as interests, priorities, and goals, the conflict management process can lead them to better outcomes than if they hadn't disagreed. But if the conflict becomes personal, the team is likely to be far less productive.

PROMOTING CONSTRUCTIVE CONFLICT

How can we engage in constructive dissent in group meetings and negotiations without being sabotaged by destructive conflict? Research and real-life conflict management examples suggest these three guidelines:

1. **Negotiate differences behind the scenes.** When negotiating with another team, your team needs to present a unified front. Conflict may be useful behind the scenes, but at the table it can be a sign of

weakness and disarray. For this reason, spend at least twice as much time preparing for an upcoming negotiation as you expect to spend at the table, advises Cornell University professor Elizabeth Mannix. Begin by debating the issues to be discussed and developing priorities. Aim to achieve consensus on the team's goals and the strategies you will use to achieve them.

2. **Assign a devil's advocate.** At Chicago-based money-management firm Ariel Investments, leaders actively promote dissent in meetings by assigning "devil's advocates" to poke holes in the decision-making process, writes Gino in her book *Rebel Talent: Why It Pays to Break the Rules at Work and in Life* (Dey Street Books 2018)[34]. Ariel's president, Mellody Hobson, kicks off team meetings by reminding those present that they don't have to be right; they just need to be prepared to disagree in order to help the team make wise decisions.

3. **Prepare for conflict.** Although team members may try to express their differences professionally and respectfully, there may be times when disagreements become personal and unproductive. In real-life examples of workplace conflict, leaders can encourage team members to reveal the hidden interests and concerns behind their accusations and demands through active listening. As they navigate real-life conflict scenarios, team members may come to view their differing preferences as opportunities for value-creating tradeoffs.

CONFLICT RESOLUTION SHOULD BE FORMALLY ORGANIZED TO MAKE CLEAR HOW TO DO IT WELL: GROUND RULES

1. **Conflict resolution strategy #1: Recognize that all of us have biased fairness[35] perceptions.** Both parties to a conflict typically think they're right (and the other side is wrong) because they quite literally can't get out of our own heads.

2. **Conflict resolution strategy #2: Avoid escalating tensions with threats and provocative moves.** When we feel we're being ignored or steam-rolled, we often try to capture the other party's attention by making a threat, such as saying we'll take a dispute to court or try to ruin the other party's business reputation.

3. **Conflict resolution strategy #3: Overcome an "us versus them" mentality.** Group connections build loyalty and strong relationships, but they can also promote suspicion and hostility toward members of out-groups.

4. **Conflict resolution strategy #4: Look beneath the surface to identify deeper issues.** Our deepest disputes often seem to involve money: labor disputes over employee wages, family conflicts over assets, for example. Because money is a finite resource, these conflicts tend to be single-issue battles in which one party's gain will inevitably be the other party's loss.

5. **Conflict resolution strategy #5: Separate sacred from pseudo-sacred issues.** Conflict management can be particularly intractable when core values that negotiators believe are sacred, or nonnegotiable, are involved, such as their family bonds, religious beliefs, political views, or personal moral code. Take the case of two siblings who disagree about whether to sell their deceased parents' farm, with one of them insisting the land must remain in the family and the other arguing that the parents would want them to sell it.

The second approach is even more powerful in uncovering hidden errors in judgment with huge potential for cost benefits to change organizational behavior as well as to help understand how risks are perceived.

DECISION AUDITS

You can't fully appreciate decision audits until you understand noise, variance, and bias. The fundamental flaws in human judgment. Coincidentally, these two errors are systemically reduced in machine learning algorithms to improve the accuracy of prediction models (judgment).[36] A prediction error in a machine learning model is the difference between *ground* truth and the learned model traditionally composed of three parts:

$$Error = Variance + Bias + Noise$$

Here, variance measures the fluctuation of learned functions given different datasets, bias measures the difference between the ground truth and the best possible function within our modeling space, and noise refers to the irreducible error due to non-deterministic outputs of the ground truth function itself.[37] Artificial intelligence (AI) is smart but has flaws. AI consists of a combination of algorithms and data; bias can exist in both of these elements. Computer scientists and programmers who produce training data constantly seek to mitigate biases that influence their machine learning systems.

There are four different types of bias that data scientists and AI developers seek to avoid and balance with variance for optimum predictive models: (a) *algorithmic bias*; (b) *sample bias*; (c) *prejudicial bias*; and (d) *measurement bias*. Data scientists are trained to determine an optimum balance in bias and variance to enhance predictive confidence. The key to successfully mitigating bias is to understand how and why it occurs. The human element is a key factor in every aspect of machine learning (ML) and AI, from data gathering and annotation to writing algorithmic code, which means AI systems *always* contain a degree of *human error*. Ignoring this basic reality puts your organization at risk of significant exposure.[38]

Decision-makers are not fed highly curated "training data" nonetheless decisions are made every day without weighing the impacts of bias and noise in the information received. Now that we know that bias and noise is not consciously recognized in judgments, we can assume there is more bias and noise than we think because there is seldom a formal process to reduce it in decision-making in modern organizations. This is a core violation in building confidence in predictive modeling and illustrates how organizations are systemically led off track in strategic planning.

Decision audits are designed to recognize the amount of bias and noise that exists in decision-making and provide a simple approach to assess the costs of these hidden flaws in judgment. How does a decision audit detect noise and bias in decision-making and why does it matter? Two examples will be provided that demonstrate both noise and bias in subjective decision-making. The first example is one that will be familiar given the attention in politics that now dominates the national discussion. Noise in criminal sentencing is not a new concern. Civil and voting rights activists have been active proponents of fairness and justice in the judicial system. However, reform came from within the judicial system in the 1970s from a judge, Marvin Frankel, who conducted empirical evidence of how noisy criminal sentencing had become among sitting judges (Kahneman, Sibony, Sunstein, ppgs. 14–22, *Noise*).

Judge Frankel was a passionate human rights advocate and founder of the Lawyers' Committee for Human Rights. Frankel's writing hinted at the noise in criminal sentencing,

> If as federal bank robbery defendant was convicted, he or she could receive a maximum of 25 years. That meant anything from 0 to 25 years. And where the number was set, I soon realized, depended less on the case or the individual defendant than on the individual judge, i.e., on the views, predilections, and biases of the judge. So, the same defendant in the same case could get widely different sentences depending on which judge got the case.

This still holds true today, and possibly more so, given the political divide in the country.

The examples used by Frankel were simple decision audits that exposed both noise and bias in criminal sentences which were compelling enough to eventually convince Congress to criminal sentencing guidelines. Here is one example used by Judge Frankel to demonstrate noise:

> Two men, neither of whom had a criminal record, were convicted for cashing counterfeit checks in the amounts of $58.40 and $35.20, respectively. The first man was sentenced to 15 years, the second to 30 days! For embezzlement actions that were similar to one another, one

man was sentenced to 117 days in prison, while another was sentenced to 20 years! These case samples were not isolated examples, there were numerous cases of this kind.

In 1981, a study was conducted involving 208 federal judges using 16 hypothetical cases with summaries of information used by judges in actual sentencing, involving criterial such as the charges in a crime, the testimony, previous criminal record, social background, and evidence related to the character of the defendant. The findings resulted in *substantial disparity* sentencing among judges. If conducted today, there is little reason to believe the same results would be much different. System noise, the unwanted variability in judgments that should be the same, creates rampant injustice, high economic costs, and errors of many kinds. More contemporary versions of these errors have been uncovered by the National Institute of Justice (NIJ) using DNA and forensic science to overturn wrongful convictions.[39]

According to the Innocence Project, "a national litigation and public policy organization dedicated to exonerating wrongfully convicted individuals, 342 people have been exonerated as a result of DNA analysis as of July 31, 2016.[40] The Innocence Project lists six "contributing causes" for wrongful convictions":

- Eyewitness misidentification.
- False confessions or admissions.
- Government misconduct.
- Inadequate defense.
- Informants (e.g., jailhouse snitches).
- Unvalidated or improper forensic science.

However, Dr. Jon Gould, who has written extensively about erroneous convictions, and his colleagues caution that "without a comparison or control group of cases, researchers risk labeling these factors as 'causes' of erroneous convictions when they may be merely correlates."[41] They designed a unique experimental strategy to study factors leading to rightful acquittals or dismissal of charges against an innocent defendant – near misses – that were not present in cases that led to the conviction of an innocent person. After identifying a set of erroneous convictions and near misses and analyzing the cases using bivariate and logistic regression techniques, Gould and his colleagues identified 10 "factors" (not causes) that led to a wrongful conviction of an innocent defendant instead of a dismissal or acquittal:

- Younger defendant.
- Criminal history.
- Weak prosecution case.
- Prosecution withheld evidence.
- Lying by a non-eyewitness.

- Unintentional witness misidentification.
- Misinterpreting forensic evidence at trial.
- Weak defense.
- Defendant offered a family witness.
- States with a "punitive" culture.

Judge Frankel was somewhat successful in bringing awareness to noise and bias in the judicial system; however, judges did not like being told how to administer sentencing. Therefore, a compromise was struck that made criminal sentencing guidelines discretionary, thus allowing more noise and bias back into judicial sentencing. An interesting point in this example is that decision-makers are unaware of or ignore the noise and bias embedded in their judgments. Judges resented taking away the discretion they enjoyed in applying more severe sentencing even though the facts and circumstances suggested a more balanced approach is fairer.

What should be taken from this is that decision-makers need a check on decisions that go off track to ensure that bias does not lead to injustice. We all have an inherent bias, but when bias and noise lead to consistently unjust outcomes, an intervention is needed. What is missing in policy compromise, like the one that Congress and the judicial system came to when making criminal sentencing guidelines discretionary, is a check on bias and noise that leads to imbalance and injustice against similarly situated defendants.

A second example that demonstrates how decision audits uncover noise in subjective judgment is one less commonly known involving risk selection in the insurance industry. Kahneman et al. were invited to consult with a large insurance firm. The company wanted to evaluate the benefits of consistency in decision-making by actuaries and claims adjusters in the selection of risk from new clients and capital allocation for future claims. The management team assumed that the processes among actuaries and claims adjusters varied very little but there wasn't agreement on the magnitude of the variance. A decision audit was proposed as a way to settle the disagreement which management accepted.

The context for how the Kahneman consulting team set up the decision audit is very interesting. Many industries rely on the judgment of a range of professionals who make judgments on behalf of the organization, a medical facility, or an organization (public sector or private). Doctors make the call on patient care, medical resources used, and diagnosis. Business executives are given wide latitude on how budgets are spent, deal-making, and risk-taking in strategic initiatives, and government policy ebbs and flows with political appointees or life-long government servants who make policy impacting large swaths of the public.

In the case of insurance, actuaries/underwriters are required to quote premiums for future financial risks and claims adjusters must forecast the cost of future claims and negotiate settlements in disputes with claimants or their attorneys. In both cases, the *random selection* of individuals who make decisions on behalf of the firm creates an artificial lottery. The concept of a lottery is important to understand in the evaluation of noise and bias. A lottery is created when a decision is made by an underwriter or claims adjuster in anticipation of a future outcome. The true value of a quote and future value of the cost of a claim is unknown at the time of the decision. If the quote is too high, it may result in a significant profit or loss of business. If the quote is too low, it may result in significant financial loss and excess claims.

The assumption in risk selection and claims adjustment is that the collective decisions made by underwriters and claims adjusters will average out over time to equal a value Kahneman calls the *Goldilocks price* (not too high, not too low), but in fact that didn't happen in this case and may not at other insurance companies. Accepted quotes above or below the "goldilocks price" are costly to the bottom line. Noise is characterized as the *variance* in different quotes given similar risk profiles in risk selection. Bias would be characterized by risk selection consistently being below or above the goldilocks price. However, since we don't know the future value of the correct price of risk in this scenario, we can still determine the impacts of the collective errors in judgment – it's the variance or noise.

The findings from the noise audit were five times greater than the median difference expected by management and in some cases larger. One would expect that similarly trained actuaries and claims adjusters would make similar judgments about risk, but a great deal of subjective decision-making goes into their analysis. The variance in judgments did not average out they accumulated resulting potentially millions in lost revenues. "The data showed that the price a customer is asked to pay depends to an uncomfortable extent on the lottery that picks the employee who will deal with that transaction."

The purpose of these two examples should demonstrate that emotions play an outsized role in judgment. Emotions are important but people have a hard time accepting when their judgments are biased or off target. The inability to recognize these errors in judgment suggests that decision-makers need help to correct course. A formal process is needed to provide constructive dissent in reaching a final decision, and structured qualifying questions give business leaders a tool for identifying bias in proposals presented to them. Finally, a periodic decision audit can be performed on strategic plans to develop confidence in the processes used to reach the best possible outcomes even when uncertainty is high. Reducing noise and bias in decision-making is an organizational imperative in order to minimize the impact of emotions in strategic planning.

NOTES

1. https://bancroft.berkeley.edu/ROHO/projects/debt/1980srecession.html.
2. https://www.federalreservehistory.org/essays/stock-market-crash-of-1987.
3. https://www.federalreservehistory.org/essays/stock-market-crash-of-1987

4. https://www.nytimes.com/1987/06/14/business/misery-on-the-meatpacking-line.html
5. S. S. Cowen, L. B. Ferreri, and L. D. Parker (1987), The impact of corporate characteristics on social responsibility disclosure: A typology and frequency-based analysis, *Accounting, Organizations and Society*, 12, 111–122. https://doi.org/10.1016/0361-3682(87)90001-8.
6. https://stmuscholars.org/the-stock-market-crash-of-1987-triggering-one-of-the-most-haunting-declines-in-the-markets-history/.
7. https://money.usnews.com/investing/buy-and-hold-strategy/articles/2017-10-12/30-years-ago-lessons-from-the-1987-stock-market-crash.
8. https://corporatefinanceinstitute.com/resources/knowledge/economics/dutch-tulip-bulb-market-bubble/.
9. https://www.history.com/topics/21st-century/recession.
10. https://hbr.org/2009/07/the-end-of-rational-economics.
11. https://fee.org/articles/predictably-irrational-the-hidden-forces-that-shape-our-decisions/
12. https://www.value-at-risk.net/risk-limit/.
13. https://www.bloomberg.com/quicktake/the-london-whale.
14. https://www.hsgac.senate.gov/imo/media/doc/REPORT%20-%20JPMorgan%20Chase%20Whale%20Trades%20(4-12-13).pdf.
15. http://files.shareholder.com/downloads/ONE/2288197031x0x628656/4cb574a0-0bf5-4728-9582-625e4519b5ab/Task_Force_Report.pdf.
16. https://www.investopedia.com/terms/s/syntheticcdo.asp.
17. https://www.wallstreetmojo.com/collateralized-debt-obligation-cdo/.
18. https://www.cfo.com/banking-capital-markets/2013/01/jpmorgan-cfos-slammed-for-risk-management-failures/.
19. https://effectivemanagers.com/dwight-mihalicz/the-top-12-fallacies-that-get-in-the-way-of-organizational-performance-part-1/.
20. https://www.ndtv.com/business/analysis-fallout-from-jpmorgan-loss-may-have-just-begun-307817.
21. https://www.demos.org/research/jp-morgan-chase-whale-trades-case-history-derivatives-risks-and-abuses.
22. M. Alvesson (2001), Knowledge work: Ambiguity, image, and identity, *Human Relations*, 54(7), 863–886. https://doi.org/10.1177/0018726701547004.
23. https://theconversation.com/a-whale-of-a-time-how-traders-cost-jp-morgan-billions-17130.
24. https://www.reuters.com/article/jpmorgan-brief-idUSL1N1KC1FA.
25. https://finance.yahoo.com/news/us-decides-drop-criminal-charges-203052177.html.
26. John C. Doyle, David L. Alderson, Lun Li, Steven Low, Matthew Roughan, Stanislav Shalunov, Reiko Tanaka, and Walter Willinger (2005), *Proceedings of the National Academy of Sciences*, 102 (41), 14497–14502. https://doi.org/10.1073/pnas.0501426102.
27. A.-L. Barabaśi and R. Albert (1999), *Science*, 286, 509–512.
28. S.-H. Yook, H. Jeong and A.-L. Barabaśi (2002), *Proceedings of the National Academy of Sciences USA*, 99, 13382–13386.
29. R. Albert, H. Jeong, and A.-L. Barabaśi (2000), *Nature*, 406, 378–382.
30. R. Albert and A.-L. Barabaśi (2002), *Reviews of Modern Physics*, 74, 47–97.
31. M. E. J. Newman (2003), *SIAM Review*, 45, 167–256.

32. https://www.mckinsey.com/~/media/McKinsey/Business%20Functions/Strategy%20and%20Corporate%20Finance/Our%20Insights/The%20case%20for%20behavioral%20strategy/The%20case%20for%20behavioral%20strategy.pdf
33. https://www.businessmanagementdaily.com/7664/encourage-open-constructive-dissent/.
34. https://www.amazon.com/Rebel-Talent-Pays-Break-Rules-ebook/dp/B071HD8589
35. https://www.pon.harvard.edu/daily/conflict-resolution/in-real-life-conflict-scenarios-promote-constructive-dissent/.
36. https://blog.dataiku.com/bias-and-noise-in-machine-learning.
37. https://insidebigdata.com/2018/08/20/machine-learning-bias-ai-systems/.
38. https://tannerabraham.com/bias-in-machine-learning-and-ai-examples/.
39. https://nij.ojp.gov/topics/articles/wrongful-convictions-and-dna-exonerations-understanding-role-forensic-science.
40. http://www.innocenceproject.org.
41. J. B. Gould, J. Carrano, R. Leo, and J. Young (2013), *Predicting Erroneous Convictions: A Social Science Approach to Miscarriages of Justice*, Final Technical Report, NCJ 241839, Washington, DC: U.S. Department of Justice, Office of Justice Programs, National Institute of Justice.

Chapter 6

Cognitive readiness – risk-solution designers

As we enter the third year of the Covid-19 pandemic, now is a time to reassess risk in a completely different way. The emotional toll on everyone feels like a national trauma that has been building since the 2008 Great Recession which accelerated the transition to a new digital operating model. Complexity is now the norm, and moments of simplicity seem scarce as we are bombarded by "breaking news," threats of political violence, social unrest, and uncertainty on a global scale.

Risk, once a distant concept that seemed abstract, is now front and center in every part of our lives. An increased frequency in climate-related events, natural disaster, cyber threats, geopolitical war, and more create the feeling of a lack of control. We need control, or at least the idea that we have control over what happens to us and for the most part we do. Organizations have spent billions on technology, infrastructure, products, and strategic plans to gain control in order to compete proactively in a global marketplace driven by digital innovation. These investments have allowed organizations to pivot during the start of the pandemic because of financial support from governmental agencies, low-interest rates, and cheap labor, but now the low-lying fruit has been picked. As organizations seek new ways to build scale and resiliency, more creative investments in staff will be needed to develop cognitive readiness.

What is cognitive readiness? Researchers, working with military leaders and other complex environments, have explored how to prepare soldiers for the asymmetric environments in the battlefield where manual and autonomous drones are used to gather intelligence and provide cover. Where information and data are being pushed onto the battlefield with real-time analysis of the threat environment and classroom training is augmented with scenarios to evaluate cognitive readiness to be successful in the war theater. In reviewing research in this space, I found an evolving field in cognitive readiness that is applicable to building resilience in the workforce in any organization.

> Cognitive readiness is the mental preparation (including skills, knowledge, abilities, motivations, and personal dispositions) an individual

DOI: 10.1201/9781003189657-6

needs to establish and sustain competent performance in the complex and unpredictable environment of modern military operations. The concept of cognitive readiness may be of special relevance and significance for those who must quickly adapt to rapidly emerging, unforeseen challenges. Both individuals and units can be prepared to perform many of the essential tasks that are anticipated as necessary for accomplishing the missions assigned to them. However, their readiness to acquire the additional capabilities needed to meet the unexpected, unforeseen challenges that inevitably arise in today's uncertain operational environment will contribute substantially to the success of their operations. Such readiness is a cognitive capability, which can be found and measured to an appreciable extent in both individuals and units.

(Fletcher and Morrison 2002)[1,2]

Research in cognitive readiness examines the human factors needed to become more effective in complex operating environments. If you are a baby boomer, your concept of change is different from Generation XYZ, millennials, and whatever generational code that followed. Those of us in the latter category experienced the civil rights movement, police violence, the Cuban missile crisis, nuclear bomb drills, fall of the Berlin Wall, and a host of technological change today's generation takes for granted. Most of us had a lifetime to adjustment to change and adapt coping skills over time. The rate of change today is unsettling to were born just before September 11th and the wars that have followed. The world seems more uncertain and unpredictable and in some cases it is, but uncertainty is not new. These factors are the subject of cognitive readiness in an uncertain world providing insights to prepare for the next evolution of technological change to come.

The corollary of cognitive readiness on the battlefield to cognitive readiness in the boardroom may not be obvious yet; however, the training and skills needed to be successful in both arenas will make more sense as we break down the science. There are ten psychological components that lay the foundation for cognitive readiness:

(1) **Situational awareness** – the ability to perceive oneself in relation to risks and the operating environment. (2) **Memory** – active processes of reconstructing what has been learned and the speed at which one can execute effectively based on acquired knowledge. (3) **Transfer of training** – the ability to apply what is learned in one performance context to another performance context. (4) **Leadership** – consist of motivational patterns and a combination of technical, conceptual, and interpersonal skills. (5) **Emotion** – possess the ability to channel and control emotions to perform complex tasks under the stress and confusion that accompany modern operations. (6) **Metacognition** – involves the executive functions of thought, knowledge, and cognitive processes toward achieving one's goals. (7) **Automaticity** – refers to processes that are performed rapidly with little forethought or

effort. (8) **Problem-solving** – techniques for solving problems is ideally suited to the goals and objectives to be addressed. (9) **Decision-making** – the selection of tactical and strategic plans primed by the recognition of learned patterns. (10) **Mental flexibility and creativity** – problem-solving: applying "strong" methods (based on acquired knowledge and skills) to well-defined, structured tasks and applying "weak" methods to poorly defined, ill-structured, chaotic tasks.

Cognitive readiness combines two complimentary concepts: *readiness* and *effectiveness*. Effectiveness is measured as an outcome relative to the success of a mission or goal. Readiness is a measure of the potential of an individual and team to perform well in a mission or goal. Thus, readiness represents an estimate or prediction of effectiveness. Developing cognitive readiness is about developing leadership skills in organizations. The military understands that leadership is not just about rank as much as it is about the preparation to lead. The goal of cognitive readiness is preparation to perform in modern competitive operating environment characterized as complex, dynamic, and resource limited (Etter, Foster, and Steele 2000).[3]

Cognitive readiness implies that executives must be mentally prepared to sustain performance while facing stressors in the workplace such as information overload, information uncertainty, fatigue, time limitations, and resource constraints. Therefore, the primary factors to determine cognitive readiness are psychological with all other factors either a catalyst or inhibitor to cognitive readiness (Fletcher and Morrison 2002).[4] Each of the components of cognitive readiness contributes to the design of leadership training toward reinforcing readiness.

Endsley (1988) provided a more detailed, three-level definition of situation awareness as "(1) the perception of elements in the environment within a volume of time and space, (2) the comprehension of their meaning, and (3) the projection of their status in the near future. Among the complex behaviors and processes involved in cognition, situation awareness represents the initial perceptual analyses that precede decision and action."[5] Traditional approaches to create situational awareness through visualization tools and displays begin by determining what data is needed, integration of data to make sense of the environment, and trending for projection of events.

Situational awareness is not just about technology, human perception, and cognition to make sense of the information presented. Today's decision support tools are becoming more sophisticated and will require more than static data sources. Information and data integration from multiple sources including media, news, and trusted data pools to create visualizations that allow the user to design real-time analysis instead of selecting predetermined outcomes.

Memory and transfer of training are central to cognition and performance under conditions that involve stress. Training for specific scenarios over periods of time reinforces the skills learned in training to apply when needed. Metacognition is the ability to be aware of conscious cognitive processes when involved in work tasks. Brown (1987) maintained that this self-awareness of internal routines is the highest form of human intelligence.[6] With reference to the relevance of metacognition for education, Hacker (2001) stated that "the promise of metacognitive theory is that it focuses precisely on those characteristics of thinking that can contribute to students' awareness and understanding of being self-regulatory organisms, that is, of being agents of their own thinking" (p. 50).[7]

Automaticity is a product of memory and training on the right skills and a focus on repetition. Each of the components of cognitive readiness complements the next. Automaticity leads to problem-solving and decision-making. Like memory and transfer of training, problem-solving and decision-making are closely related areas of research that have similar implications for cognitive readiness. Mental flexibility and creativity tap into training in specific learned skills but adds another dimension when combined with creativity. The ability to bring new ideas and solutions to traditional problems that do not follow the playbook in a complex business environment are attributes of mental flexibility and creativity. Learning to improvise is a critical skill as long as it is done within acceptable limits.

Leadership is not simply the next component of cognitive readiness, it embodies the previous components into a multifaceted behavioral skill set. Yukl (1989) summarized such research by observing that successful leadership in large hierarchical organizations is characterized by a dominant concern for socialized (as opposed to personalized) power. This motive puts organizational interests above personal interests. Further, the leader motivated by socialized power is more likely to use a participative, coaching management style as opposed to authoritarian, coercive style.[8]

And finally, emotions. Emotional intelligence has garnered a great deal of attention more recently as an attribute of new leadership modeling. Emotional intelligence is a type of social intelligence that involves the ability to monitor one's own and others' emotions, to discriminate among them, and to use the information to guide one's thinking and actions (Salovey and Mayer 1990).[9] The scope of emotional intelligence includes the verbal and nonverbal appraisal and expression of emotion, the regulation of emotion in the self and others, and the utilization of emotional content in problem-solving (Mayer and Salovey 1993).[10] Emotions, or emotional intelligence, is the summation of the components of cognitive readiness training in preparation for navigating the complex new operating environment that exists today. While a lot has changed in terms of technology and skills in many organizations, the biggest challenge in making things work well is the human element.

Cognitive readiness is a dynamic and evolving discipline of study, but the point of this discussion is that these skills can be learned and by extension training can be designed to develop cognitive readiness. The idea of connecting emotions to intelligence comes with its own set of disagreements.

We (Mayer and Salovey 1993) have been criticized for connecting emotion and intelligence, both in anonymous reviews of our initial articles and in a symposium where we employed the construct (Wegner 1990; cf. Mayer 1990).[11],[12]

Such criticisms raise important issues. They state: (a) that intelligence is an inappropriate and misleading metaphor, and we are redescribing social intelligence, as well as perhaps falsely casting dispositions such as interpersonal warmth as abilities; (b) that there are no important abilities connected with emotion, or at least no unique abilities; and (c) finally, there is an objection that we might be "rocking the boat" by connecting a heretofore less controversial area (emotion) with a controversial one (intelligence).

The idea of "feelings" in a business context is often fraught with judgment and some cases misconceptions about intelligence, but from a research standpoint, the topic is not settled science to be sure.

The review suggests that cognitive readiness is an integrative concept that pulls together diverse themes related to performance improvement and sustainment. It also suggests that cognitive readiness is a serious candidate for inclusion in routine measures of readiness in so far as it can be trained and measured. It may be essential in determining the capabilities of individuals and units to adapt rapidly to the unpredictable exigencies and challenges of modern asymmetric military operations (Mayer and Salovey 1993).

The psychological preparation for cognitive readiness also includes the integration of networked systems at the individual level. No executive is expected to carry 70 pounds of equipment, connected helmets, Kevlar jackets, and long rifles with them into corporate battle but today's warfighters have become accustomed to the rigors of modern battlespaces. In this section, we will discuss what a future networked environment might look like as a supplement to cognitive readiness.

The term network-centric operations refers to military operations enabled by networking the military force.[13]

> Networking has multiple meanings, but in the network-centric context it means computer network based provision of an integrated picture of the battlefield, available in detail to all levels of command and control down to the individual soldier. The latter is achieved through command post, vehicle, and helmet- or head-mounted displays, and individual soldier computers, all linked by radio-frequency networks.

As stated in a 2001 Defense Department report to Congress, "Network-Centric Warfare is to warfare what e-business is to business."

As noted above, organizations have been networked for years and has deepen as new digital strategies have emerged. The design of organizational network analysis evolved as a theoretical construct in the study of communications and socio-technical networks within organizations. "This technique creates statistical and graphical models of the people, tasks, groups, knowledge, and resources of organizational systems. It is based on social network theory and more specifically, dynamic network analysis."[14]

Research conducted by Price Waterhouse Coopers revealed that employees are more responsive or less resistant to change initiated and managed through informal structures. This study encourages organizations to shift from the traditional formal hierarchical networks to the contemporary informal networks. Thus, *organizational network analysis* (ONA) is essential in:[15]

(1) Revelation of the actual emerging relationships in an organization to identify, assess, and streamline information flow in an organization.

(2) Identification of key players and most influential employees to enhance communication flow and improve business results.

(3) Identifying strategy and innovation groups to help you tap into them and find key resources to increase the competitive advantage for the business.

(4) Establishing the new and more efficient way to coordinate and communicate with employees for better response. This is necessary particularly when initiating change like adopting new technology, culture, or any restructuring.

(5) Identification of sustainable linkages in a firm and how to improve such linkages.

The basic premise of ONA is that a better understanding of the organic exchange of information and informal networks in an organization can help leverage strategic goals and objectives. ONA describes these channels of communication using terms that mimic systems. *Central nodes* are described as people who seem to know everyone. *Knowledge brokers* are considered bridges between people and groups. *Peripherals* are high potential talent with easily transferable skills who can leave the organization without transferring skills to others. And *ties* are the connections between central nodes and knowledge brokers. Some have described ONA as simply a diagnostic tool to measure the "relationship capital" of individuals, teams, groups, or departments across an organization.

Organizational Network Analysis (ONA) is a scientific methodology that makes visible information and communication flows across work networks in an organization. By providing a lens into the inner workings of the organization, ONA enables HR and People Analytics leaders to analyze and understand value-creating networks that are vital for knowledge sharing, team collaboration, individual productivity, customer engagement, and innovation.

Traditionally, ONA has used surveys to collect information illustrating relationships between individuals and groups in an organization. The results of the surveys, while still highly insightful, have limitations because they provide a singular view based on an employee's perceptions and biases at a single point in time. Implementing surveys at an enterprise level is time-consuming and suffers from limited responses, making the results less than optimal.[16]

Tools such as ONA are useful in providing new insights into an organization but are too narrow a view of human interaction. In addition, these tools can be misused by creating unintended perceptions and biases of individuals who are considered "outside" these rigid structures of behavioral norms. The most troubling aspect of these tools is the impersonal and academic grouping of individuals into categories that have nothing to do with the actual work being performed.[17]

The most promising aspect of ONA that I found is related to patient care. The transition in patient handoffs and patient outcomes has informed best practice in patient care.[18] An abstract from the US National Library of Medicine, National Institute of Health, provides research on ONA's application at the tactical level.

> Communication during patient handoffs has been widely implicated in patient safety issues. However, few studies have actually been able to quantify the relationship between handoffs and patient outcomes. We used ORA, a dynamic network analysis tool, to examine handoffs between day and night shifts on seven units in three hospitals in the Southwest. Using *ORA's visualization and analysis capabilities we examined the relationships between the handoff communication network metrics and a variety of patient safety quality and satisfaction outcomes. Unique network patterns were observed for different types of outcome variable (e.g., safety, symptom management, self-care, and patient satisfaction). This exploratory project demonstrates the power of *ORA to identify communication patterns for large groups, such as patient care units. *ORA's network metrics can then be related to specific patient outcomes.

Other tactical approaches to ONA have been applied to projects related to digital transformation.[19] Digital transformation provides organizations with an opportunity to reimagine how technology can be used as a network between employees, customers, and external stakeholders. A well-designed organizational network analysis combined with feedback from internal and external partners provides an effective roadmap for designing digital transformation. An analysis gleaned from communication channels combined with insights from respective stakeholders using visualization tools creates insights into gaps and opportunities to enhance collaboration and reduce risk. An ONA project is useful in identifying obstacles to a successful digital transformation.

According to the Academy to Innovate HR, "awareness of possible obstacles of any kind of digital transformation approach increases successful outcomes." Marcus Blosch, Gartner's research vice president, warns about six barriers to become a digital business. There are different names for it (mostly organizational culture), but with all fingers pointing in the same direction, *the biggest obstacle seems to really be – the human aspect.*

(a) Barrier No. 1: A change-resisting culture.
(b) Barrier No. 2: Limited sharing and collaboration.
(c) Barrier No. 3: The business isn't ready.
(d) Barrier No. 4: The talent gap.
(e) Barrier No. 5: Current practices don't support talent.
(f) Barrier No. 6: Change isn't easy.

Research in networking has broad implications for enhanced organizational performance through technology and human-centered design.[20] According to a Harvard Business School blog,

> Human-centered design is a problem-solving technique that puts real people at the center of the development process, enabling you to create products and services that resonate and are tailored to your audience's needs.
>
> The goal is to keep users' wants, pain points, and preferences front of mind during every phase of the process. In turn, you'll build more intuitive, accessible products that are likely to turn a higher profit because your customers have already vetted the solution and feel more invested in using it.

The idea is drawn from marketing;[21] IDEO, a global design firm, popularized the term "human-centered design" by stressing three central themes: *inspiration*, *ideation*, and *implementation*. The concepts in human-centered design also apply to organizational network analysis and cognitive readiness. However, human-centered design is conceptualized more broadly in organizational networks. Let's first explain the three themes and then broaden them to incorporate how the next generation *risk-solution designers* will evolve from the multidisciplinary practices introduced in this book.

Human-centered design starts with inspiration. *Inspiration* is not the textbook definition but involves deep listening to the needs of others. Deep listening is a trained skill that involves turning off the noise in our heads and any preconceived notions of what the answer is. Deep listening is a process of probing to fully understand what is needed, why it is needed, and how it makes a difference.

The process of deep listening is described as a form of empathy for what others feel and a desire to understand the pain points that hinder performance.[22] For the purposes of this book, deep listening is presented as a tool to learn or be inspired by understanding how workflows, governance, communications, tools, and teamwork hinder performance. The goal in deep listening is to validate how pervasive the scope of pain points is in achieving organizational success. This is the first step in data gathering in the risk-solution design process.

Step #2 is Ideation. *Ideation* requires validation through quantifiable data analysis, if possible, or building consensus from independent sources that the problem exists and is pervasive, even when it may be in isolation of one group, department, or operational division. The process of ideation is iterative, meaning that initial observations must be tested and challenged before moving forward with a proposed solution.

Alternatives must be carefully considered and informed by feedback throughout the process to ensure rigor in the brainstorming process is supported by data. The goal of ideation is to develop the best available solution that is possible given time and resource constraints. Contingencies must also be included in the process by considering scenarios not contemplated in the design ideation phase. And finally, Step #3, Implementation.

Implementation is the final phase of the process. *Implementation* does not suggest that all needs are met, but it does mean that a solution meets the key expectations and objectives of the participants impacted. The implementation process requires an understanding of how to build scale, anticipated maintenance, changes in operations, business contingencies, and more. Implementation is not the end of the process but is the beginning of visualizing how the solution works in real time. A human-centered design process is an evolution from risk management to risk-solution design.

So why is thinking outside the box so hard? There are lots of large successful toothbrush companies but only one thought to study how children brush their teeth. This is not an isolated problem. Most organizations assume they already know what their customers need, what their employees need, but fail to anticipate these needs consistently. Typically, the solution to the problem is a simple one but seldom are the simple solutions anticipated. There is safety in staying inside the box, but when we stay too long, that is when failure is more likely. I think what we too often forget is that the "box" was designed to fit a specific problem, at a singular point in time, and was never intended to become the only way of solving all problems.

In psychology, rigid thinking is considered a personality disorder in which a person has a rigid and unhealthy pattern of thinking, functioning, and behaving. A person with a personality disorder has trouble perceiving and relating to situations and people that do not see the world as they do.[23] Clearly, there are degrees of rigid thinking that inhibit thinking outside of the box. For one, there is safety in numbers for personality types who like rules, order, and comfort in doing things the same way. There is also a sense of normalcy that is created by consistently following established processes. Rules ensure that expectations are clear, and outcomes are somewhat predictable. However, too much rigidity creates inflexibility in thinking and innovation.

In researching rigid thinking, I found that blame and rigid thinking are somewhat correlated. According to Exploringyourmind website,[24] blame and rigid thinking are two elements that make us ruminate, "a psychological concept referring to the inability to stop thinking about something. Excessive rumination has been associated with psychotic disorders, neuroticism, eating disorders, and more." If we look for commonalities in all the times we've felt blue, we'll see blame and rigid thinking at the top of the list. We could even say that's where the lion's share of our negative thoughts originate.

Rigid thinking means an inability to change one's mind when all signs point to a change of mind. It also implies an inability to see a situation from a different point of view.[25] People with rigid thinking see life with blinders on, perceiving only one out of the countless nuances there are. Thinking outside the box requires risk-taking that some may find hard to adapt to. Human-centered design must account for individual differences as well as the need for uniformity. The opportunity in human-centered design is that most organizations don't see how new approaches in organizational design can produce profound performance outcomes.

Building cognitive readiness is about developing a new set of skills and thinking that exceeds the dogma of risk management. Risk management is formulaic. Risk management assumes that by following a few prescriptive steps a "risk" is mitigated. In reality, risks exist in degrees of mitigation that are seldom measured by risk professionals. Residual risks are empirical evidence that risks exist in degrees of mitigation. The goal is not risk elimination. The goal in human-centered risk design is a better understanding of acceptable risks by designing solutions to enhance performance.

Cognitive readiness is a trainable skill that changes how organizations execute governance, manage risks, and seek better performance. Risk-solution design is a product of cognitive readiness and a new approach to designing an organization that learns continuously. The example used in the Harvard Business School blog offered a short use case to exemplify human-centered design for products.[26]

> A great example of human-centered design is a children's toothbrush that's still in use today. In the mid-nineties, Oral-B asked IDEO to develop a new kid's toothbrush. Rather than replicate what was already on the market—a slim, shorter version of an adult-sized toothbrush—IDEO went directly to the source; they watched children brush their teeth.

They realized in the process that kids were having a hard time holding the skinnier toothbrushes their parents used because they didn't have the same dexterity or motor skills. What children needed were toothbrushes with a big, fat, squishy grip that was easier for them to hold onto.

"Now every toothbrush company in the world makes these," says IDEO Partner Tom Kelley in a speech. "But our client reports that after we made that little, tiny discovery out in the field—sitting in a bathroom watching a five-year-old boy brush his teeth—they had the best-selling kid's toothbrush in the world for 18 months." Had IDEO not gone out into the field—or, in this case, children's homes—they wouldn't have observed that small opportunity, which turned a big profit for Oral-B.

Reimagining organizational performance and governance will require a multidimensional approach. Cognitive readiness, organizational network analysis, human-centered design, and risk-solution design are examples of new disciplines that will be needed as organizations prepare for Industry 4.0. But how will organizations tie these new disciplines together to form new operating environments? How will organizations deconstruct hierarchical governance to flatten 19th century models of span of control? Researchers have explored network-centric models in anticipation of digital transformation in the form of information sharing at every level of the organization.[27]

Network-centric models of operation depend on the availability of information at the individual level that creates situational awareness in performance. A general assumption in network-centric operation is that transparency, information, and data encourage "self-synchronization" of behaviors in shared goals and objectives. The general concept of *being on the same page* is taken to a new level of understanding. Network-centric operations create access to information in order to make informed decisions in a timely manner and delegates authority to execute more effectively within a channel of accountability. Structured channels of accountability are determined by roles within the organization, but a common set of information is available for completing the objectives of the firm.

The idea is to drive performance accountability down to the individual level by creating cognitive readiness based on the actions, decisions, and behaviors that contribute to organizational performance. Instead of a focus on sales goals, every person in the sales department understands how each customer contributes to bottom-line performance based on long-term profitability versus short-term sales. Operations is provided information on costs and opportunity for efficiencies instead of production to encourage continuous improvement in efficient operations. Management will have access to quantifiable risk data to make informed decisions about how to mitigate organizational behaviors that cause risk. And board of directors and senior executives will have access to real-time performance and operational data to query to inform strategic planning.

Self-synchronization does not happen in a vacuum. The drivers of organizational behavior are typically profits, purpose, opportunity, customer satisfaction, and rewards.[28] Yet, many organizations go through the motion of engaging employees in understanding how they contribute to the success of the firm. Most employees want to have a better understanding of their role, how the firm achieves success, and how they can contribute, even if their contribution is a small one. A good friend and well-known business leader in self-synchronization described the process as "creating a stake in the outcome."

Jack Stack and Bo Burlingham wrote about these concepts in their book, *A Stack in the Outcome.* The authors did not use the term self-synchronization but instead called their process, A Culture of Ownership. SRC Holdings Corporation (formerly Springfield ReManufacturing Corporation) is a small manufacturing operation in Springfield, Missouri where I attended college at Drury University. The factory specialized in remanufacturing engines and engine components that were used as replacement parts for construction equipment made by International Harvester.

Jack Stack was the plant manager of the firm with about 230 people in 1981. A major recession was starting, and International Harvester was in debt and recovering from worker's strike as demand for their equipment began to wane. Wages were frozen and unemployment rose nationally causing a significant cut in production at Springfield ReManufacturing Corp. Jack and his management team knew that layoffs and potential closure of the plant were a real possibility if International Harvester decided they needed cash to repay their loans and whether the economic recession was starting.

The controller of production operations for International Harvester's Construction Equipment Group floated the idea of buying the plant from Harvester to Jack Stack. Neither of the two men had any money to buy the factory nor knew if Harvester would take them seriously if they approached the company to buy it. Undeterred, the two men enlisted the head of production operation to help develop a proposal to senior executives at Harvester. The initial proposal went nowhere with management not ready to decide as the recession grew worse, as layoffs had begun. Harvester began restructuring to stave off creditors and reduce costs with the Springfield plant left intact but on tetters as a succession of new bosses came and went as cuts in staff grew. However, the adversity of the recession and Harvester's financial problems created a spirit of mutual self-sacrifice at the Springfield plant.

After one significant budget cut, everyone at the Springfield plant got together and agreed to close the factory for one day a week in order to avoid having to lay anyone off. This meant a 20% reduction in wages on top of the erosion of income brought on by the wage freeze. Yet, no one complained.

Instead of playing defense, the management team went on the offense. Jack and his team had no salespersons on staff but found new customers enough to generate additional work to keep everyone employed. They also began looking for investors and met with dozens of potential investors. What Jack and his time learned in the process of pitching the firm to investors was they weren't interested in his background, the team's experience, or how smart they were. What investors cared about was how they were going to grow the business and how their percentage in the business would provide them with the return they were seeking. Return on equity!

The management team had to learn the language of finance and how to pitch the factory as a value proposition that investors understood! The next challenge was finding the right investors who believed in building long-term value versus an investor whose values did not align with the vision Jack and his management team were developing. Rejection after rejection rolled in over the months, but the process was teaching them how to run a company and think like owners. Two years after the start of the recession and the dream to buy the factory, the vision for their company began to take shape. The vision started with a focus on the fundamentals. As the plant manager, Jack Stack's vision centered on the people in the plant. He wanted to create a place where mutual respect existed within a healthy environment where people liked their work and one another.

Money was not secondary, but the goal was to create wealth for employees and management shared in the wealth. Jack decided that giving employees an ownership stake in the company would give him a competitive advantage. Success would depend on everyone contributing, otherwise the whole experiment would fail. Ownership also meant that a shared responsibility would be created instead of it being just a job and someone else's responsibility to be successful. What Jack wanted mainly was to make people successful, feel a sense of accomplishment, ownership, and meaning in work and in life! This is not the typical story of survival because this idea of success evolved while the company was still seeking a financial lifeline.

And it almost didn't happen! While Jack was dreaming of his ideal company, International Harvester tried to sell the Springfield plant. Jack wasn't told by his management team, he found out from a friend who read about it in the Wall Street Journal. The announcement drew a great deal of interest and interested investors came to Springfield, Missouri to see the plant. The Wall Street Journal article led Jack to another story about asset-based lending, financing for cash-strapped firms was a new lending vehicle the Bank of America had begun to offer. The bank secures the loan based on the assets, receivables, facility, equipment, etc. and in turn receives a higher-than-market interest rate. This high-risk loans include "loan covenants" that monitor the financial performance of the creditor. Failure to maintain strong financial controls may result in the bank seizing assets to recover its money.

The financial lifeline Jack was looking for was the Bank of America asset-backed loan. Timing was opportune on two counts. They needed the money asap! Secondly, International Harvester was running out of options to repay its debt and was close to filing for bankruptcy. However, at the last moment a buyer, Dresser Industries, made an offer of $100 million for the entire division, including the Springfield plant! Fortunately, Dresser Industries had only given a letter of intent which Harvester could give to its bank to buy time. This also gave Jack and his team time to negotiate while Harvester and Dresser worked out the terms and assets to be included in the sell. The negotiating teams from Dresser had planned to liquidate all of the assets in Springfield and use the funds elsewhere. This infuriated the negotiators at Harvester and the team called Jack and asked if he still wanted to buy the plant. Jack finally saw his dream beginning to come alive again, but he had to act fast to secure an agreement and arrange the financing.

SRC Holdings Corporation was born out of a dream, now Jack and his team had to design the business they wanted. According to Jack Stack, *"a good company, I've learned, is like a good car: It begins with a good design."* The company you end up with reflects the concepts and principles you incorporate at the very beginning. SRC Holdings needed a new design because the old operating model depended on International Harvester and now the factory needed new customers and streams of revenue. The problem was no one had any idea how to develop a new design – so they had to figure it out!

In describing the SRC Holdings story, the term is seldom used but Jack faced a mountain of risks he did not realize existed before completing the buyout of the company. The first risk hurdle was securing financing to acquire the firm. Next Jack had promised that, if successful, everyone would become owners of the firm. The firm had to figure out a legal way to do so without violating regulatory rules. Becoming a public company would have been too costly and time consuming. That is when the idea of an employee stock ownership plan or ESOP was formed. The ESOP allowed Jack to fulfill his promise of employee-ownership and avoid legal issues.

The next step involved the design of control of the company versus ownership. Two classes of stock were issued; one with voting stock to elect a board of directors and the other class of nonvoting stock was also owners. SRC Holdings is a story of bootstrapping at every level. Jack Stack started out in the mail room, worked on the shop floor, and finally plant manager but still had no idea how to properly design the new firm. Working as an employee, Jack had to think as an owner now. He learned from his experience at International Harvester that even the top executives at large firms fail to anticipate risks. Executives make mistakes more often than not and Jack realized he needed a team around him to help prevent making similar mistakes. What Jack realized is a valuable lesson for all firms. Concentrating power and decision-making at the top creates risks, it doesn't mitigate risk.

He wanted something more, and alternative to a top-down, command-and-control business structure which is still the norm today.

SRC Holdings had to begin the process of educating employees on their role as owners. All shareholders have a legal right to vote on the issues that impact owner's interests. The valuation of shares, issuance of stock, purchase, and sale of major assets. Employees were taught how the board of directors operated and how the directors were elected. The duties of the board were explained to employees as well as state law governing the type of voting shares were used to elect directors to the board. Outside directors were brought in to provide appropriate expertise not available in the management ranks to create a framework of ownership. Employees were also taught how to read and analyze the income statement and balance sheet of the company so that they could see how the money the firm made was used to grow shareholder equity. Imagine spending time explaining the financial statements and who the board of directors are at your firm and the role they play in managing the firm. Most firms don't take the time to explain how their firm operates nor believe employees care, but they do.

SRC was still in survival mode as the fledgling company emerged from Harvester's corporate structure. Few people at the factory understood the arcane language of finance, corporate governance, and the role of the board of directors or how money would be spent in operating the firm. Trust became a huge issue when the two classes of stock were issued. The two classes of stock appeared to create two classes of employees on the surface both on the management team and between management and line employees. Initially, the focus was on how the stock would be divided up, but soon the realization that the value of the stock depended on the success of the firm. Another lesson Stack learned is that everything management does sends a message to employees whether intentional or not. Communicating how and why stock distributions were made helped refocus attention on running the business.

Finally, SRC had to figure out cash flow analysis, how to cash out stockholdings when someone leaves the firm, valuations, and provisions for uncertainty. Design does pay off is the final lesson from SRC. SRC is still a 100% employee-owned company today. It ranked in the top 25 best small companies in America by Forbes. SRC Holdings has grown to 2,000+ associates, 3.8 million square feet in manufacturing and warehouse space, $3 million in charitable giving, and spun-off 60 individual businesses since 1983. I served on the board of trustees at Drury University with Jack Stack, and he was part of my "kitchen cabinet" when I asked to chair the search committee for a new president at Drury University. Jack was an invaluable ally through the 18 months it took to search and vet the next president and to engage the business community in the process.

Here are just a few additional lessons Jack learned through his journey of building an employee-owned company. The foibles of human nature and employee thinking – lesson #1. Changing old habits is hard. Stock owner-ship is more than equity; it requires a new mental attitude about the big pic-ture of running a company. Shared sacrifice was a challenge when managers had to cut staff to save the company and one department head refused to make any cuts. The damage in trust created was felt across the firm and was a sign that the real risk was human behavior inside the organization was more important than external factors. Short-term thinking as an employee almost killed the experiment before it could get off the ground. One exam-ple was leaders who focused on protecting their own fiefdom over the needs of the firm failed to grasp the strategic imperatives in the short-term. Jack had to override some managers, but the damage had been done.

Lesson #2 – Open book policy and ownership culture. Explaining how a firm makes money and how each part of the business contributes to the success of the firm is critical to instilling an ownership culture. Who are the biggest customers? Who are the most profitable customers? What is impor-tant to each customer in the top, middle and bottom group? It takes a team to build equity and value in a company. Knowing where to focus attention and what work to avoid can be material in performance management.

Lesson #3 – Manageable failures lead to success as long as the organization is learning from small failures. Small failures can strengthen organizational performance therefore minimizing failure is key. Lesson #4 – Individual superstars are the enemy of long-term performance. Competition among star performers hurts the culture of ownership. Single-minded success lim-its the growth of the firm for many reasons including employee morale, star performance is cyclical and returns to mean performance over time, and favoritism hurts organizational culture. The myth of the best athlete is just that. Any manager who focuses on hiring the best athlete has probably not been one themselves. Phil Jackson, the legendary coach of the Chicago Bulls, often asked Michael Jordan, "what will make you a superstar?" Michael would answer, "not being the star." Valuing teammates and allow-ing others to share in the glory is what made Michael Jordan the greatest of his time. The same is true with Tom Brady with the New England Patriots and later with Tampa Bay. The team creates the superstar, not the other way around.

The last lesson that I will share with you is lesson #5 – The Dream Matter. Jack Stack assumed that ownership would overcome all other obstacles, but it didn't. It wasn't enough to share equity. Ownership, by itself, is not enough to give an organization the edge. Some people won't get it or buy in, even really smart people. Handing out stock wasn't enough. A process was needed to teach people what ownership meant and why equity was worth building over time. People need to understand how to increase the value of their equity and see how the big picture comes together. They need to believe in the dream to make it come true. Otherwise, it is only a job. Without belief and commitment in building a dream about what is possible, your organization becomes just another firm in the middle of the pack. That may be enough for some firms, but it may not be enough to survive as competition heats up in the new digital global economy.

One last observation, Jack Stack wrote two books about the success of an ownership culture: *A Stake in the Outcome* and *The Great Game of Business*. One of the things that was never mentioned in either book, employee performance evaluations! In *The Great Game of Business*, Jack has a message to middle managers, appeal to employees' best instincts. Managers were expected to require employees to "think at their highest level and use all their intelligence, ingenuity, and resourcefulness to help each other achieve the common goals of the organization." When employees act as owners or are taught to act as owners, performance evaluations are not needed. What company that you know of has credited their employee performance evaluation program as the key to their success? Name one? The annual employee performance evaluation is dreaded for several reasons.

Employee evaluations have become a tool to get rid of employees. This model was created by General Electric and unfortunately became a model across many companies in America and may have been emulated broadly in other countries. GE's model became known as "rank and yank" in the 1980s and is still practiced today.[29] It is a purely punitive approach to employee performance and does little to encourage better performance and serves mostly as a tool for middle managers to get rid of people they don't like instead of making middle managers responsible for the success of employees. The main reason most employees leave an organization is because of a bad boss. Most organizations cannot provide a justifiable reason for its "rank and yank" program other than other companies are doing it and it was a best practice they adopted from GE.[30]

Here is what Deloitte says about the employee performance assessment program invented by GE.

> The human resource function is at a crossroads. People are the heart of our organizations, yet many fundamental management and HR practices are based on outdated ideas of human psychology and organizational design. Often they are rooted in stories about successful business leaders operating in specific places and times (for example, Jack Welch at GE in the 1980s and '90s). These anecdotes and examples evolve into management trends and, later, received wisdom that executives try to implement—at least while they're on bestseller lists and magazine covers.
>
> But it is rare for such practices to be rigorously evaluated. To paraphrase a well-known psychologist, they lack the character of scientific knowledge: "They tend neither to be refuted nor corroborated, but instead merely fade away as people lose interest."[31]

According to Laszlo Bock, "You spend more time working than doing anything else in life. It's not right that the experience of work, even at some of the best employers, should be so demotivating and dehumanizing." In other words, there is no evidence employee evaluation programs are predictive of employee performance. They are based on subjective evaluations of performance which is ripe for bias. The measures for performance may even ask an employee to evaluate their own performance, then given zero weight in their own weights by being over-ruled by the middle manager.

Research has documented gender difference which results in woman being underpaid versus men and people of color are routinely evaluated lower than their counterparts. Human resource managers must be able to develop evidence-based performance programs that reduce bias and subjective evaluations or eliminate them altogether. If employee performance evaluations cannot empirically demonstrate how they add value to the employee and company performance, what is the purpose? HR resources would be better spent on development of people, skills, and aligning roles with the contributions needed for organizational success.

If a small manufacturing plant in Springfield, Missouri, can grow its business ten-fold in just a few years with employee evaluations, we must ask what is everyone else missing? More on this topic later but now is the time to reimagine organizational behavior that distracts from performance as opposed to contributing to performance. Employee performance evaluations is a great place to start.

NOTES

1. J. Morrison and J. D. Fletcher. (2002). Cognitive Readiness.
2. https://apps.dtic.mil/sti/pdfs/ADA458683.pdf.
3. https://apps.dtic.mil/sti/pdfs/ADA458683.pdf.
4. C. Fletcher (2002), Performance appraisal and management: The developing research agenda, *Journal of Occupational of Individual*, 74, 473–487.
5. M. R. Endsley (1988), Design and evaluation for situation awareness enhancement, *Proceedings of the Human Factors Society Annual Meeting*, 32, 97–101. https://doi.org/10.1177/154193128803200221.
6. A. Brown (1987), Metacognition, executive control, self-regulation, and other mysterious mechanisms. In: F.E. Weinert and R.H. Kluwe, eds., *Metacognition, motivation, and understanding*, Hillsdale, NJ: Lawrence Erlbaum Associates, 65–116.
7. D. J. Hacker (2001), *Metacognition: Definitions and Empirical Foundations* [On-line Report]. Memphis, TN: The University of Memphis. Retrieved May 30, 2001, from the World Wide Web: http://www.psyc.memphis.edu/trg/meta.htm.
8. G. A. Yukl (1989), *Leadership in Organizations* (2nd ed.), Englewood Cliffs, NJ: Prentice-Hall.
9. P. Salovey and J. D. Mayer (1990), Emotional intelligence, *Imagination, Cognition and Personality*, 9(3), 185–211. https://doi.org/10.2190/DUGG-P24E-52WK-6CDG.

10. J. D. Mayer and P. Salovey (1993), The intelligence of emotional intelligence, *Intelligence*, 17(4), 433–442. ISSN 0160-2896, https://doi.org/10.1016/0160-2896(93)90010-3 (https://www.sciencedirect.com/science/article/pii/0160289693900103).

11. A. Wegner (1990), Brief history of the Glen Canyon environmental studies, in *National Research Council, Colorado River Ecology and Dam Management Proceedings of a Symposium*, May 24–25, 1990, Santa Fe, New Mexico.

12. Salovey and Mayer, Emotional intelligence.

13. US Department of Defense, Command and Control Research Program, Network Centric Warfare, report to Congress, 27 July 2001, Washington: GPO, 2001. http://www.dod.mil/nii/NCW.

14. J. Merrill, S. Bakken, M. Caldwell, K. Carley, and M. Rockoff (2005), Applying organizational network analysis techniques to study information use in a public health agency (summary), *AMIA Annual Symposium Proceedings 2005*. American Medical Informatics Association. p. 1052. PMC 1560595.

15. https://seity.com/transform-your-company-with-organizational-network-analysis/.

16. https://www.trustsphere.com/organizational-network-analysis/.

17. https://www.sciencedirect.com/science/article/pii/S1048984310000901.

18. https://www.ncbi.nlm.nih.gov/pmc/articles/PMC4156878/.

19. https://info.microsoft.com/rs/157-GQE-382/images/Digital%20transformation-%20seven%20steps%20to%20success.v2.pdf?aliId=860635945.

20. https://online.hbs.edu/blog/post/what-is-human-centered-design.

21. https://www.designkit.org/human-centered-design.

22. https://jedfoundation.org/news-views/ask-the-expert-deep-listening-skills/.

23. https://www.mayoclinic.org/diseases-conditions/personality-disorders/symptoms-causes/syc-20354463.

24. https://exploringyourmind.com/blame-rigid-thinking-mental-health/.

25. https://www.psychologytoday.com/us/blog/making-sense-autistic-spectrum-disorders/201608/cognitive-rigidity-the-8-ball-hell.

26. https://humancentereddesign.org/.

27. https://www.academia.edu/15594889/Cognitive_readiness_in_network_centric_operations.

28. https://www.loc.gov/extranet/cld/workforce-performance/PerformanceDrivers.pdf.

29. https://www.performyard.com/articles/how-does-ge-do-performance-management-today.

30. https://www2.deloitte.com/us/en/insights/deloitte-review/issue-18/behavioral-economics-evidence-based-hr-management.html.

31. Laszlo Bock (2015), *Work Rules! Insights from Inside Google that Will Transform How You Live and Lead*, New York: Twelve.

Chapter 7

The human element

Throughout the book, we have examined the human element indirectly, but now we need to take a deep dive to further clarify and explain what is meant by the human element, human factors, and the attributes of human factor risks that lead to errors in judgment in organizations from corporate governance down to errors on the shop floor and cubicle alike. Not surprisingly, the term *human element* is more complex than anticipated. When the term *human element* is used, we instinctively know we are talking about people, but what does this really mean? Overwhelmingly, there are many definitions used to describe the various complexities of the human element.

In fact, the human element is defined by different industries very differently. Different definitions are used but the following definition is illustrative of the scope of the human element. "The work environment and conditions that lead to human error, safety issues, questions of judgment and failure will determine a focus on human elements. The Human Element is a holistic and comprehensive methodology for improving the way people work together, leading to better individual, team, and organizational performance and rate of goal achievement. The goal of The Human Element is to reduce unproductive behaviors and achieve better business results. By dealing with root causes rather than superficial behaviors, The Human Element helps individuals, teams and organizations eliminate the behaviors that sabotage, undermine relationships, and lower motivation."[1] For example, one version of the human element from cybersecurity is focused on social engineering. There are several authoritative books on this subject, and I have witnessed live examples of how effective social engineers are at conducting reconnaissance on a target firm prior to launching a full-blown cyber-attack.[2,3] Social engineering is the psychological manipulation of people into performing actions or divulging information through various techniques.

The maritime industry has developed an exhaustive definition of the human element to address the risks associated with the shipping industry. According to a study by the UK Maritime and Coastguard Agency,

> The shipping industry is run by people, for people. People design ships, build them, own them, crew them, maintain them, repair them, and

DOI: 10.1201/9781003189657-7

salvage them. People regulate them, survey them, underwrite them and investigate them when things go wrong. While these people vary in all sorts of ways, they are all, nevertheless, people – with the same basic set of capabilities and vulnerabilities. The "human element" is misnamed. It implies something that happens at the sidelines – a piece of the picture that is hopefully being dealt with by some specialist or other. Or else it implies that it's "just one of those things" – a bit of a mystery about which we can do little more than shrug our shoulders and hope for the best. But humans are not simply an element like the weather. They are at the very centre of the shipping enterprise. They are the secret of its successes and the victims of its failures. It is human nature that drives what happens every day at work – from the routine tasks of a ship's rating, right through to the policy decisions of the IMO.

The human element is prominent in the healthcare industry. A *Forbes* article describes the human element this way:[4]

> Xerox has new evidence to suggest that there are still some sizable gaps in at least one critical element of our healthcare transformation – and it's that human element. A recent survey of 2,147 U.S. adults, conducted for Xerox by Harris Interactive found that only 26% want electronic health records (EHRs).[5] Even beyond that surprise, only 40% of respondents believe that EHRs will deliver better, more efficient care – and that's down 2% from last year's survey. About 85% also said they have privacy concerns about EHR systems generally. Those concerns aren't unfounded. An online site, ModernHealthcare, reports that over the last 3 years there were over 470 healthcare data breaches that involved the medical records of over 20 million people.[6]

> Much of that human element relates to a variety of customer experiences around all the different dialogs in healthcare (physician to hospital, hospital to payer, patient to doctor etc...). In this context, consumers are really all of us – regardless of any healthcare affiliation. Fundamentally changing these experiences isn't as simple as slathering on a glitzy web design – or racing full throttle to the cloud and mobile. Recent headlines certainly aren't conclusive – but they do suggest ample room for innovation and improvement – especially around that human element.

These issues are significant but don't fully address the broad human element issues that result in patient outcomes due to miscommunications in handoffs between nurses, doctors, and other healthcare caregivers within and adjacent to medical facilities writ large.

Each industry has its own set of common and unique human element challenges including the military, manufacturing, retail, the judiciary, aerospace, government agencies, corporations, and more. The common denominator in all organized endeavor is human behavior or the human element. Not surprisingly, must of the literature is focused on the negative side of the human element equation. Human nature is fixated on what and how things go wrong so that it can be "fixed" theoretically in order for it not to happen again. Yet, we humans tend to find new ways to circumvent the fix and make new errors. The question this chapter poses is, does our search for quick and easy answers give rise to the circumvention of the solution to our own detriment?

The human element consists of various human factors. Examples of human factors include: (1) cognitive functions of decision-making (attention, detection, perception, memory, judgment, and reasoning, including heuristics and biases), (2) cognitive systems (system 1 – intuition, system 2 – reasoning), (3) types of performance (rules-based, knowledge-based), (4) error types (mental lapses, mistakes, etc.), (5) physical functions and quality (speed, strength, accuracy, balance, reach), (6) behaviors and skills (situational awareness, teamwork, skills), (7) learning domains, (8) physical, cognitive, and emotional states (stress and fatigue). This list is not exhaustive and different human factor practitioners may use different human factors in response to specific circumstances under investigation.[7]

This kind of human factors is emphasized in a definition provided by human factors pioneer Alphonse Chapanis (1991): "Human Factors is a body of knowledge about human abilities, human limitations, and other human characteristics that are relevant to design." Human factors represent the limitations and capabilities of human characteristics. Therefore, these factors of humans are of interest in the pursuit of performance in a specific domain. Better patient care in medical settings. Safety in the cockpit of a plane. Driver safety in cars, and more. The intent of human factors engineering and human factors analysis is ultimately to inform front-line professionals with non-technical skills on design and performance outcomes.

According to Steven Shorrock, who is an interdisciplinary humanistic, systems and design practitioner, Chartered Psychologist (CPsychol), and Chartered Ergonomist and Human Factors Specialist (CErgHF),

> Decades of scientific research have produced a plethora of empirical data and theories on factors of humans, along with a sizeable corpus of measures. Arguably, literature is far more voluminous for this kind of human factors than any other kind. We therefore have a sophisticated understanding of these factors. Much is now known from psychology and related disciplines (including human factors/ergonomics) about sustained attention (vigilance), divided attention, selective attention, working memory, long term memory, skilled performance, 'human error', fatigue, stress, and so on.

The challenge in the analysis of human factors is the narrowing into one or two characteristics such as situational awareness or cognitive load and not capturing the full human experience within specific domains of operation. Too narrow a lens into human factors results in missed opportunity in understanding the full picture. A concept that is central in humanistic psychology is, the whole person is greater than the sum of his/her parts; therefore, analysis of one or more parts will not be sufficient to evaluate performance in isolation. But this begs new questions about what is enough? What is the right combination of analysis in hard quantitative data and soft qualitative analysis?

To partly answer these questions, we must look at the factors that affect human performance. This perspective provides a rich array of options to analyze the factors that affect human performance; the workflow of planned and organized work activities, instruments of governance, supervision and monitoring, design of work processes or team coordination, flow of informal and formal communication channels, and the tools used to process, maintain, and share work product are a short list of options for evaluation.

Shorrock provides further insight in the role of design and performance,

> While the "factors of humans" perspective goes down and in to the cognitive, emotional, and physical aspects of human nature, the "factors affecting humans" perspective extends also up and out into the system, environment, and context of work. This acknowledges the influence of factors outside of humans on human performance, and therefore helps to explain it. "Human error" is not usually "simple carelessness", but a symptom of various aspects of the work situation. This acknowledges an important reality for any of us; our performance is subject to many factors, and many of these are beyond our direct control.

> This kind of human factors therefore more clearly points to design as a primary means to influence performance and wellbeing, as well as instruction, training, and supervision. The view of factors affecting humans also mirrors to some degree the way that organisations are designed and operated, as functional specialisms (e.g., training, procedures, design).

Shorrock's observation makes clear that complexity in the real world cannot be fully analyzed in simplified academic models with one or two controllable variables as compared to potentially unlimited and dynamic variables in the real world. Given this, we must accept that the complexity that exists is of our own making; therefore, there is resistance to reassess legacy decisions that created complex work environments. The tendency to expect people to adapt to complexity as opposed to making reduction in complexity creates tension and hesitancy in tackling human factors as effectively possible.

> Ergonomics (or human factors) is the scientific discipline concerned with the understanding of interactions among humans and other elements of a system, and the profession that applies theory, principles, data, and methods to design in order to optimize human well-being and overall system performance.

The three main bodies have adopted the following definition of human factors, the International Ergonomics Association, Human Factors and Ergonomics Society, and Chartered Institute of Ergonomics and Human Factors.[8,9,10]

A simple case study provides a lens into how the human element can become disruptive and impact organizational performance in ways many do not anticipate or resist addressing in a proactive way.

HUMAN ELEMENT IN THE WORKPLACE – PART I

This case study is about the alleged misconducts of Governor Andrew Cuomo and his brother Chris Cuomo. The facts and circumstances of the case are based on reports that are the subject of dispute; therefore, my focus is not on the details or specific allegations but on the impacts of the human element on the office of the New York governor, the CNN's president, and a high-profile reporter in prime time. None of this case study will dwell on fault and instead demonstrate how known behaviors became the source of controversy and ultimately lead to high-level resignations. Some of the details are relevant only for context in the case.

By now, unless you have not read any newspapers or social media or watched cable news, you are painfully aware that Governor Andrew Cuomo was accused and ultimately resigned because of allegations of unwanted sexual conduct by several female accusers. After an investigation on sexual harassment brought by several women regarding Governor Andrew Cuomo, Letitia James, the 67th Attorney General of the state of New York, issued a report that suggested the governor had engaged in these acts on October 22, 2021.

Governor Cuomo had already resigned on August 10, 2021, under tremendous political and public pressure in anticipation of the investigation by Attorney General James. Kathy Hochul, the Lieutenant Governor, assumed the office of Governor after former Governor Cuomo resigned. Ultimately, the case was taken up by David Soares, the Albany, New York District Attorney who concluded,

> The Westchester County District Attorney's Office announced late last month that it had concluded a thorough investigation into two sexual

misconduct allegations against Cuomo and that while "credible evidence" was found, there would be no forthcoming charges against Cuomo.[11]

"Our investigation found credible evidence to conclude that the alleged conduct in both instances described above did occur," Westchester County District Attorney Mimi Rocah said in a statement. "However, in both instances, my Office has determined that, although the allegations and witnesses were credible, and the conduct concerning, we cannot pursue criminal charges due to the statutory requirements of the criminal laws of New York. This conclusion is unrelated to any possible civil liability which is beyond the scope of a District Attorney's jurisdiction, which focuses solely on criminal laws."

However, in the process, Governor Cuomo's brother Chris Cuomo had been serving as an unpaid adviser of sorts during the investigation in support of his brother, the governor. The fact that Chris Cuomo chose to help his brother navigate the allegations is unremarkable the fact became a problem when Chris did not disclose his role either publicly or presumably internally to CNN. Chris had a very high-profile role as one of the most popular anchors of a prime-time show, Cuomo Prime Time, at CNN and had hosted Governor Cuomo several times during the start of the pandemic when Andrew Cuomo was leading the charge in the fight against the Covid-19 pandemic.

Chris Cuomo acknowledged it was a mistake to have participated as an adviser to the governor and only wanted to help. The problem was that Chris did not tell CNN what he was doing on his brother's behalf and the lack of disclosure became the sticking point.[12] Chris Cuomo's communications, text messages, and calls to Governor Cuomo's staff members were caught up in the investigation of the governor. CNN was likely blindsided by the disclosure and the lack of transparency of Chris's involvement. According to NBC News, "state prosecutors shed light on CNN anchor Chris Cuomo's involvement in managing the response to the sexual harassment scandal surrounding his brother, N.Y. Governor Andrew Cuomo."[13]

Chris might have survived that event had it not been for a new allegation that he, Chris Cuomo, was the subject of a sexual harassment complaint himself. On December 1, 2021, CNN announced they had suspended Chris Cuomo for his involvement in defending his brother against sexual harassment allegations. Days later Chris Cuomo was abruptly fired, "we retained a respected law firm to conduct a review, and have terminated him, effective immediately," the network said. "While in the process of that review, additional information has come to light."

That new information came in the form of a letter from attorney Debra S. Katz, who said she was representing an anonymous client who worked with Cuomo at ABC News, The New York Times reported, citing interviews with Katz, Chris' accuser, and other sources. Addressed to a CNN lawyer, the letter stated that the woman was a temp at ABC in 2011 but was looking for permanent employment when she accepted an invitation to have lunch with Chris, who had previously offered her career advice, according to the Times.[14]

In the course of the investigation into Chris Cuomo, Jeff Zucker was asked about and acknowledged a relationship with his closest colleague, Allison Gollust, the chief marketing officer for CNN. There is no reporting on how CNN learned of the relationship, so presumably someone raised the issue or emails disclosed the matter, but either way Jeff Zucker admitted he violated company policy by not disclosing the relationship.

Nearly two weeks after Zucker handed in his resignation, Allison Gollust resigned as well.[15] Gollust's relationship with Zucker appears to have been an issue internally based on Gollust's response as she left the firm. Gollust called Warner Media's statement "an attempt to retaliate against me and change the media narrative in the wake of their disastrous handling of the last two weeks." Katie Couric weighed in as well after Zucker's resignation, "The following day, Couric, 65, spoke out on the matter in a statement as part of her 'Wake-Up Call' newsletter and claimed that many people 'turned a blind eye to inappropriate behavior.'"[16]

In announcing the latest departure, WarnerMedia CEO Jason Kilar wrote in a memo to employees that an internal investigation "found violations of company policies" by Cuomo, Zucker, and Gollust, according to the *Times.* "I realize this news is troubling, disappointing and, frankly, painful to read," Kilar wrote.

Why is it important to bring up corporate gossip? The human element is a broad set of behaviors and attributes of decision-making on the part of executives and subordinates alike. The facts and circumstances from this event are still unfolding, and based on comments from Chris Cuomo and Allison Gollust, legal redress may be sought further dredging up more attention and repercussions for the cable news network. Further, the personality picadilloes pale in comparison to the corporate governance issues that will be discussed in part 2 of this case study. The purpose for providing context to this case will become self-evident in the second part of the case when the full drama at CNN and future strategic vision is provided.

More importantly, the human element is a major factor in corporate governance. Internal relationships, political maneuvering in divisions, concentration of power, and other human factors either distract from performance or contribute to performance. The issues at CNN are not unique or novel but have led to the early departure of many highly successful business leadership too often to detail at this point. This is a common problem that has been perennially difficult to address but is well known in most organizations where it occurs. This case, like many others, became an issue after an unrelated incident and then snowballed into something bigger. As you will see in part 2, the details matter because the larger story has yet to unfold at CNN.

Before we move to part 2 of this case, it is important to show how involved Chris Cuomo was in defending his brother, Andrew Cuomo. According to media reports,

> The bombshell report by the office of New York attorney general **Letitia James**, which concluded that New York Governor Andrew Cuomo sexually harassed multiple women, revealed that his brother, CNN host **Chris Cuomo**, testified as part of the investigation about his role in advising the governor on how to respond to the allegations.[17]

According to the same report,

> The *Washington Post* had previously reported that Chris Cuomo participated in "strategy calls" with his brother. "Cuomo, one of the network's top stars, joined a series of conference calls that included the Democratic governor's top aide, his communications team, lawyers, and a number of outside advisers," the paper reported in May.

At the time, CNN said in a statement that "it was inappropriate to engage in conversations that included members of the governor's staff, which Chris acknowledges." The network added that Chris Cuomo would "not participate in such conversations going forward," but did not discipline the host [MEDIAite.com, by Aidan McLaughlin, August 3, 2021]. Chris Cuomo acknowledged that he could not comment on-air about his Andrew Cuomo's legal issues.

Chris Cuomo and Jeff Zucker were close friends forged in a relationship where Cuomo joined Zucker on walks in Central Park while Zucker recovered from heart surgery. The close relationship between Zucker and Chris Cuomo may have initially shielded Chris from scrutiny until the details burst into public headlines by the New York State Attorney General's office. Chris Cuomo has always maintained that Jeff Zucker knew of extent to which he had helped his brother while he was in office with the network boss ignoring calls to fire him for months. Zucker and Gollust were apparently supportive of Chris's involvement not fully aware of all the details.

The issue for TimeWarner become a conflict of interest between CNN, Chris Cuomo, Allison Gollust, Jeff Zucker, and the level of support and guidance CNN provided to the embattled governor of New York, Andrew Cuomo.

> Utilizing her [Gollust] connections from her time in the Governor's office, Gollust was reportedly "instrumental" in having the Cuomo

brothers appear on the network during the early stages of the pandemic in 2020. Together with Zucker, she lobbied Andrew Cuomo to appear on their network, allegedly violating company policy and calling into question their own condemnation of Chris Cuomo's actions.

The relationship between Zucker and Gollust was also allegedly an *open secret* at CNN and could have been easily resolved had it been disclosed.

The *New York Times* story points to bigger issues facing CNN. The sordid stories and resignations foretell a far greater challenge facing the cable news network.[18]

> CNN had skidded into third place in cable news ratings. A key investor had criticized the network's opinionated, personality-driven programming. Mr. Zucker had clashed with a top executive at CNN's parent company. And he had made powerful enemies out of Mr. Cuomo and his brother, the former New York governor.
>
> By the time of Mr. Cuomo's ouster, the law firm that had been hired to investigate his behavior had turned its attention to Mr. Zucker and his management of a network where his intimacy with sources and employees had been both his calling card and Achilles' heel. Mr. Zucker's abrupt departure has thrown the future of CNN into chaos, just as it was poised to introduce a highly anticipated streaming service and to come under new corporate ownership. Mr. Cuomo is hoping to extract tens of millions of dollars from CNN. Star anchors are revolting. Employees are wondering whether, without Mr. Zucker at the helm, the network's soon-to-be-owners at Discovery Inc. will fundamentally change CNN's sprawling news operations.

The scandal and the fallout of the public unraveling of a president and top anchor in prime time demonstrate how the human element can be devastating for all involved and impact all aspects of the operations of an organization. It is now time to review the cognitive map of CNN and where the root cause of the tensions existed at CNN.

COGNITIVE MAP: JOHN MALONE, THE CONSUMMATE DEAL-MAKER – PART 2

The details of this part of the story have been pieced together mainly from a piece written by *The New Yorker*'s Claire Malone, no relation to John Malone and partly from the *New York Times*.[19] Media companies have been consolidating for decades now and many now view streaming as a way to monetize content and intellectual property. John Malone, chairman of Liberty Media, has been at the center of consolidation in the cable business and is widely recognized as a consummate operator and deal-maker and spent decades and billions buying cable operations in the US and abroad. Malone has owned large stakes in Murdock's NewsCorp, is the largest shareholder in Discovery, and is one of the largest private landowners in the US.

However, Netflix and other media franchises have created a juggernaut in streaming that has forced cable operators like Malone to rethink the value proposition in his cable assets. Disney, ESPN, HBO, Amazon, and a host of others have deftly switched from subscription-based cable offerings to streaming alternatives giving subscribers more choice and options to pick and choose the services they want as opposed to buying bundled programming, the vast majority most people don't watch or want to pay for.

According to *The New Yorker*,

> soon, WarnerMedia, which is currently owned by A.T. & T., will merge with Discovery, and make David Zaslav, Discovery's current C.E.O., the head of a new company, with properties that include Warner Bros., HBO, and CNN. "John Malone is David Zaslav's mastermind," one TV-industry insider told me. "John Malone is the brains of the operation."

AT&T announced in May of 2021 to merge WarnerMedia with Discovery for $43 billion.[20] Discovery shareholders will own 29% of the combined company. What John Malone gets is access to 400 million households for new streaming services and the ability to compete with Netflix and Disney, the two behemoths in streaming services. AT&T gets to streamline assets for cash and receive 71% ownership in the new company. This is a merger of titans with potential intrinsic value of $150 billion if the parties and work together to grow the respective assets. AT&T has struggled with mergers in media more recently, so they need a big win in their deal-making as well.

According to a CNBC report,

> Zaslav said on the press call that he believes the combined company will be able to differentiate itself from top streaming services like Disney+ and Netflix by offering a combination of news and sports on top of its entertainment properties like "Game of Thrones" and Harry Potter. Zaslav also expressed confidence in CNN, which some had speculated would be spun off from WarnerMedia. Zaslav said Monday his new company plans to keep CNN with the intention "to take everything we have in news, combine it with CNN and be a world leader in news."

According to *The New Yorker*'s report, "Malone gave up super voting shares in Discovery to form the new company but will be the largest shareholder in Warner Bros through Discovery who will become Advance

Publications, the parent company of Condé Nast and *The New Yorker.* But people I talked to said that Malone's close relationship with Zaslav and his acumen in the television business mean he will have an influence on the future of the new company that exceeds his ownership stake (which will be less than 1%) and his single seat on the board of directors." If you watch CNN, you may have noticed CNN+ services being promoted with various anchors who will stream new content in line with Zaslav's vision to compete against the other giants in streaming services.[21]

Jeff Zucker, as chairman of WarnerMedia, News and Sports and president of CNN Worldwide, was expected to head up the transition to CNN+ and the merger with Discovery. The departure of Zucker doesn't upend the merger but it does make the transition and strategic execution harder the longer it takes to replace him. CNN staffers have been upset by the resignations and the behavior of Zucker and Gollust's involvement with the coaching and support Andrew Cuomo received during the pandemic broadcasts chaired by Governor Cuomo. Jason Kilar, CEO WarnerMedia, terminated Gollust after learning of the roles of Zucker, Gollust and Chris Cuomo with Andrew Cuomo. Zaslav believed Zucker would be able to protect CNN after the merger of Discovery, but the new company would have tens of billion in debt and cuts would be needed to pare costs down in order to realize the strategic goals in streaming content and CNN had been spending heavily on content and talent. The cuts are expected to be significant, and CNN is not contributing enough profit to help pay down the debt on its own.

According to reporting by *The New Yorker,* Zaslav was both "flabbergasted" by the costs of production at CNN as compared to Discovery and "enthralled" by the glamor of the new business he was entering. But the focus has remained on streaming content, the movie production business and TV production with news at CNN seen as business model in decline.

> [Zaslav] told *Variety,* adding that movies were "the top of the funnel" for driving new subscribers to its platforms, which the company hopes will reach two hundred million subscribers. In a 2019 interview with CNBC, Malone described the elements that would eventually lead to a winning streaming bundle. "As those new packages are created, the guys who have uniqueness will start extracting more and more share, the prices will go up, and we will see this play again," he said. That "uniqueness" is likely not going to come from the news.

It is not clear from Zucker's viewpoint if he was on borrowed time but clearly the guy that matters, John Malone, had a vision that was very different than the one Zaslav envisioned given CNN's small footprint versus the value anticipated in creating value through unique offerings. CNN+ must be able to add subscribers and attract advertising dollars on a massive scale or be scaled down in size and scope. CNN+ is thought to be the training ground for how cable transitions to streaming content and the talent who attracts the most money. John Malone has also made clear that he sees CNN changing its focus and the tone of its reporting to become more "unique and refreshing." However, the longer view is that Malone sees WarnerMedia, Discovery, and CNN as chips that he can trade as streaming evolves over time. None of this speculation would necessarily have included or excluded Jeff Zucker but the pressure to grow an audience, revenue, and profits was likely growing.

The bigger picture from Malone's standpoint is the Warner Bros. Discovery deal is just a piece on the chessboard that can be bartered from more valuable options later. Media assets are fungible and will be put in play when needed. *The New Yorker* summarizes the long game succinctly, "There's going to be winners and losers," Malone said, last year, of the transition from cable to streaming. "We're only in the third inning of this nine-inning game." It's one he'll want to win, if only for the hell of it. "I have earned so much money that money doesn't interest me," he told the German publication *Der Spiegel*, in 2001. "Now it is only the love of the game that drives me." While he's not the only powerful player at the new Warner Bros. Discovery table, he will undoubtedly still have a voice. "If you invite an eight-hundred-pound gorilla to lunch, he's going to eat what he wants," the person familiar with Malone said. "He has a seat at the table, and he's very good at expressing his opinions."

Given this context, Jeff Zucker, Allison Gollust, and Chris Cuomo are collateral damage in the long game. The CNN story is a complex one but not an isolated story of empire building, egos, and performance. The human element is equally complex and layered depending on where one sits in the pecking order. The media industry like so many other industries is in flux as technology influences and separates the winners from the losers. The short-term distraction at CNN is only that, a minor distraction, in the game that players like John Malone are involved in. In the meantime, pundits and news analysts will dissect the CNN drama but miss the larger picture and forces in play. The bigger picture is who will win the media asset battle from consumer attention and revenue to entertain the masses. I wouldn't bet against John Malone. To wrap up the human element, let's review the lessons learned at CNN in part 3.

DECODING THE MISCALCULATION BY JEFF ZUCKER AT CNN – PART 3

Jeff Zucker was the youngest executive producer of NBC's "Today" and steered the show "near-irrelevance into dominance, but Jeff Zucker's track record is 'mixed' at NBC and CNN.[22] Industry observers credit Jeff's greatest success to the show, *The Apprentice*, starring Donald Trump which revived The Real Donald Trump's career by churning out millions in advertising revenue for the network and the former president. Zucker also was the head of NBC when '*The Office*' and '*30 Rock*' hit their stride but there were many who blame him for a number of missteps at NBC and CNN."

Katie Couric, who led *Today* has become a major critic after Jeff did not hire her at CNN and instead hired Allison. "When we worked together at NBC, she and Jeff cooked up even bolder ways to draw attention to *Today* and later Jeff himself when he moved to Entertainment," Couric, 65, details. "They were joined at the hip." Couric adds, "The problem was, we'd already hired a PR person for the show. There wasn't a role for Allison. Jeff asked me to meet with her anyway."[23] There were other missteps at NBC. Critics blame Zucker with keeping Jay Leno in his slot for too long over Conan O'Brien. Zucker closed "Friends" and launched Joey one of the characters from the show in a failed attempt to leverage the franchise. Zucker also brought onboard Don Lemon while Chris Cuomo joined CNN at about the same time in high-profile anchor roles in prime time.

Zucker was considered a superstar when he joined CNN, a major news brand in need of repair, in 2014. Zucker laid off journalist and cut expenses to redefine 24/7/365 news in the digital age. CNN's ratings were dropping, and the network had no real strategy to turn things around.[24] Zucker is credited with increasing "breaking news" coverage, investing in digital assets which grew a huge online audience. CNN was earning money and under Zucker's early watch moved from the number 3 position to number 2, so the early success was paying off for the network. Cable news viewership had declined significantly from 2009 to 2014, and MSNBC and Fox News were also looking to turn around the bleeding to maintain ad revenue and viewer attention.

Zucker expanded news coverage and covered most major events and made investments in alternative programming to attract a more diverse audience mix. Shows like Anthony Bourdain's travel adventures and other personalities lifted ratings and grew audience share. Zucker's relationship with Donald Trump was a godsend when the candidate garnered attention from every news network. Zucker again transformed the programming at CNN to feature liberal pundits in shouting matches over anything Trump. Zucker invited Trump allies on the show as contributors to balance the discussion between liberals and conservatives. Clearly, Jeff Zucker knew that controversy and political fireworks would draw attention, and audience and ad revenues to CNN. This was less about news and more about punditry by design and Trump delivered the goods by saying and doing things other candidates never would. Counterintuitively, when Trump branded CNN as "fake news," it helped CNN, which increased coverage by pitting Trump loyalists against the liberal pundits.

CNN grew in the Trump era along with Fox News changing "news" forever to infotainment pitting one side against the other. This is the legacy of Jeff Zucker at CNN but what must be understood is it's all about the ratings, viewers, and advertising revenue today in a digital streaming environment that is constant and continuous. This may say more about how the American public views news today than the foibles of Jeff Zucker. Zucker simply provided the audience what they wanted and did what he had to do to compete in the marketplace. Even more interesting, the post-Trump era has resulted in a massive drop in ratings at CNN.[25]

In one year, CNN has lost almost 50% of its daily viewers from June 2020 to June 2021. CNN has lost the most viewers of all three major news networks and 37% of its total audience since June 2020. CNN ratings dropped 70% along with MSNBC which had also dropped significantly. In comparison, Fox News was down on 14%. The bleeding hadn't stopped by January of 2022, after high viewership in the coverage of the January 6th insurrection on Congress viewership has dropped 90%, according to media reports.[26] The January 6th coverage was the highest ratings event since Ted Turner's ownership of the network. Some of the audience has moved to Fox during the ratings drop but the audience is fickle and the most recent invasion and bombardment by Russia into Ukraine on February 24, 2020, will undoubtedly return viewers to CNN.

Jeff Zucker has been praised and vilified depending on the audience and distractors of the CNN network. Undoubtedly, the ratings and ad revenues are sustainable only when major networks appeal to the infotainment of the viewing audience and events either real or concocted by coverage. The point is that the product of news has changed, and CNN has to adapt to more controversial coverage and punditry by its anchors or become more normalized around stories that appeal to specific markets. It seems that Jeff Zucker attempted to do both and may not have found the right balance needed to maintain CNN's leadership role. CNN has also made some missteps in the selection of some anchor positions although their anchors had maintained loyal followers, if only for their human foibles than from being likable as newscasters.

As a result, the scandals surrounding Chris Cuomo and sudden spotlight on Zucker's relationship with Allison Gollust were simply the last straw for the network. This is one example of the complexity of the human element and provides some insight into why it is important to address human behavior before events become untenable. The red flags were evident long before the events unfolded at CNN but may have been overlooked for reasons the human element is often overlooked. Dealing with the human element is uncomfortable and involves personal and intimate conversations about a person's affairs that executives would rather avoid. However, overlooking personal indiscretions in the C-suite can and often does result in lawsuits, reputational damage, lost business, and employee morale issues that only come to light after the damage is have been done.

The human element is messy and requires a deft touch by a team of advisers, a culture of constructive dissent, and organizational design that levels the hierarchical decision-making to benefit the long-term strategic objectives of the organization. When executives are whispering about personal affairs and rumors performance will be hurt. Allowing similar personal indiscretions means that more capable employees leave the organization because they no longer see fairness in promotion and opportunities. Although senior executives may not have been as attuned to the issues within the CNN network, they should have been because the rumors were rampant.

Jeff Zucker, Allison Gollust, and Chris Cuomo will now be the storyline for years to come if CNN is sold as a product in the next merger or reduced to a second-tier network by leadership to cut costs. Almost no one believes that today's talent at CNN will be able to produce a streaming product that saves the network from itself. More importantly, John Malone has already decided that cable news is not a unique product in the long-term future for media assets. That is bad news for viewers who may want alternatives to tabloid news and especially when the country is divided politically as it is today and would like an unblemished version of the truth.

NOTES

1. https://thehumanelement.bconglobal.com/what-is-the-human-element/principles
2. https://en.wikipedia.org/wiki/Social_engineering_(security).
3. https://docs.google.com/viewer?a=v&pid=sites&srcid=ZGVmYXVsdGRvbWFpbn1Y3M0MDJ8Z3g6MmZiYzA4YjdmYmM4NDgwOA.
4. https://www.forbes.com/sites/danmunro/2012/08/02/healthcares-often-missing-element-the-human-element/?sh=6f5bcc7a3a88.
5. http://news.xerox.com/pr/xerox/Xerox-Surveys-Americans-Electronic-Health-Records.aspx.
6. http://www.modernhealthcare.com/article/20120801/NEWS/308019974/large-medical-records-breaches-affect-nearly-21-million-ocr.
7. https://humanisticsystems.com/2017/08/12/four-kinds-of-human-factors-2-factors-of-humans/.
8. https://iea.cc/.
9. https://www.hfes.org/.
10. https://ergonomics.org.uk/.
11. https://www.dailywire.com/news/district-attorney-no-charges-against-cuomo-over-sexual-allegations-despite-credible-evidence.
12. https://abcnews.go.com/Entertainment/wireStory/details-chris-cuomos-role-advising-brother-andrew-81450669.
13. https://www.nbcnews.com/news/us-news/new-details-emerge-about-how-cnn-anchor-chris-cuomo-advised-n1275839.
14. https://www.nytimes.com/2022/02/15/business/jeff-zucker-cnn.html?smid=tw-share.
15. https://people.com/tv/allison-gollust-resigns-from-cnn-violated-company-policies-with-jeff-zucker-chris-cuomo/.

16. https://people.com/tv/katie-couric-speaks-out-about-jeff-zucker-resignation/.
17. https://www.mediaite.com/tv/chris-cuomo-appears-to-have-helped-draft -brother-andrews-response-to-harassment-allegations-ag-report-reveals/.
18. https://www.nytimes.com/2022/02/15/business/jeff-zucker-cnn.html.
19. https://www.newyorker.com/news/annals-of-communications/cnns-prob-lems-are-bigger-than-jeff-zucker.
20. https://www.cnbc.com/2021/05/17/att-to-combine-warnermedia-and-discov-ery-assets-to-create-a-new-standalone-company.html.
21. https://www.cnn.com/2021/07/19/media/cnn-plus-launch/index.html.
22. https://www.salon.com/2022/02/03/jeff-zucker-cnn-history-nbc/.
23. https://people.com/tv/katie-couric-mentioned-jeff-zucker-relationship-in-her -book-before-he-resigned/.
24. https://www.nytimes.com/2014/10/04/business/media/at-crossroads-cnn -seeks-to-reassert-itself.html?ref=television.
25. https://www.msn.com/en-us/tv/news/cnn-loses-nearly-half-its-viewers-in -post-trump-network-ratings-bloodbath/ar-AALBCKu.
26. https://nypost.com/2022/01/12/cnn-sees-ratings-dive-by-90-from-2021 -coverage/.

Chapter 8

Cognitive risk governance
Advanced ERM and cybersecurity

Corporate boards have been around for decades allowing for a great deal of literature and research on the operation of corporate boards but given the volumes of academic literature on how boards work, board governance is still a blackhole of insight into board performance and the methods boards use to influence the right behaviors toward risk management, strategic objectives, and organizational performance. Measurements of board performance are also inclusive with a focus on ex-anti board structure (size, diversity of experience, and expertise), or ex-post financial results (easy credit, stock price, profit margin, return on capital, or other ROI metrics).

These anecdotal criteria do not explain how board structure and board processes lead to failure or success. This same phenomenon is prevalent in the performance of the President of the United States (POTUS) where the populace attributes success by the ex-post results or predict ex-anti performance based purely on campaign promises. Both criteria are flawed given the many variables in the economy that are completely out of the control of the president. The same is true with measuring corporate performance. Favorable product trends, changes in demographics, inflation, and thousands of independent variables can impact the performance of a board of directors in positive or negative ways.

Board performance is therefore measured by previous performance in financial conditions, stock price, change in revenue, and so forth. Given the attention board governance has attracted in research and literature, one would expect a plethora of best practice that is evidence-based and shared with other organizations. However, there is a widespread disparity in organizational performance even with, and especially in, mature organizations that enjoyed great success but more recently have faltered badly. Why has the board structure evolved to become the dominant structure for overseeing organizational performance and has this structure lost its relevance for achieving sustainable performance?

There is a wide gap between the expectations in the role of the board of directors to preside over the operations of organizations and the reality of the obstacles in executing governance on most boards. The risks in board governance are squarely in the human factors realm which we have seen is

DOI: 10.1201/9781003189657-8

extremely difficult to manage if left to the devices of management alone but can be more proactively addressed as we have pointed out along the way in each chapter. Before we describe an alternative to traditional board governance, it is important to understand why and how board governance has become the default for managing organizational performance.

A matrix of board governance models was discussed in detail in previous chapters; therefore, we will avoid redundancy in explaining specific board models. Instead, a little historical context may help demonstrate that over time the original intentions of board governance have evolved without a change in commensurate best practice in board governance. First, a centralized board of corporate governance, with minor variations, has become the universal model in the US and around the world.[1,2] The board governance model is premised on three underlying concepts. The three concepts are interrelated or have become so over time starting with, first, the relationship between the board of directors and shareholders of the corporation; secondly, the relationship between directors on the board themselves; and lastly, the relationship between the board directors and senior executives of the organization.

In the first instance, shareholders or the "owners" of the corporation do not manage the day-to-day operations of the organization. Shareholders delegate the responsibility to manage or place under the direction of the organization to the board of directors who are selected by the shareholders. The board hires the senior executives and members of the management team as agents who manage the day-to-day operation of the organization and report to the board of directors in periodic board meetings. The directors then hold one another accountable for overseeing a section of the governance model through specifically designated committees. Typical committees consist of administrative and operational areas of significance, such as audit, compensation, performance, and strategic planning. The board is also responsible for monitoring its own performance and that of the senior executives of the organization. The long-standing corporate law rule is that individual directors have no authority to act alone and are expected to exercise governance through consensus with other members of the board.[3]

A comprehensive analysis of the impacts on the board relationships noted above (Turley and Zaman 2004) indicates,[4]

> It is clear that there is no automatic relationship between the adoption of audit committee structures or characteristics and the achievement of particular governance effects, and caution may be needed over expectations that greater codification around factors such as audit committee members' independence and expertise as the means of "correcting" past weaknesses in the arrangements for audit committees. The most fundamental question concerning what difference audit committees make in practice continues to be an important area for research development.

In other words, there is little to no correlation between the contributions made by an audit committee and increased enhancements in corporate performance.

This finding may be both confusing and appear contradictory to norms and expectations in corporate governance. There are a number of reasons that board governance is not material to enhancements in corporate performance that are counterintuitive to conventional wisdom. Confirmation bias is one of the reasons! The current model of board governance (audit committees) provides limited evidence that it contributes to corporate performance.

> It is argued that there is only limited and mixed evidence of effects to support claims and perceptions about the value of audit committees for these elements of governance. It is also shown that most of the existing research has focused on factors associated with audit committee existence, characteristics and measures of activity and there is very little evidence on the processes associated with the operation of audit committees and the manner in which they influence organizational behaviour.

The absence of evidence is not conclusive but does suggest there is very little substance from which evidence can be derived to prove the contributions to corporate performance.

Confirmation bias in the adoption of the current model of board governance has been created by the misleading perception that the audit committee and hierarchical structure of board governance are contributing factors without any empirical evidence to prove it is true. There has been growing degree of codification and harmonization of best practice. In other words, adoption has grown simply because there is global acceptance of the audit committee as the de facto governance structure model because others have adopted the model. This has been reinforced by regulatory language and literature that describes the audit committee and governance model using aspirational taxonomy but fails to provide little evidence for how the structure of a board through the audit committee format makes such contributions to corporate performance.

A lack of evidence and continued poor outcomes as reflected in current financial fraud through repeated history of failure in corporate governance has not been abated as demonstrated by COSO's own research. More importantly,

> while no *a priori* position on the efficacy of audit committees (ACs) for alleviating weaknesses in corporate governance as adopted in this paper, it can be noted that regulators, governmental bodies, and researchers in many countries have raised questions about ACs' effectiveness and their contribution to governance (Wolnizer 1995).[5]

The incidence of high profile corporate failures, notably in the period since 2000, involving fraud, poor accounting and failure of internal control have provided at least anecdotal evidence to support concerns about the adequacy of the monitoring provided by ACs. Such events have accentuated concerns that have been expressed over a somewhat longer period.

Financial fraud, earnings manipulation, and corporate failure are being corrected not by regulatory bodies or a more robust governance model but by disruption from private equity investors in order to protect their investment. We discussed this dynamic in Chapter 3, but it is important to note that external sources or market dynamics are the catalyst for change, not a best practice model of enterprise risk or board governance.[6]

An article in *Financier Worldwide* explains the transition taking place currently,

Within the private equity (PE) industry, corporate governance has become more important than ever, for both institutional investors and fund managers. When a PE firm invests in a company, important questions need to be addressed. Such as, in the interest of creating value for investors, how should the decision-making process be managed across shareholders, the board of directors, and management? To what extent should PE be represented on the board? It is becoming clear that building strong governance and expert boards within portfolio companies is crucial to returning value to investors.

It is clear that change has not happened within industry leading to a status quo that is corrected primarily by activist investors or a crisis. Resistance to change and complacency in board governance is caused by insular incentives at the board level and with the agents (senior executives) of the firm leading to risk aversion. The idea and concepts behind Board 3.0 are interesting but are equally limiting and not robust enough to be sustainable because it concentrates decision-making in hierarchical structures similar to traditional board governance. As a reminder, "Board 3.0, as an option for public company boards. The goal is to develop a model of *thickly informed, well-resourced, and highly motivated* directors who could credibly monitor managerial strategy and operational skill in cases where this would be particularly valuable. Unlike the present board model of *thinly informed, under-resourced, and boundedly motivated* directors. Board 3.0 accurately lays out the challenge in traditional board governance. Generally speaking, traditional board governance driven by an audit committee is *thinly informed, under-resourced*, and *boundedly motivated* lacking the skills and capability to drive long-term sustainable growth."

An alternative model is offered here, described as a cognitive risk framework for enterprise risk and cybersecurity that includes cognitive governance. What is a cognitive risk framework and why is it needed as an alternative to existing traditional governance or emerging proposed models to address organizational performance and board governance? It is important to note that none of the existing or proposed governance models are rooted in evidence-based science. The reason that today's traditional board governance model represents a "black-box" in performance metrics is because it is based on prescriptive principles of governance.

Regulatory guidance and so-called "best practice" assume the principles of *homo economicus* are still alive and well. You may recall, homo economicus is a flawed belief in the portrayal of humans as agents who are consistently rational and narrowly self-interested, and who pursue their subjectively defined ends optimally. I have dubbed this bias *homo periculum*, a fallacy in judgment that an organizations' subjectively defined pursuits in risk management are conducted optimally. Human nature is inherently bounded, a concept created by Herbert Simon, the first political scientist who influenced the fields of computer science, economics, statistics, and cognitive psychology.[7]

A true renaissance man in his time. Much of Simon's work is seldom leveraged in contemporary organizational science or corporate governance, but his thesis is still as relevant today as it was in the 1950s when he first presented *Administrative Behavior*, his seminal book on decision-making processes in administrative organizations. Daniel Kahneman and Amos Tversky built on Simon's work in a new multidisciplinary body of work in behavioral economics, cognitive science, decision science, and more in *Prospect Theory*

The cognitive risk framework incorporates as its foundation the concepts of Herbert Simon, Paul Slovic, Frank Knight, Kahneman and Tversky, and more. Corporate governance has continually failed because we have largely ignored the *science* of decision-making and human behavior. Decision-making under uncertainty is not an exact science, but the core of this body of work is an understanding of the errors in judgment that lead to poor or suboptimal outcomes. These concepts recognize that reliance on subjectively pursued means leads to suboptimal outcomes, but it does not suggest a purely analytical alternative. Decision-makers must balance data analytics with subjective values and stakeholder interests as well. As I have proposed in previous chapters, balance is best struck through a collaborative approach by weighing the interests and value to the organization after being informed by data. Developing alternative approaches and evaluating the probability of various outcomes.

The cognitive risk framework and five pillars program components include the following pillars. Each will be discussed in detail:

1. Cognitive governance.
2. Intentional controls design.
3. Cybersecurity and enterprise risk management – asymmetric risk.

4. Human factors and socio-technical risk.
5. Cognitive risk mitigation – bias and noise.

The cognitive risk framework and five pillars have been revised and updated since the original publication in 2016 in *Cognitive Hack: The New Battleground in Cybersecurity and Enterprise Risk Management.* Additional research and collaboration with behavioral scientists and human factors academics have expanded the role and scope of the revised five pillars.

COGNITIVE GOVERNANCE

So how is this achieved without the process becoming a process of analysis paralysis? A cognitive risk framework includes five pillars of maturity with each pillar an advanced approach based on design principles, behavioral science, and other multidisciplinary approaches. The first pillar is cognitive governance. Cognitive governance is based on a simple principle created by Paul Slovic in his seminal paper on "The Perception of Risk."[8] Slovic examined how people respond to and make decisions around highly complex risks such as nuclear and chemical waste. Most complex business decisions do not evolve such life and death choices but the challenge in making rational decisions under uncertainty for complex risks provides insight into the vagaries of discernment regarding the emotional response to complex risks versus the ability to make reasonable choices using risk analysis derived by risk perceptions.

The intellectual process of risk assessment has become very muddled and opaque in most organizations and the purpose of designing *cognitive governance* as the first pillar is presented to clarify how decision-makers should organize the process for better decision-making on complex and residual risks that seldom get re-examined in a systemic way. A secondary purpose is to improve the quality of risk communications between laypersons, technical experts, and decision-makers so that all have a common understanding of how to evaluate complex risk. Cognitive governance is a formal process of continuous analysis and evaluation of risk within a firm as well as external risks that may have an impact or be impactful to the operations of an organization.

Cognitive governance would replace the audit committee on all boards of directors for the reasons we have elucidated throughout the book. Audit committees are point in time checks on subjectively defined risks without an analysis of quantifiable levels of confidence in the outcomes presented to the board of directors. There are an endless number of "what-if," subjectively defined issues presented to the board that take up valuable time but offer any real insight or value-added objectives to strategic goals. Cognitive governance is designed to be strategically targeted at defining confidence in

risk assessments that have the potential to be most impactful to the organization. An example would be helpful in clarifying how this would work
in practice.

Let's say that a hospital has defined a goal of improving patient care
or patient outcomes. This is a typical, and very vague goal-setting process. Instead of conducting a survey of subject matter experts or canvassing
external experts on patient outcomes or care, an extensive analysis can
be conducted on the frequency and severity of poor outcomes within the
hospital would replace subjectively defined survey measures of patient care
or outcomes. Once the data is captured, a statistical analysis is conducted
to determine a level of confidence in the data as well as the variable used
in the modeling of the results. Lastly, secondary set of data is captured to
determine the root cause and finally subjective data is gathered to vet the
two data sets to balance out the human impact to address the problem in a
sustainable way.

A host of hidden issues will undoubtedly become exposed in this process
versus the usual process where people are afraid to speak their mind or
expose bad behavior of others. Starting with real data avoids the messy
human element issues that inevitably derail risk assessment and risk management initiatives. When people are presented with the facts, it is much
harder to come up with excuses and alternative narratives. Instead of an
audit, conduct a data-driven analysis of errors, events, or corrective actions
resulting from existing internal controls. Auditors do not perform statistical analysis of internal controls over financial reporting or any other control operations, but they should. This is the only way to create a realistic
baseline of operation from which to begin to develop a better understanding of risk. Once firmly established, the new baseline can be monitored or a
decision can be made to reduce risk through automation, training, or better
design of internal controls. Cognitive governance does not blame people.
The approach is designed to develop a single and reliable source of truth
about the effective operations of the firm.

So why is it important to replace the audit committee with cognitive governance? Cognitive governance provides a fuller more robust lens into the
actual performance of the organization as opposed to the opinions of an
audit department or senior executives. Opinions are fine for less critical
areas of operation, but if you want to understand the truth about how well
the organization is performing in key areas of operation data, real-time
data is the only way to get a better understanding. The interpretation of the
data is where opinions can be expressed. Challenges of the data, results,
and conclusions must also be formalized with equally robust methodologies
that can be supported by data then reconciled as needed.

The cognitive governance team then is a multidisciplinary group within
the firm who is independent of management and is responsible for providing
the directors on the board and senior management with high-quality insights
on the key risks that have the most potential to operational excellence or

that could derail performance. Cognitive governance product(s) would be designed as a decision support platform, customized to increase efficiency in operations or clarity in strategic planning or to better understand residual risk exposures in each area of the business where line of sight is obscured from board of directors and senior executives. Cognitive governance could also be used in Board 3.0 as the deal team responsible for analyzing how well an activist strategy would be performed or how well an acquisition would fit in the financial accretion of a new firm.

The point is to raise the bar at the board of directors level to become "a model of thickly informed, well-resourced, and highly motivated directors." Some may suggest that the data does not exist to keep a cognitive governance team busy or enabled to provide new insights. I would suggest from personal experience that there is more data available to actively pursue cost savings, strategic and operation efficiency goals indefinitely. The problem is not sufficient data, the problem is that most organizations have not taken the time to find the data that could make themselves more productive or the data has not been captured in ways that make it hard to develop insights that can be used as powerful tools for innovation within the firm. These are easily solvable problems to overcome but require a change in culture within the firm that must be driven by senior executives. Transparency is one of the cultural challenges that must be addressed right up front.

As Paul Slovic explains,

> these perceptions and the opposition to technology that accompanies them have puzzled and frustrated industrialists and regulators and have led numerous observers to argue that the American public's apparent pursuit of a "zero-risk society" threatens the nation's political and economic stability.

Wildavsky (3, p. 32) commented as follows on this state of affairs. "Slovic proposes that are perceptions of risk are based on our training to analyze risk." A layperson experiences *risk as feelings* and a researcher experiences *risk as analysis*. Slovic and a small team of researchers sought to examine what people mean when they describe something as risky or not risky. In the process, Slovic and researchers developed methodologies to evaluate risk as feelings and to study the underlying factors that contribute to these perceptions.

Douglas and Wildavsky (1982) found that "people acting in social groups, downplay certain risks and emphasize others as a means of maintaining and controlling the group."[9] We see this playing out in the divided response to the Covid-19 guidance and challenges to the CDC and medical professionals. This is no coincidence and demonstrates that these behaviors are predictable. The science behind perceptions of risk is deep and multidisciplinary incorporating studies on human behavior, sociological studies, probability assessments, utility assessments, and decision-making processes.

Slovic's research with Dan Kahneman and Amos Tversky goes even further,

> Although these rules are valid in some circumstances, in others they lead to large and persistent biases, with serious implications for risk assessment. In particular, laboratory research on basic perceptions and cognitions has shown that difficulties in understanding probabilistic processes, biased media coverage, misleading personal experiences, and the anxieties generated by life's gambles cause uncertainty to be denied, risks to be misjudged (sometimes overestimated and sometimes underestimated), and judgments of fact to be held with unwarranted confidence. Experts' judgments appear to be prone to many of the same biases as those of the general public, particularly when experts are forced to go beyond the limits of available data and rely on intuition.[10,11]
> Research further indicates that disagreements about risk should not be expected to evaporate in the presence of evidence. Strong initial views are resistant to change because they influence the way that subsequent information is interpreted. New evidence appears reliable and informative if it is consistent with one's initial beliefs; contrary evidence tends to be dismissed as unreliable, erroneous, or unrepresentative.[12] When people lack strong prior opinions, the opposite situation exists-they are at the mercy of the problem formulation.[13] Presenting the same information about risk in different ways (for example, mortality rates as opposed to survival rates) alters people's perspectives and actions.

This research and its findings were developed long before "fake news" was popularized by politicians and used to manipulate the public in ways and on a scale never seen before. Cybercriminals have used the digital version of these concepts and now people are more aware that Russia and other nation states have become active users of misinformation and disinformation to divide countries politically and socially. The research has been weaponized in very subtle ways but has tremendous power because it works by seeping into the subconscious tricking our minds into thinking and believing it is real or there is truth in misinformation and disinformation.

Cognitive governance is a powerful antidote to these cognitive risks as well because leaders of powerful organizations are prone to be impacted and influenced in their beliefs easily as other laypersons. Unfortunately, when positions of power use these techniques, they are participating in spreading misinformation and disinformation making it harder for laypersons and experts alike to know the difference between what is real and what is false. This is not a political statement, it is evidence-based research! I found these risks while conducting research for my first book in 2017,

Cognitive Hack: The New Battleground in Cybersecurity and Enterprise Risk Management. I have attempted to warn the risk community about these risks for the last six years and continue with this book!

Paul Slovic may not be a household name but in the behavioral science community he is revered. Slovic has warned researchers about the perception of risk challenges. An unrealistic expectation of a "zero-risk society" has permeated America and boardrooms where risks are perceived as a negative reflection of management. Audit, risk, and compliance professionals are expected to address all risks to prevent "surprises." Risk is inherent in any pursuit where the outcome in uncertain. However, without risks there is little to no opportunity for innovation or gains. With that said, transparency into risks in an organization is the beginning of the exploration of the hidden vulnerabilities that have not been fully addressed. Instead of avoiding risk as a four-letter word not to be discussed, a new curriculum on the opportunities in risk must be ingrained in oversight best practice. This is the ultimate outcome of cognitive governance. The opportunity side of risk is about discovery, learning, and transformation, not obfuscation. Too often, risk "experts" use confusing terms like systems thinking and design thinking to explain risks when these terms are about a mindset, not a risk discovery process.

Cultural resistance to risk discovery is itself a risk. Senior executives must learn to embrace the two sides of risk. There are two kinds of risks that exists in all organizations – known inherent risks and unknown residual risks. The vast majority of risk oversight groups spend upward of 90% of their time and resources on known inherent risks yet fail to make an informed decision about what, if anything to do about them. These risks are known because they present themselves daily and for the most part are frequent but not impactful. This ineffective waste of risk resources, time, and reporting on perennial risks has failed.

A risk inventory is the greatest evidence of that failure. If a risk (small or large) impedes efficiency, creates material loss over time, or results in hindering strategic objectives, it must be addressed to enhance performance. A certain amount of pain is tolerated in all organizations and few, if any, take the time to analyze the small pain points that accumulated over time dragging down productivity. All risks require an informed response, but key risks must be prioritized. Risks that impede human performance appear to be insignificant because we largely blame the person but for those who overcome the impediment are equally impacted by slowly them down or making work harder than it should be. We ignore these inconveniences until they result in a major error, loss, or worse. The failure to understand and analyze risk as a performance inhibitor is one of the reasons cybersecurity risks, operational risks, and ethical behavior are ignored or hidden until they become a headline event. We know these risks exist but simply fail to address them before it is too late. This is why everyone knows why it [a risk] occurred after the fact. In reality, it was hiding in plain sight!

Risks that impede human performance are broad in all organizations; therefore, it is important to clarify what this means and how to scope human performance risks specifically. Obviously, where human life is at risk or has been exposed to injury or harm remediation is paramount; however, human performance risks are specifically directed at optimizing the remediation of human error, human skills, execution of strategic initiatives, and at each level of the organization including the board of directors down to the person on the shop floor or cubicle. There are three strategic areas of focus in cognitive governance: (1) *decision risk management*, (2) *operational risk management*, and (3) *human risk management*.

Decision risk management addresses the two flaws in decision-making: *bias* and *noise*. Operational risk management addresses enhancements in *workflows* across the organization, and human risk management addresses the board area of *human factor* risks. One of the reasons that enterprise risk programs fail is because the programs are siloed along risk lines of discipline, such as market risk, credit risk, operational risk, and cyber risk for example. In other cases, ERM programs are even more generic base on the three lines of defense creating different types of silos between audit, risk, compliance, and management. The problem with these approaches is there is no real alignment between how work is structured in traditional management spans of control and how risk is originated in the organization. In other words, decision risk, operational risk, and human factor risks exist in all lines of work not just in silos but across the organization in interrelated ways, and are sometimes correlated, but often uncorrelated by specific risk disciplines.

An error in coding systems used to process new products and services can ripple through an organization and impact multiple systems, departments, and strategic initiatives if not detected or remediated in a timely manner. Therefore, dividing traditional risk disciplines into silos ensures that risk oversight groups never have a full picture of the enterprise risks that exist within the organization. The structure of risk management and oversight is broken by aligning risk by discipline into separate ineffective silos. Risks don't care what your organizational chart looks like! Enterprise risk is about ensuring that performance is sustained over time and improved by having clear insight into the overall health of all components that contribute to success or could impede it.

Another example is social engineering. A skilled social engineer is someone who knows how to conduct reconnaissance on an organization to gather intelligence about the training and awareness of the people on the front line in organizations. A skilled social engineer has learned that busy complex organizations that failed to train all points of contact such as receptionist, assistants, admins, and others to detect these callers will expose a firm to more risk than a phishing attack, but most organizations fail to conduct this type of training. The goal of social engineering is to evade all cybersecurity controls using nothing but a phone call. Few, if any organizations, have detailed training in place to thwart social engineering attacks but many have adopted training to recognize phishing attacks even though this training is ineffective. Cognitive governance is about hardening the human element in the firm to be resilient at the enterprise level.

There are several misconceptions about risks that have been ignored for too long. The process of risk discovery is simple. First, a cost-benefit analysis of known inherent risk mitigation must replace risk inventories. Management must participate and sign off on the cost-benefit analysis. Second, a risk budget must be established to address known risks and to explore residual risks. Third, residual risks are the most pervasive and frequent contributor to tail risk events and "surprises" in operational risk. This is the cognitive governance model. Seventy-five to eighty percent of oversight must be focused on risk discovery, not risk monitoring. This is also how organizations reduce the growing cost and bureaucracy in compliance, risk, and audit. If a risk needs monitoring, it also needs to be minimized to an acceptable level. We will discuss how to do this later as this is a behavioral failure and not a risk failure.

Cognitive governance flips the practice of how risks are managed. Traditional governance and risk oversight simply babysit risks, it does nothing to manage risk. A risk inventory is a risk babysitter which adds no value. Sarbanes–Oxley stipulates that management is responsible for risk management; however, risk experts have not been empowered to conduct robust analysis of risks so that management can make an informed decision about how to manage known inherent risk and unknown residual risk. A more robust discussion on unknown residual risk will be addressed later in this chapter. Counterintuitively, management has been allowed to delegate risk management to oversight groups who lack the authority to make any decisions that effectively manage risk, nor should they. Risk, audit, and compliance must be reimagined along two objectives – *robust risk analytics* and *effective risk communications framing*.

Cognitive governance is an advanced approach that replaces the audit committee by informing the emotional side of risk awareness with the scientific analysis of risk. A cognitive governance approach is responsible for framing risk communications in terms of a design of cost-effective risk solutions. A simple example of the two risk objectives becomes apparent in the Covid-19 response. Scientists were extremely effective at developing highly effective risk mitigation solutions (RNA viral vaccine platforms) to minimize illness and death but failed at framing effective risk communications the public was able or willing to adopt. Cognitive governance addresses both the design of effective risk solutions and the human behavioral components that determine how effective risk solutions are implemented. If risk mitigation does not take into account the human element, the best risk assessment will often fail its objective.

People are the solution, not the problem, but effective risk communications is the tool used to activate the problem-solving that is needed to address risk. This requires risk professionals to become designers of risk solutions through creative and effective ways to frame the solution to fit the cultural norms and behaviors in each organization. This is why a cognitive governance approach is the first pillar of a five-pillar cognitive risk framework. Cognitive governance requires a diverse, multidisciplinary group of risk professionals with different analytical skills and backgrounds.

Using a professional sports team analogy, every member of the team must play his or her part in harmony or disharmony, toward the team's overall objectives. Today, there are too many competing oversight teams within organizations with competing objectives. Hierarchical organizations have formed silos that are counterproductive to the overall objective of oversight. Risk oversight teams will never advance if members of each respective oversight function; risk, audit, compliance, and management (three or four lines of defense) are on different teams with competing and opposing strategic objectives! There should be one team with complementary skills who contribute to the success of organizational goals. Do more with less! Stop the checkboxes! Start prioritizing! Enterprise risk should have one overarching objective to find and minimize the risks and hurdles (design solutions) that hinder organizational performance. Risk management must become performance based!

Cognitive risk governance is about defining selective risk treatments based on evidence it impacts or could impact performance. Performance-based risk includes ensuring compliance, policies, procedures, and meeting strategic goals as well. The difference in traditional risk frameworks and a cognitive risk governance framework is that CogRisk looks at how these processes impact people and impedes their performance. In other words, CogRisk is human-centered. If cybersecurity practices become too cumbersome to effect situational awareness, it must be redesigned. If operational risk is less effective, it must be redesigned. The difference is the end goals must be well-defined and measurable to allow for reductions in risk to be measured with a higher level of confidence. If existing risk practice is not defined by levels of confidence in risk impacts, the program is simply guessing about assurance. Risk professionals must be able to say with confidence how effective a risk program is operating with evidence. Not doing so is malpractice.

Cognitive governance requires an honest assessment of key risks, how much is known about the probabilities of key risks, and how material to operating effectiveness are key risks. This requires simplification of risks through robust analysis and a data-driven approach to measure risk behavior is paramount. Wherever there is human decision-making and performance, there is risk data. It may require risk professionals to seek out new and alternative ways to evaluate performance. However, performance-based risk programs demonstrate how they contribute to the performance of an organization in dollar terms. The key risk indicators are different than traditional risk KRIs. CogRisk indicators are metrics of change in behavior, performance, intelligence, and maturity.

Simple example

A large insurance company in Boston with a commercial vehicle line of business was experiencing a sudden and unexpected hike in auto and truck claims. Nationally, highway vehicle fatalities and accidents had declined for almost 20 years; however, this insurer was experiencing excessive losses and paying large claims for catastrophic accidents across the country. Actuaries within the firm were flummoxed about the spike in accident rates, but none of their historical databases or actuarial tables reflected the trends they were experiencing. I was asked to conduct an external risk analysis of highway accidents to find anecdotal and quantitative evidence to help underwriters understand and explain the change in accident rates to determine how to address the troubling trend in claims and large losses with clients and brokers.

In order to find data that would be credible and insightful, I started my research by searching for vehicle accidents across the country in local and national online news stories that reflected the states and localities of loss events by the insurer. Secondarily, after narrowing the list of states down to the ones with the highest incident of losses, I started to pull data from state highway department of transportation. Using qualitative data from news articles combined with analytical data from state and federal agencies, general themes emerged wherever there were large oil fracking operations along with corresponding news stories of major accidents which coincided with events in counties specific to oil fracking. A compelling story emerged that specific counties were experiencing massive damage to county roads and increased catastrophic accidents between trucks and civilian cars and commercial vehicles. Fracking is an oil drilling process where companies drill sideways into bedrock to break up rocks to find oil and gas deposits not captured in traditional drilling. The process requires more vehicles than normal drilling because water is a big component. The trucks are heavier than normal and fracking fields are in remote locations resulting in abnormal traffic on small country roads.

I found data that pinpointed the exact counties and local towns where the department of transportation experienced higher spikes in accident rates than neighboring counties and town and was able to identify high levels of traffic on old county roads with an increase in oil fracking activity in each state. Lastly, I was able to use local news accounts of increased spending to repair roads in local communities where fracking was active as well as tie in supporting documentation related to spikes in oil and gas production by county across the country. What I found was a shortage of qualified truck drivers, lack of pipeline to move the oil to refineries further south near coastlines, drivers exceeding work limits set for driver safety, and correlated increased oil production by increased vehicle accidents in the regions reporting higher losses and claims to the insurance company. The report changed how actuaries viewed the risk consulting group because it was a project unlike any other they had produced, and we were able to provide context beyond simply data trends and analysis. I provided a comprehensive story that anyone could understand and develop solutions to address the loss trends.

The point here is there are times when new approaches are needed to reimagine how risks are assessed in order to understand the unanticipated changes that occur. No one at one of the largest insurance companies in the country had ever conducted such a study of losses and claims with this level of context! I was able to demonstrate that there are credible data sources outside of the firm to better frame the problem and use that information to inform their clients to change their behavior. More could have been done but the firm was satisfied with the results. They immediately started a campaign to address their risks. The data was also accurate enough to predict the top in oil prices based on US historical data of past oil production trends. Actuarial methods fail to solve risks that fall outside of their predetermined loss models. I also learned that actuaries have limited risk tools to help them think outside the box!

Similar stories are now playing out in many industries where past experience is not a predictor of future behavior. Risk professionals cannot rely on the fallacy that the past is a prologue of the future. As technology advances, the past is no longer relevant because of the speed of change and dynamic leverage technology affords companies in comparison to the past. In fact, in some cases, technology accelerates risk or can mitigate it. The problem for humans is our inability to process subtle changes and explain what is happening when we still rely on tools that have limited capacity to anticipate change. Change is the mother of new risks whether we know or believe it or not. Covid is a wakeup call to change how we think about risk. One-hundred-year events are happening more frequently than in the past and with more damage, but these events are evident long before they become pandemic if we are willing to look for clues or signals. The signals are there we fail to pay attention.

Risk doesn't announce its presence as it accumulates and must be discovered through active measures or by accident. Cognitive governance focuses on developing active measures. Risk professionals must anticipate that residual risks are hidden and must be discovered using different tools and processes depending on the nature of the event, positive or negative. This is the opportunity in cognitive governance! Organizations must begin to reconcile their different views on the concept of risk and weigh the benefits of risk performance versus a risk aversion approach. Cognitive governance goes beyond developing a risk appetite statement. Cognitive governance operationalizes risk appetite into action and changes behavior. Risk appetite statements are similar to risk inventories. Neither is important or effective without a change in behavior or actions taken to address risk.

In other words, we have learned to tolerate some risks without a full understanding or comprehension of the extent of known risks. The conflicts over risk are the result of different definitions between novice and expert risk decision-makers for measuring risk. Risk perceptions are complex and are often influenced by social groups, media, beliefs, and past experience. Differences in risk perceptions must be taken seriously in order to develop a constructive dialogue about what to do about risks where conflicts prevent forward progress. We have discussed constructive dissent as one way to address different perceptions of risk, but the most effective approach is to formalize the process of risk discovery, assessment, and remediation that impedes performance. Cognitive governance is proposed as an independent, formal methodology to address complex risks that have broad organizational implications.

Returning to unknown residual risks and the role they must play in cognitive governance. As noted in an earlier chapter, wherever there are subjective decisions in an organization, there is noise and bias. Any organization that has achieved a modicum of success has also experienced failures as well. Few organizations are able or willing to make an honest assessment of the bad decision-making that led to past failure. Everyone wants to move past failure and move on to the next "big" thing, but failure is a gold mine of lessons if we are willing to explore them properly without pointing fingers of blame. Operational failures, cyber breaches, and strategic and product failures all have lessons that can inform new initiatives. However, my experience is that the goal of an assessment of failure is primarily to assign blame or fault. This is counterproductive on so many fronts because the truth will seldom be discovered in a culture of blame.

Why is a blameless environment important in assessing unknown residual risks? We don't live in a zero-risk environment. We live in a residual risk environment called uncertainty. As opposed to COSO's definition of inherent and residual risk, residual risks are not risks after we have imposed controls, residual risk is the reality of uncertainty. The organization is not a static environment where equilibrium is constant. Every year new products are launched, new initiatives are planned, new regulation is introduced, people come and go, and new systems are implemented. Digital strategies are just the latest continuum of change that has become a constant in every organization. Every year unknown residual risks are added to the equation no matter how many controls you have in place. This is why risk inventories and risk appetite are ineffective! Uncertainty is seldom captured in risk inventories or appetite in actionable plans. Unknown residual risks are created by change. Therefore, change must trigger an initial understanding of how residual risks may form in the vacuum of change.

Legacy systems, legacy processes, legacy products, legacy controls, etc. may be impacted by change including the manual workarounds and interdependencies that were needed to support the legacy practice. Employees stop complaining when management stops listening about ineffective legacy processes; therefore, when those processes change, new residual risks may accumulate resulting in a major event. I experienced such an event at a major financial services firm.

Senior executives made a strategic decision to move operations out of a major New England town to locations in the south that were not customer facing. In the move, operations in New England were moved to the Southwest, but because New Englanders hate moving, new employees were hired in the Southwest and had to be trained. The operations that moved were responsible for manually processing transactions to account for money flows into and outside of different fund accounts. However, a new team and inexperienced analysts were left alone over a holiday weekend. The policies and procedures available to the new team had not been developed for the new employees to handle exception processing and the holiday left too few senior executives around to respond in a timely manner. A simple error in recording transactions between accounts with inexperienced staff led to the largest error the firm had ever made in excess of $24 million dollars! The first conversation that I had with the head of the department was who should be blamed? Not, let's look into how this happened and determine how we support the team. By the way, insurance companies don't like to pay for big operational errors like this.

Everyone knew this risk existed (legacy risk from manual processing) but management was very short-sighted in not providing support to mitigate this risk because a loss of this size had never happened before. This is the nature of residual risks. Instead, everyone wanted to point fingers and blame. That behavior does not fix the problem, it makes risk aversion a real factor going forward. I am sure this firm is the only one this kind of behavior occurs. The problem was amplified by a lack of control over spending by junior staff traveling to India to set up operations there as well. A host of issues led to the error, but human behavior was the key cause.

Now let's turn to the second pillar in the cognitive risk framework – intentional control design.

INTENTIONAL CONTROL DESIGN

The five pillars of a cognitive risk framework are designed to provide a three-dimensional view of enterprise risks. In the last installment, cognitive governance (CogGov) was introduced as the first pillar. Its five disciplines reimagine risk governance as a path toward enhanced assurance through a more rigorous view of the dual roles of risk assessment and risk management.[14] Cognitive governance is the driver of the other four pillars through a continuous process of exploration of risk behavior and uncertainty.

Think of CogGov as a formalized Kaizen approach to improving risk governance:

1. CogGov is structured to clarify the roles of risk governance and recognize that new processes are needed to reconcile inherently different perceptions of risk.
2. The new insights that emerge from this approach inform the other four pillars in ways that are dynamic, simple, and based around the human element.
3. CogGov is responsible for developing templates for sustainable solutions to complexity in operations, people, and technology risks using a multidisciplinary lens on blind spots that lead to errors in judgment.

The next four pillars are additional levers of risk governance.

The worst-kept secret in many organizations is the lack of forward-looking investment in back-office operations. Legacy infrastructure, manual risk processes, layers of confusing policies and procedures, and changing demands from management make operations less nimble and resilient over time, requiring a series of "break-fix" maintenance actions simply to maintain the status quo.

Unfortunately, organizations become accustomed to workarounds, building them into operational preparedness as opposed to evaluating the net impact on long-term performance. Intentional controls design (ICD) is a cognitive risk governance lever to build nimble and resilient operational excellence into risk management.

A FUNDAMENTAL APPROACH TO REDUCE RISK

Intentional control design (ICD) is not a branch of design research, which originated out of a need for new methodologies to solve increasingly complex problems in organizational design.[15] Intentional design is a more fundamental approach that involves reducing risks by relieving cognitive load, streamlining processes, and enhancing situational awareness in business performance. Emerging research in design highlights the opportunity as summarized by Bruce Archer, "the most fundamental challenge to conventional ideas on design has been the growing advocacy of systematic methods of problem-solving, borrowed from computer techniques and management theory, for the assessment of design problems and the development of design solutions."[16] Intentional control design is a deliberate process of anticipating change and creating flexibility to respond to the environment.

Archer's challenge is no less daunting today. As organizations seek to integrate competing mandates that streamline security, enhance human decision-making, and reduce operational complexity, *good design becomes critical.* The good news is, advanced technology is evolving to achieve breakthroughs in smart design to empower employees with situational awareness, risk management tools, and straight-through processing workflows. Intentional controls design, like any creative process, requires a clear vision of strategic objectives, which will be different for all organizations. Why position strategic objectives as key outcomes? Because when organizations fail to direct the right level of energy to achieving strategic objectives, outcomes become less certain over time.

The purpose of this view of risk is to provide a multidimensional approach to risk management and move away from one-dimensional solutions driven purely either by data analytics or qualitative evaluations of risk. Combining the two views of risk assessment is not sufficient. Risk professionals must become designers of risk solutions that facilitate risk awareness in each layer of the organization. Designing situational awareness in business operations reduces risk through insights into data with tools that anticipate and respond to emerging and present threats.

I offer an example of resiliency not as a standard, but to present a model for thinking about defining outcomes. Resiliency is one of many attributes used in considering intentional design.

ACHIEVING RESILIENCY

Resiliency is developed through a consistent focus on the following elements: (*Quo Vadis*)

1. Clear goals and objectives that optimize performance.
2. Investment in people.
3. Nimble operations.
4. Financial agility.
5. Smart IT/cybersecurity.
6. Appropriate and balanced risk-taking/management.
7. Risk management tools.
8. Stable and robust relationships (customers/stakeholders).
9. Strategic analysis.
10. Ethical behavior.

The design of elements in an intentional design model should be formed through a rigorous process of collaboration within the organization. Each element is a design project and will require scope development. In the process of developing a scope strategy, the following steps should be considered:

- What are the synergies among all elements?
- What are the bottlenecks to building synergy among elements?

- What conflicts exist among or between the elements?
- Which element(s) impact resiliency – positively or negatively?
- What are the considerations around a full or partial implementation of each element?
- Which element depends on support from one or more other elements?

Pay attention to and leverage each intersection between the key elements.

Intentional design represents a range of solutions designed to manage risks writ large and small. Intentional design begins with a clear set of strategic objectives, leverages empirical risk-based data, then clarifies optimal outcomes. Simplicity in design is the guiding principle in intentional design.

I earlier referred to cognitive load and situational awareness as outcomes of intentional design. Very few will be familiar with the term cognitive load, but if I mentioned the impact of stress on performance, you would understand the concept that developed out of a study of problem-solving (Sweller, 1988).[17]

Stress is created by situations requiring task completion under tight or shortened timelines in which the consequences are significant, resulting in either peak performance or failure. Stress factors increase the risk of failure when normal operating procedures must be discarded, and improvisation is required. However, lessons can be learned – from design solutions to situational stress – to improve performance when the real thing occurs. In other words, performance is a product of good design.

More current research is needed on the impact of job performance and the design of the work environment. Studies have, however, found correlations between job performance and satisfaction and poor design of work processes. Most of these studies have focused on workplace ergonomics, health impacts, and insurance costs, yet missed opportunities to evaluate how good workplace design contributes to better efficiency and work performance overall.

The synergy between the five principles of cognitive governance and intentional design becomes even more powerful when taking work design into account. A simple example may help clarify the point. For the first time in history, the medical industry is transforming into a digital environment. Medical data is revolutionizing how doctors diagnose patient care and monitor patients remotely. Patients are also benefiting by being empowered with medical devices, reducing visits to the doctor for routine checkups.

As data continues to be democratized across industries, workers will be empowered to manage risks in real time with access to a range of data to support better decision-making about risks and performance. Collectively, these processes improve situational awareness of risks and responses to risks much more proactively. The synergies must, however, be designed specifically to address risks that matter by creating tools to respond in kind.

The same types of models can and should be deployed to provide stake-holders – from front-line managers to the board of directors – with the same level of situational awareness to address threats in organizational fields of operation.

THE SCIENCE OF COGNITIVE CONTROL

Understanding how people guide their thoughts and actions is a long-standing challenge in psychology and neuroscience. Being able to behave in accordance with current intentions is suggested to depend on dedicated neurocognitive control mechanisms.[18] These control mechanisms allow us to sustain focus on the information relevant to the behavioral goal we wish to achieve while competing with possible distractions, and to change focus when required. In other words, cognitive control allows for goal-directed and flexible behavior in a dynamically changing environment. When this top-down control fails – due to some temporary distraction or a permanent deficit – behavior is expected to be governed by habitual or recently acti-vated pathways. Even with top-down input, performance is expected to be less efficient if our current behavioral goals conflict with habitual patterns of behavior.

Processes involved in cognitive control have often been investigated exper-imentally by asking people to switch between different cognitive tasks.[19] Participants would for instance be required to switch between responding to the color and responding to the shape of geometric figures. In these well-established task switching paradigms, tasks are mostly specified by a task cue provided on each experimental trial or by predefined task orders. The large number of studies conducted within this research field has provided empirical evidence that people are indeed able to switch quickly and flexibly from one task to another.

People, however, experience cognitive limitations while doing so: they slow down and make more errors when switching. Surprisingly, this switch cost is reduced but not abolished when providing ample time to prepare for the required switch. The ability to switch tasks as well as the reduction of switch costs with ample preparation time are typically taken as a clear expression of top-down intentional control, whereas the residual cost is attributed to different bottom-up effects disrupting goal-directed behavior. So far, a broad consensus has been reached that performance in instructed task switching experiments reflects a complex interaction between top-down control and bottom-up interference.

Intentional control design evaluates the impacts on people as they conduct their jobs with an informed lens on the risk profile of accurately completing the tasks in question. Human factors experts use ergonomics to accomplish similar goals, but ergonomics is the applied science of equipment design to maximize productivity and minimize worker fatigue and discomfort. Intentional control design is a much more expansive concept that I created that looks at workflows, communications, access to pools of data, and organizational governance to account for the systemic risk of organizational behavior.

Many of today's controls are external to the organization due to data transitioning to the cloud or a host of other third-party service providers. In the past, contractual agreements and service-level agreements were considered sufficient to managing the risk of outsourcing. The contractual language itself poses risks because it does not contain sufficient language to respond to human behavior by third parties. We now know that cybercrime has recognized that external service providers have weak controls and are an entry into a target firm.

This is why the "E" in ERM is no longer relevant in a digital economy. Enterprise risk represents an increasingly smaller part of the risk picture. Business is conducted today with borders and boundaries; therefore, we must reimagine the scope of risk management in a digital era. The "Exoprise" more accurately describes risk management in the digital economy. Exoprise is a new term that I created that broadly encompasses networked systems via Internet of Things (IoT), internal controls, cloud services, vendors, off-shore contractors, contracts, insurance, and third-party providers who handle customer and company proprietary data through custom arrangements.

The "Exo" includes external risk and internal controls and other controls inside and outside the firm. The Exo incorporates the risk of human behavior across the "robust yet fragile" spectrum of risks. Robust yet fragile was discussed in an earlier chapter but it is timely to return to the topic now. Just as the Internet is robust yet fragile so is the extended enterprise risk footprint. Networks like the Internet are complex systems with nodes of fragility but collective robustness with massive scale. Organizations have not reached the level of scale as the World Wide Web but that is largely because businesses don't understand fully where they are robust and how they are fragile.

Apple computers is robust. Steve Jobs created an ecosystem with the Apple Store, iTunes, smart phones, and devices, but Apple is fragile in its dependence on iPhones for growth. Google is robust as the largest purveyor of online ads and search but is still fragile to competitors who may create search capability that creates an alternative to advertising for revenue growth. Intentional control design is a deep dive assessment of robustness and fragility in organizations to ensure long-term sustainability because all organizations have strengths and weaknesses that have not been fully exploited or experienced yet.

Risks evolve and change but risk practice has not kept pace. The fact that many risk professionals believe that enterprise risk management is state of the art is testament to how broken risk practice is today. Risks are not static as anticipated in ERM doctrine. Risks are three-dimensional in nature because they are the product of people, behavior, and decisions that happen each and every day. Intentional control design takes into account what is needed to get the job done but also incorporates risk, compliance, and impacts on human performance. Internal control design is ideally suited for the digital era emerging in business and automation with machine learning and other artificial intelligence.

Intentional control design evolves with risk and requires risk professionals to become risk solution designers. Risk management is the responsibility of management which means senior executives are the principals of the firm who select the risks they want to optimize and select the risks they want to minimize. The job of the risk professional is to design the right solution to create the opportunity to maximize risk and minimize the impacts of risk. That is how intentional control design plays its most powerful role. Risk assessment facilitates the scope and blueprint for the design of a solution. Just as the architect starts with a blueprint to build any building or a car designer starts with a conceptual design, risk professionals need to develop a blueprint for the design of risk solutions needed to help the organization optimize human performance.

In order to demonstrate how to operationalize intentional control design, the asymmetric risk of cybersecurity is an excellent example for demonstrating how a cognitive risk framework and its five pillars are used to mitigate this risk through intentional controls design and supported by cognitive governance.

CYBERSECURITY AND ENTERPRISE RISK MANAGEMENT – ASYMMETRIC RISK

Cyber risk is the most complex facing organizations today and will continue to become a critical challenge in a digital business environment. Cybercrime is estimated to be in the trillions of dollars annually and continues to grow unabated and has become a tax on businesses, small and large. As the scope of cybercrime grows from ransomware, viruses, phishing attacks, and other methods, the cost of defending against theft and data exfiltration has skyrocketed alongside insurance premiums and losses. The cyber paradox is the conundrum of cyber theft increasing faster than cyber defenses to deter intruders. No entity is exempt, with federal government agencies, corporations, military defense contractors, and private enterprises all experiencing impacts. There are no simple solutions to the threat of cyber risk, but there is an opportunity to rethink how security can be implemented to narrow the gap in security against the threat.

There is a saying in cyber security that the human element is the greatest vulnerability, but that statement does not provide context for the scope of the opportunity to leverage the human element to mitigate cyber risk.

Information security officers have begun to adopt the language of risk management in response to the growing threat. One of the hottest trends in cybersecurity is the adoption of a zero-trust posture. This was discussed in earlier chapters but is noteworthy now not as pillar in the cognitive risk framework but as context from what else is needed to ensure zero-trust methodology works as expected.[20] Zero trust and the cognitive risk framework share concepts that are important and diverge where there are gaps. Zero trust is a long-term, transformational commitment.

Zero trust requires organizations to re-architect how information security is conducted. The third pillar of a cognitive risk framework is focused on re-architecting how people interact with technology. Both are radical changes in how traditional security is implemented, and both rely on people executing the re-architecture of systems and people in new ways. Both must reflect the fluidity of business operations and be responsive to change as well as recognize that progress is incremental, not a plug and play with a new app or new policy and procedure. Both require radical change in mindset in the CISO suite and with management.

Zero trust is prescriptive, meaning there is a great deal of guidance provided by the National Institute of Standards and Technology (NIST). The third pillar of a cognitive risk framework is not prescriptive, it is based on assessing the risk probabilities of threats and vectors where the intersection of humans and technology poses the greatest risk. A cognitive risk framework recognizes the lack of high-quality actionable pools of data to make accurate assessments but like zero trust, following the zero trust guidance takes time to develop and does not guarantee success. Both practices require exploration for what works in a specific operating environment and anticipates learning best practice over time as opposed to implementing one-time solutions. The sources include guidance from NIST 800-207: Zero Trust Architecture,[21] DoD's Zero Trust Reference Architecture,[22] NSA's Embracing a Zero Trust Security Model,[23] CISA's Zero Trust Maturity Model,[24] CISA's and NSA's 5G Cloud Security,[25] and OMB's Federal Zero Trust Strategy.[26]

Zero trust requires a well-articulated implementation plan that defines the scope of the change and what will be covered. This is not a technology product approach, zero-trust is a mind shift in security just as a cognitive risk framework changes how security professionals must consider the roles of people, including security professionals, trust in access to critical data, new approaches to identify and authenticate users who are authorized to conduct business, and validate who has authority to make changes. Again, the key difference is in a focus on technology versus a focus on people, but both are needed and the exclusion of one is a detriment to the success of the other approach. Zero trust proposes a five-step process: (variations may apply) (1) define your protest surface, (2) map the transaction flows, (3) build a zero-trust architecture, (4) create zero-trust policy, and

(5) monitor and maintain the network. Zero trust doesn't specifically say this, but it relies on the execution of human actors to successfully execute and zero trust environment. The third pillar of a cognitive risk framework is designed to enable human performance in building zero trust.

Zero trust must be aligned with compliance requirements. A cognitive risk framework is not based on compliance but anticipates compliance requirements without stringent adoption. This is because compliance standards and the adoption of compliance standards must align with mitigating risk and avoidance of hindrance in human performance. Flexibility in compliance, instead of rigidity, is a core element of cognitive controls in a cognitive risk framework. Over-reliance of compliance is a double-edged sword that must allow for good judgment and risk-based data analysis. The final three zero trust principles, shared-services in zero trust, cloud-based use for zero trust implementation, and identity management, also depend on a robust cognitive risk approach.

Zero trust assumes that all organizations have the requisite skills, capabilities, expertise, and experience to develop and implement zero-trust architecture at the same level of proficiency. That is the risk of zero-trust. A cognitive risk framework assumes that the organization must prepare not only its security staff but all other personnel beyond security for a zero-trust environment to operate as effectively as expected. This is the vulnerability that cyber researchers refer to when they call the human element the greatest vulnerability in cybersecurity.

Almost all organization underestimate the effort of big transformational technology projects and especially ones related to information security. It is human nature to take people for granted in complex projects. However, there is sufficient research and data to demonstrate that we must harden people for change as well as the infrastructure of the operating environment. Yet, each time this step is short-changed as organizations rush ahead without conducting an assessment for of the human element impacts in change.[27,28,29,30,31] Organizations often overlook the human element but those that are attuned to these risks view it in the narrowest of forms, the insider threat. The reality is information security officers have bought into the "Snowden Effect," based on confirmation bias but lacking a full understanding of the influence factors that cause human error and mistakes, the larger component of the human element risk.

The disconnect between the novice and the expert is how "noise" and "bias" are treated in risk analysis and how subjective risk analysis leads cybersecurity professionals astray. A big part of the problem is a risk communications problem as well. Terms like the insider threat have been adopted without robust definition or quantifiable characteristics. Different people define the insider threat differently and that is a big part of the confusion and gap in how to mitigate the problem. There is a saying, "if you don't trust your people, they become untrustworthy." That saying rings true in the insider threat anecdotal use of the term. When terms like the insider threat is used to describe all human element risks, you have defeated the purpose of the definition. Humans are not one-dimensional, and neither are the errors they make. More definition and detail is needed to assess the risk of the human element.

The title of the third pillar of a cognitive risk framework explains the broad scope of the human element risk in cybersecurity and enterprise risk. An organization of 10,000 employees do not operate in lock-step no matter how well-intended they all are. The reality is that each person is an individual with strengths and weaknesses in performing their jobs on any given day. The expectation of zero risk is a fallacy in assuming risk can be avoided even in a zero-trust environment. In reality, the goal should be to minimize the impact of risks that occur over time.

When organizations fail to accurately define risks, like the insider threat, they will fail to define the solution needed to address this vulnerability. This is why technology vendors who sell behavioral analytics platforms have not been effective at mitigating the human element. Behavioral analytics platforms can be gamed once everyone learns the system's blind spots and weaknesses. Single point solutions implemented without a holistic plan is contributing to vulnerability instead of addressing it.

Zero trust, cybersecurity, information security, and enterprise risk management all depend on the same thing, the human element. Yet, the failure is not technology, per se. The real failure is the misdiagnosis of the role of the human actor in the execution of risk governance writ large. Cybersecurity and enterprise risk suffer from the same errors in judgment. The errors include a lack of rigor is risk assessment of asymmetric risks. You can't address asymmetric risks with subjective risk assessments. Color-coded risk matrices are subjective risk assessments. High, medium, and low are subjective risk assessments. Subject matter expert opinions are subjective risk assessments. Subjective risk assessments are effective at socializing with other executives their *perceptions* of risk, but the process is not predictive of risk. That is the difference!

Imagine addressing the Covid-19 pandemic with the collective opinions of uninformed professionals with little to no experience in infectious disease? Why do we think that subjective perceptions of risk will be more effective? Risk assessments are not perfect; however, there are processes that possess the rigor needed to make more informed decisions not being used by cybersecurity professionals. Instead of using traditional risk practice as "best practice," use statistical analytics,[32] data science, build models with internal and external data,[33] game theory, and hire or develop risk analysts. Cyber risk analytics should not be thought of as a platform that you buy but is a discipline you must develop in-house.

The same skills needed to solve life-saving problems in medicine, healthcare, science, and space travel are the same skills needed to understand the complexity of technology in modern organizations with networks in, across, and beyond the four walls of the enterprise. The best cyber adversaries are computer scientists and mathematicians, not hackers, and they design the products that are sold to novice hackers in the dark web. To compete with top talent in cyberspace, you need to hire or develop top talent in diverse, multidisciplinary disciplines in information security and network architecture.

When Wall Street needed talent to manage complex trading risks, they hired PhD physicists and mathematicians. They didn't ask a subject matter expert what they thought. Physicists with programming skills and the math ability to advance the science of trading. Computer scientists and network engineers are the new skill sets needed to address the challenges of modern cybersecurity. A small team of physicists, computer scientist, network engineers, and human factor experts will be needed as the cost of cyber losses continues to mount. Protecting the enterprise is as important as generating revenue, and in many cases, leveraging these skill sets will allow forward-looking firms the ability to create new opportunities and products that will compete with adversarial talent. This talent must be developed in-house and nurtured so that a baseline knowledge base is developed across industries with spin-offs and start-ups that assist smaller organizations.

A cognitive risk framework is about learning what you do not know or may not fully understand about risk. I am an advocate of zero trust concepts and methodology, but the cybersecurity industry must be honest about its ability to build robust zero trust capability at the high levels of expectation assumed in the guidance. The risk to zero trust adherents is the failure of firms with zero trust methodology if severe breaches are still rampant. Zero Trust is one of many approaches that will be relevant, but standards of excellence must be established based on evidence-based outcomes. A cognitive risk framework is a vehicle for development and experimentation (skunkworks).[34] A *skunkworks* project is a project developed by a relatively small and loosely structured group of people who research and develop a project primarily for the sake of radical innovation.

What is the role of the board and senior executives in supporting the way forward?

The framework is simple: board of directors and senior executives

a) Define the risk profile of your cybersecurity and enterprise risk program.
b) Conduct a gap analysis of skills and capability to mitigate risk.
c) Define the goal and objectives of cybersecurity and enterprise risk to help achieve the organizations strategic objectives.
d) Develop a plan to close the gap.
e) Communicate the plan and get buy-in across the firm.
f) Assign accountability and responsibility to a small team with the requisite skills to execute the plan.
g) Have the team report to the board on progress.

h) Develop deliverables and expectations for the team.
i) Give the team 3 –5 years to produce results.
j) Refine the process each year and expect results annually.
k) Stop expecting easy solutions with technology, but search for simple solutions with people.

The board of directors and senior executives are responsible for setting the strategic direction of the cybersecurity and enterprise risk team. The talent and team must be aligned with the risk profile of the organization. Early expectations must be centered around gaining insight into the vulnerabilities where the firm is fragile and strengths where the firm is robust. The team must assess channels of communication, governance processes, integration of technology and people, and external networks with customers, vendors, and solution providers and provide a robust assessment of the gaps that exist in the first 18 months. The third year will pivot to remediation and enhancement. Each subsequent year will involve refinements and enhanced security processes.

Cybersecurity and enterprise risk needs an upgrade from generalist to specialist status. This is a competition that will only become more intense as the digital operating environment accelerates and will be won with advanced practice not subjective analysis. Organizations that see the future have already begun to make the transition to upgrade or build the talent needed for competition in the 21st century.

This brings us to the fourth pillar of the cognitive risk framework: human factors and socio-technological risk.

HUMAN FACTORS AND SOCIO-TECHNICAL RISK

Human factors is the scientific discipline concerned with the understanding of the interactions among humans and other elements of a system, and the profession that applies theoretical principles, data, and methods to design in order to optimize human wellbeing and overall system performance. A socio-technical system is a network of interconnected elements comprising groups of people and technology that functions as one simple or complex system designed to achieve specific goals.

For a socio-technical system:[35,36]

- **Error** is the variance between expected outcomes and the actual outcomes.
- **Redundancy** in a high-reliability socio-technical system is designed to have little to no errors in operations or redundancies to recover.
- **Regulation** refers to the process of detecting and responding to system errors, including those caused by surprising disturbances in the

operating environment. Self-regulation is a key feature of high-reliability socio-technical systems.

- **Resilience** is a *social* concept that refers to the adaptability of a socio-technical system to respond to a significant failure of the system and resume the achievement of its goals, or alternatively set new goals.

What does this mean in plain English? Well, we should start with a layperson's definition of human factors and why it is important. According to Michigan Tech,

> The field of human factors combines a number of related specializations, such as human-computer interaction, usability, UI/UX, human-centered design, engineering psychology, human-systems engineering, cognitive engineering, ergonomics, and industrial/organizational psychology. While many human factors professionals specialize in either **psychology** or **engineering**, others take a more balanced approach and are trained equally in both.
>
> The field dates back to World War II, when an interdisciplinary group of experts teamed up to improve airplane safety. Since then, the field has continued to grow, and human factors professionals are in high demand across a variety of industries. As technology advances and becomes more and more prevalent in our daily lives, it's critical that new technologies continue to work for and with us.[37]

Human factors has expanded in healthcare, manufacturing, maritime industry, insurance, and many other areas where safety is important but has failed to gain traction in cybersecurity or risk management. The reasons that risk professionals have not employed human factors into their practice is simply a matter of a lack of exposure and training, but much of human factors science is very common sense and easy to grasp if you take the time to understand what it is and how it can improve performance in the workplace. You don't have to be a human factors scientist to adopt these practices and a few simple steps can go a long way to build more resilience into your cybersecurity or enterprise risk management program.

There is some confusion in the terminology used to describe the human factor versus the human factors among researchers and laypersons. The term, the human factor, has been adopted by information security officers to describe the errors, mistakes, non-compliant behavior, or the insider threat. This negative connotation of the human factors has become a catchall phrase for *what when wrong as opposed to what could be better*, leading to confusion about the role of human factors methods and obscures the upside of human factors in enhancing human performance. The success of human factors science is subtle that we take it for granted every day, but it has transformed a host of industries and saved countless lives and reduced injuries on the job.

When you get in your car, you don't have to think about arriving at an unknown address. You simply enter the address into your navigation system and arrive approximately the time the GPS says so. When you back out of the driveway, the rearview camera provides a clear picture of what is behind the car allowing you to avoid an untimely accident. The dashboard is ergonomically designed to place the dials and buttons that give you access to a suite of electronic tools to help you enjoy your ride. All of these features are based on human factors design concepts. They seem common sense now, but I remember the bench seats in the front where three people could comfortably ride it with seat belts on. The design of cars today and the corresponding drop in highway fatalities is the product of human factors design. The smart phone has changed that dynamic by incorporating your phone into the dashboard, but people still drive and text to this day, namely the millennials and Gen Zs.

Car manufacturers responded to safety issues and redesigned the cockpit of the car and passenger seats into an experience that improved the drudgery of driving and safety at the same time. Human factors design was used to solve safety issues but has also created value in cars. I am convinced that similar concepts and practices can be developed to reduce risk in cybersecurity if the same attention to problem-solving is adopted by information security officers. Before we get into the weeds, let's take a step back to understand better the positive side of human factors.

Human factors refer to environmental, organizational, and job factors, and human and individual characteristics which influence behavior at work in a way which can affect health, safety, and situational awareness. A simple way to view human factors is to think about three aspects: the job, the individual, and the organization and how they impact on people's health, safety, and behavior. The workflow in any organization is a reflection of human factors in action and is often used as a tool in risk assessment and risk analysis, although attention to the impacts on humans is more often than not ignored in traditional risk and control self-assessments (RCSA). Unfortunately, this simple adjustment to RCSAs is overlooked and misses the contextual information that could inform the analysis of risk and controls. With that said, traditional workflow analysis is too narrow to fully comprehend the influence factors in the job, the organization, and individual characteristics.

To correct this oversight, risk professionals in audit, risk, compliance, and information security must map out a human factors workflow diagram that includes the span of control, governance, tools, technology, people, data sources, skills and capacity, and communications along with predictive risk data. As you can see, the most detailed RCSA of risk and controls has lost the context of the influence factors that create or mitigate risk. Residual risks are seldom if ever considered in RCSAs but would be captured in human factors workflows. The fallacy of subjective risk analysis and assessment is the lack of real context and partly explains the failure of traditional risk practice. RCSAs are prescriptive; therefore, they are simple to follow but fail to force risk professionals to think deeply about risk. Unfortunately, these failures are considered "best practice"; without any evidence, they work as expected in predicting risk outcomes or comprehensively enhance human performance.

This approach does take more time upfront, but the real savings is on the back end. Performing a quick and simple RCSA is more costly because they fail to fully address the fragility that is hidden in most organizations in repeated errors, employee morale, mistakes, reduced productivity, and rework which is never quantified. The failure of poor risk practice is felt but never analyzed as residual risk.

This is why you must incorporate human factors analysis into your risk and information security programs. Subjective risk assessments are sufficient for getting a picture of the perceptions of risk, while a human factors workflow analysis and risk data analytics is the confirmation or disconfirmation of the perceptions of risk. Said a different way, perceptions of risk are the null hypothesis which requires advanced procedures to prove or disprove the null hypothesis. Traditional risk practice treats the null hypothesis as true without conducting any procedures to test its proof. I learned this the hard way by following the prescriptive methods of tradition risk practice and watching it fail in real time and dealing with the fallout. Unfortunately, these failed risk practices have only spread and become the dominant risk practice. Risk management is not respected as a discipline that adds value and it is true because of the lack of rigor in risk management. Managing risk is not about reducing risks to zero because risk management is about people.

The Great Resignation in corporate America is a symptom of the failure to understand and address human factors. The symptoms are rampant: mental health issues, employee morale, high levels of staff turnover, behavioral and performance issues, complaints about working conditions, promotional opportunities, and more. We have failed people and ignored the greatest resource in the organization, the human element. Equally important, we have failed to recognize the risk in not addressing human factors. To solve this problem is not about work-life balance or perks on the job. To make real progress as an organization, human factors must be part of the analysis of any project from the start. Whether it is on-boarding new hires, design of a new system, bringing on contractors, new vendors, third-party providers, launching a new product, or creating a career path and promotional opportunities for staff. Human factors analysis must become ingrained in all human resource management initiatives.

The perception is that this approach will be costly and add a lot of work, but in reality the real cost is not doing so and hiding the cost in turnover, errors, mistakes, and poor productivity. The costs of not paying attention to human factors are far greater and higher than the small investment needed to get it right the first time. This concept may feel counterintuitive because most executives have never considered the cost of human factors risk.

Here are examples of how simple human factors led to disaster but could have been avoided:

Accident, industry, and date	Consequences	Human contribution and causes
Three Mile Island, Nuclear industry, 1979	Serious damage to core nuclear reactor.	Operator failed to diagnose a stuck open valve due to poor design of a control panel, distraction of 100 alarms activating, inadequate operating training. Maintenance failures had occurred, but no steps had been taken to prevent them recurring.
Union Carbide, Bhopal India, Chemical processing, 1984	The plant released a cloud of toxic methyl isocyanate. Death toll of 2,500 and one quarter of the city's population was affected by the gas.	The leak was caused by a discharge of water into a storage tank. This was the result of a combination of operator error, poor maintenance, failed safety systems, and poor safety management.
Space Shuttle Challenger, Aerospace, 1986	An explosion shortly after lift-off killed all seven astronauts on board.	An O-ring seal on one of the solid rocket boosters split after take-off releasing a jet of ignited fuel. Inadequate response to internal warnings about the faulty seal design. Decision-making of conflicting scheduling/safety goals, mindset, and effects of fatigue.
Chernobyl, Nuclear industry, 1986	1,000 MW reactor exploded releasing radioactivity over much of Europe. Environmental and human costs.	Causes are much debated but Soviet investigative team admitted deliberate, systemic, and numerous violations of safety procedures by operators.
Texaco Refinery, Milford Haven, Chemical processing, 1994	An explosion on the site was followed by a major hydrocarbon fire and a number of secondary fires. There was severe damage to the plant, buildings, and storage tanks. 26 people sustained injuries, but none were serious.	The incident was caused by flammable hydrocarbon liquid being continuously pumped into a process vessel that had its outlet closed. This was the result of a combination of: an error of control system reading of a valve state, modifications which had not been fully assessed, failure to ensure operating with the necessary process overviews and attempts to keep the system running when it should have been shut down.

Source: https://books.hse.gov.uk/

The risk of human factors has become normalized, and the cure is often to bring in an executive to "fix" the problem. A new highly energized senior executive comes in, makes changes, reorganizes, and gets promoted and moves on, but the root cause and underlying problems are never fully addressed. In other words, organizations have become lazy and complacent, but will it change because of competition, disruption, and digitization? American business has enjoyed unprecedented growth and success, but mergers, acquisitions, and activist investors have begun to reduce yesterday's market leaders to second-class actors on the global stage. The list of American iconic organizations bought by foreign owners or removed from the Dow Jones has accelerated and will continue to accelerate in the future.

The tech companies that enjoy success today must learn this lesson or they too will be relegated to second-class status along with traditional manufacturing and retail company failures if they ignore the human element. Talent is fungible in the digital age and mobile. Today's top talent will have no problem leaving high-flying firms and finding funding for new opportunities or new roles with competitors. The competition for top talent has already begun and will only become more fierce. The good news is that the solution is simple. Involve people in the process, think about the impacts on humans, and validate these impacts with the people on the front lines of work and continuously search for data and answers that give you insights into anything that hinders performance. You don't need a PhD to add a human factors practice, but you should be aware that human failure is predictable and avoidable. The science of human factors has codified different types of human error which makes human failure both predictable and systematically corrective.

The codification of human failure is straightforward. Human failure is the result of either errors or violations of judgment. Errors are further categorized by skill-based errors and mistakes. Skill-based errors result from slips of action or lapses of memory. Violations are the result of routine, situational or exceptional. Human *error* therefore is an action or decision which was not intentional, which involved a deviation from a standard, and resulted in an undesirable outcome. A *violation* is a deliberate deviation from a rule or procedure.

Human factors research allows us to understand that humans are prone to make errors but makes clear when deviations from protocol are intentional or not. In both cases, this knowledge gives risk professionals a guide for designing controls to account for both types of human failure. In fact, financial fraud and financial mismanagement can be addressed by using these same concepts. Human factors provides a variety of influence factors that can be used to mitigate human failure. Therefore, challenge is to develop effective influence factors, not the ability to influence the right behaviors. Secondarily, the primary influence factor used by organizations is one-dimensional – punishment. Punishment should be the last resort after all other influence factors have been used. In other words, positive influence factors and even benign influence factors can be used as alternatives to punishment (Figure 8.1).

First, we must conduct a human factors workflow analysis to identify the stressors in human performance and develop or design solutions to relieve these stressors including decision-making stressors. The type of remedial controls that can be put in place include changing the conditions that lead to errors, redesign the work or processes that cause errors, and ensure the tools and work design are sufficient to help enhance performance. This can be effective in cybersecurity as well. Human factors research is a guide and is not prescriptive as a result the final solution must be developed in collaboration with the people involved in the processes that need correction and senior management.

Influence factors can be both positive and negative. Stressors are negative influence factors and can contribute to mistakes, errors, and poor decision-making at all levels of the organization. Some influence factors are intrinsic to the job, such as workload, short time spans to complete projects, introduction of new duties, and change in technology create stress. In addition, ambiguous role definitions, micromanagement, conflicts in assignments between departments, poor management, and general disorganization in the workplace create distractions and stress that contribute to inattention

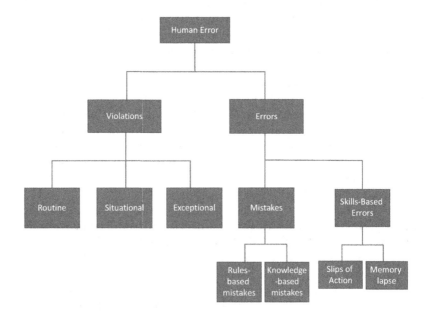

Figure 8.1   Cognitive readiness.

blindness to risks and can lead to mistakes. Research has demonstrated that turnover is often the result of poor management than any other factors.

More importantly, poor management is a leading cause of human factor risk. The board of directors and senior management have a responsibility to not only be aware when poor management is contributing to poor performance but should also play an active and engaged role to ensure that employee satisfaction is not being adversely affected. There are many ways to accomplish this without interfering with the day-to-day responsibilities of management. Glassdoor is an independent website that allows employees to provide feedback on employers, independently survey companies where names and departments are filtered out, and regular feedback surveys where management is not allowed to interfere are preferred. But honest feedback is hard to get. A secondary way to measure employee satisfaction is to monitor trends in employee turnover in specific departments and especially top talent and senior and mid-level executive departures.

Organizations that develop a plan to incorporate human factors analysis make progress in reducing risk, improving productivity, and employee morale. Some organizations have developed cultures that intuitively consider the human element but don't have a comprehensive program to address human factors risk. All organizations will benefit by being more aware and conscious of human factors risk as well as being sensitive to human performance as a risk management goal. A hidden cost and cause of human factors risk is bias and noise in decision-making. Bias and noise are baked into the legacy decisions that have created organizational culture. Who gets promoted, who is in leadership positions, how goals are established, how performance evaluations are used, how bonuses are awarded, how technology projects are implemented, and so forth?

Bias and noise are not about discrimination, per se. Organizations that do not overtly discriminate still have a bias and create noise in decision-making; therefore, it is a critical pillar and must be understood as a cognitive risk that is like subconscious in nature. It is important to separate discrimination from bias and noise for many reasons, but the most important is to understand how to measure bias and noise as opposed to discrimination which has been defined in terms of quotas. Discrimination is wrong on many levels but is very difficult to minimize. Bias and noise can be measured and mitigated in ways that reduce the impacts of discrimination in the workplace without focusing on defining discrimination of any kind. Cognitive risk mitigation is an organizational goal about making more informed decisions that lead to productive organizational goals while achieving more balance in fairness because it is an objective measure of performance as opposed to subjective measures of performance.

COGNITIVE RISK MITIGATION – BIAS AND NOISE: THE FIFTH PILLAR

Most organizations establish an explicit goal of performance but lack a structured approach to achieving the goal. When organizations talk about performance, the metrics are financial in nature; revenues, profit margin, lower costs, customer satisfaction, value-add products, etc. but human performance is seldom an explicit goal but is implied by the top-line goals that are established. This may seem an innocuous point but is one of the reasons bias and noise is a critical concept to understand.

Senior executives receive constant feedback from shareholders, analysts, customers, vendors, and the markets about their products and financial performance of the firm but most often do not get unfiltered feedback from employees on the performance of the firm. Employees are on the front line and are closest to the leading indicators of the goals and objectives established by senior management but are the least likely to contribute insight in intelligence they receive from the employees of their counterparts in the field. A counterintuitive bias is only listening to feedback on the current financial performance of the firm. Current financial performance is an important criterion, but it is not indicative of future performance.

Customer tastes change, vendors get disrupted, customers and partners can change abruptly due to mergers and acquisitions, and competitor's products may add new features that make existing products obsolete overnight in a digital economy. It is important for senior executives to get feedback from multiple sources inside and outside the organization in a structured way. A robust cognitive governance program can assist with this process, but only senior executives and the board of directors can decide the importance of including this process in decision-making. Listening to both sides of a story is one way to address bias and noise in strategic decision-making. The goal in pillar five is to establish formal processes to mitigate bias and noise.

To recap, the two flaws in decision-making, bias and noise: bias is a systemic error in judgment and noise is variability in judgment. Bias has garnered the most attention in the media and in academic circles because it is associated with negative impacts on certain demographics of people, particularly people of color, underrepresented communities, and other minorities. However, the damage done by bias and noise in the workplace is more widespread and potentially damaging than discriminatory workplace practice. Bias and noise impact all employees in systemic ways. For example, if new hires are predominately from one or more Ivy League schools, or certain customers get discounts because of size and not profitability. These kind of judgment errors may be as damaging over time as fraud because they happen unconsciously and therefore are not viewed as a risk.

This happens more often than one may think. A few simple examples are offered to illustrate the point more clearly. The first one represents sales goals in the mutual fund industry: There is a rule of thumb in the mutual fund that retention of a customer takes approximately seven to achieve profitability from each customer. However, mutual funds often use sales incentives based on growth in assets from existing institutional customers instead of net new assets. The distinction can be material. Let's say that the stock and bond markets are experiencing a rapid rise in price. Mutual fund assets will grow in size without any material change in sales staff ability or persuasion. Net new assets based on sales activity is a better way to measure growth. The difference becomes clear as soon as a market correction reveals the flawed strategy.

Secondly, a sales contract may be designed to provide discounts to large customers, but the overall relationship may be a loss leader for the firm. An arbitrary policy that appears to make sense does not hold up under analysis. Both of these scenarios are real-world examples that I had to explain to senior management with data from an analysis that no one had thought to provide before. Lastly, a problem that is endemic across organizations is the decision to maintain and build workarounds onto legacy systems that has created technical debt in most organizations. Technical debt, or design debt, is the implied cost of additional rework caused by choosing an easy (limited) solution now instead of using a better approach that would take longer.[38]

Technical debt adds up like interest rates on financial debt. If you don't repay more than minimum to repay financial debt, then actual cost is a multiple of the original amount borrowed. The same is implied in technical debt. The cost of maintenance, repair, mitigation, and integration increases the cost of systems over time that exceed the value legacy systems. Technology obsolescence is a real problem for cybersecurity as well and creates hidden fragility in security controls over time. Tech debt is one of the key reasons vulnerabilities contribute to exposure in cybersecurity. Predecessor decisions that become legacy systems are now the areas of vulnerability that must be maintained to execute strategic goals. System networks are a patchwork of fixes and workarounds that hurt performance. I have seen this problem firsthand in some of the largest financial services firms that have attempted to reduce tech debt and given up and instead built in more tech debt because the cost of remediation had become too great and disruptive to fix. The bias to build solutions in-house or outsource both contribute to tech debt leaving organizations in a constant flux to keep pace with change in the operating environment.

Bias in decision-making is the result of noise in the executive suite. Noise is the variability in decision-making in strategic planning. There are two ways that noise accumulates in organizations. The first cause of noise is widespread subjective decision-making to achieve objective strategic goals, and the second is ambiguity in corporate policy resulting in different interpretations of the policy directive. There is noise in every organization and within every organization there is noise at every level of the organization.

When a policy is vague and subjective decision-making is allowed to become the norm, the costs of subjective decision-making will accumulate over time and not be observed in financial results. In other words, noise is often hidden beneath the surface. Noise audits are the only way to undercover the costs of noise to an organization but is seldom, if ever, performed in a structured way or audit.

Noise happens in internal audits, external audits, risk management, in performance management reviews, at the board level in strategic planning, and in cyber security. Anywhere where subjective decision-making takes place noise is present. The cost of noise is hidden because audit of decision-making is not in the scope of traditional risk management, but these costs exist whether they are examined or not. The opportunity in noise is to learn how these costs accumulate and to measure its impact to organizational performance. Noise audits are the way forward-looking risk professionals examine the health of the organization and how effective the other four pillars are working. In this way, the five pillars are self-healing and perpetually seeking ways to drive performance.

The board of directors and senior executives may use pillar five as a diagnostic tool to evaluate cognitive risks across the firm. Everything starts with a decision; however, there exists no diagnostic tools until now to evaluate how the collective decision-making leads to success or failure prospectively. Computer scientists understand that reducing bias and noise in machine learning algorithmic models enhances the outcome of solutions; therefore, there are lessons for senior executives in the process. This does not mean that machine learning should replace executive decision-making. What it means is that executives can learn from their own decision-making to make better decisions or at least improve the outcomes in a structured way that had not existed before.

The five pillars of a cognitive risk framework for cybersecurity and enterprise risk management are complementary and build upon each other to enhance performance, create sustainable practice, and harden the softest vulnerability within organizations, the human element. Adopting a cognitive risk framework is not a major shift or some new transformational project. It is also more than a change in mindset. Choosing to adopt a cognitive risk framework is a formal and proactive way to simplify and validate the choices that have already been made. Choices that contribute to performance are maintained, but more importantly, the choices that hinder performance are identified and reduced to an acceptable level.

Secondarily, now is the time shift from traditional risk practice in preparation for new risks in a digital operating environment. Traditional enterprise risk is no longer applicable in an extended operating environment with no boundaries. The "E" in ERM doesn't describe the scope of risks today's risk professionals will need to better assess and design solutions to address. The vast majority of resources and time spent on enterprise risk represents the least impact on organizational performance. A cognitive risk framework has no boundaries and is focused on the *exoprise* representing a three-dimensional hybrid environment of digital and physical risks with more time allocated toward reducing residual risks, noise, and bias.

The fifth pillar of a cognitive risk framework is an extension of half a century of research on intuitive human judgment. There are no existing risk frameworks that have been studied as extensively by Nobel Prize-winning researchers as the concepts in this cognitive risk framework. In fact, the cognitive risk framework is not based on one concept, it is based on a multidisciplinary body of research and discipline into what I call a three-dimensional risk framework that unifies risk analysis, human behavior, technology, and decision science.

COSO's ERM framework is one-dimensional with singular focus on internal controls, ISO 31000 is based on risk generally but does not encompass human behavior and only recently in 2019 added a generic risk analysis addendum. NIST is one-dimensional and is focused on prescriptive guidance. Each of these risk frameworks is considered "best practice" by novice risk professionals. Why? Because others have adopted them as a pseudo standard that lacks rigor simply because they are easy to implement and there are no metrics to measure success. Open-ended subjective frameworks provide little confidence they will perform as expected. These frameworks can only be tested in binary form. They are either in compliance or not in compliance, and that binary state is subjective because there are no thresholds provided to judge completeness.

You may be asking yourself, if the concepts behind a cognitive risk framework are more effective why isn't anyone using it? I have never heard of a cognitive risk framework and no one that I know has either so what is the big deal? Those are great questions, and the answer is very simple. Most professional researchers, quantitative risk analysts, scientists, doctors, lawyers, computer scientists, engineers, physicists, mathematicians, military leadership, data scientists, and anyone serious about saving lives or is concerned with accuracy, prediction, and positive outcomes do use it. The question is why don't you know about it and why aren't you using it? That is the real question.

This is a conundrum in risk practice today, and why I named this fallacy in thinking homo periculum, a fallacy in believing that using subjective approaches to risk management is optimum. The fallacy is widespread even in the face of failure after failure well-meaning risk professionals and their organization have defaulted to generic, compliance-based, prescriptive, check-the-box risk processes. After almost 40 years of failure, it is time for risk management to grow to the level of maturity organizations need and deserve. Herbert Simon, Dan Kahneman, and many other Nobel Prize winners demonstrated the fallacy of homo economicus, economic man/woman/person. Homo periculum is the exact same fallacy, risk man/

woman/person. This book is only an introduction to the science of risk. The five pillars are presented to show the depth and breadth of the disciplines involved and many others will expand and refine these scientific principles and practices over time, including the author.

As Kahneman says,

> the invisibility of noise is a direct consequence of causal thinking. Noise is inherently statistical: it becomes visible only when we think statistically about an ensemble of similar judgments. Indeed, it then becomes hard to miss: it is the variability in the backward-looking statistics about legacy decisions. It is the range of possibilities when you and others consider how to predict a future outcome. It is the scatter diagram of random events and accidents that occur in all organizations but seldom are evaluated systemically. Causally noise is nowhere, statistically, it is everywhere if you look for it.

(Kahneman, Sibony, Olivier, *Noise*, p. 219)

The fourth industrial revolution has ushered in new technologies, new means of communication, entertainment, and research on human performance but the potential will be reached only by those who are open to pushing the boundaries of thinking. The digital economy is both exciting and terrifying as technology exceeds the human mind's ability to keep pace. Disinformation, misinformation, cyber wars, social media, virtual reality, and artificial intelligence blur the lines between what is real and what can be dreamed up in Silicon Valley and by adversaries in the digital, cyber sphere. Are you cognitively ready?

NOTES

1. Richard M. Buxbaum and Klaus J. Hopt (1988), *Legal Harmonization and the Business Enterprise: Corporate and Capital Market Law Harmonization Policy in Europe and the U.S.A.* 182-84 (describing the role of boards of directors in Europe); Christopher L. Heftel (1983), Survey, corporate governance in Japan: The position of shareholders in publicly held corporations, *University of Hawai'i Law Review*, 5, 135, 138–40, 153–54 (explaining the Japanese requirement that each stock company have at least three directors); Howard Gensler (1995), Company formation and securities listing in the People's Republic of China, *Houston Journal of International Law*, 17, 399, 420–21 (discussing the requirements for boards in China). An important caveat to this statement comes from the German two-tier board model under which there is both a supervisory board and a management board. See Thomas J. Andr6, Jr., Some Reflections on German Corporate Governance.
2. MODEL. Bus. CORP. ACT § 8.01 (2002); DEL. GEN. CORP. LAW. § 141(a).

3. See Baldwin v. Canfield, I N.W. 261, 270 (Minn. 1879). A minor variation on this rule exists under common corporate statutes which allow board action through unanimous written consent. See MODEL BUS. CORP. ACT § 8.21 (2002). Also, directors might be allowed to act through committees. See MODEL Bus. CORP. ACT § 8.25 (2002).

4. Turley, S., & Zaman, M. (2004). The Corporate Governance Effects of Audit Committees. Journal of Management and Governance, 8, 305-332. https://doi.org/10.1007/s10997-004-1110-5

5. P. W. Wolnizer (1995), Are audit committees red herrings? *Abacus: A Journal of Accounting, Finance & Business Studies.* https://doi.org/10.1111/j.1467-6281.1995.tb00354.x.

6. https://www.financierworldwide.com/private-equity-governance.

7. https://www.nobelprize.org/prizes/economic-sciences/1978/simon/biographical/.

8. https://www.researchgate.net/publication/325954197_The_perception_of _risk.

9. M. Douglas and A. Wildavsky (1982), *Risk and Culture,* Berkeley: University of California Press.

10. D. Kahneman, P. Slovic and A. Tversky. (1982) *Judgment under Uncertainty: Heuristics and Biases.* Cambridge University Press, Cambridge. https://doi .org/10.1017/CBO9780511809477.

11. M. Henrion and B. Fischhoff, *American Journal of Physics,* in press.

12. R. E. Nisbett and L. Ross (1980). *Human Inference: Strategies and shortcomings of social judgment.* Englewood Cliffs: Prentice Hall.

13. A. Tversky and D. Kahneman (1981), *Science* 211, 453.

14. https://www.corporatecomplianceinsights.com/cognitive-governance-5 -principles/.

15. https://www.corporatecomplianceinsights.com/intentional-control-design -crf/#_edn1.

16. https://www.corporatecomplianceinsights.com/intentional-control-design -crf/#_edn1.

17. J. Sweller (1988). Cognitive load during problem solving: Effects on learning, *Cognitive Science,* 12(2), 257-285, ISSN 0364-0213, https://doi.org/10.1016 /0364-0213(88)90023-7.

18. https://www.frontiersin.org/articles/10.3389/fpsyg.2012.00436/full#B150.

19. https://www.frontiersin.org/articles/10.3389/fpsyg.2012.00436/full#B191.

20. https://www.csoonline.com/article/3652339/8-takeaways-for-cisos-from-the -nstac-zero-trust-report.html.

21. https://csrc.nist.gov/publications/detail/sp/800-207/final.

22. https://dodcio.defense.gov/Portals/0/Documents/Library/(U)ZT_RA_v1.1(U) _Mar21.pdf.

23. https://media.defense.gov/2021/Feb/25/2002588479/-1/-1/0/CSI_ EMBRACING_ZT_SECURITY_MODEL_UOO115131-21.PDF.

24. https://www.cisa.gov/sites/default/files/publications/CISA%20Zero%20Trust %20Maturity%20Model_Draft.pdf.

25. https://www.cisa.gov/uscert/ncas/current-activity/2021/10/28/nsa-cisa-series -securing-5g-cloud-infrastructures.

26. https://www.whitehouse.gov/wp-content/uploads/2022/01/M-22-09.pdf.

27. https://csrc.nist.gov/CSRC/media/Events/FISSEA-30th-Annual-Conference/documents/FISSEA2017_Witkowski_Benczik_Jarrin_Walker_Materials_Final.pdf.
28. https://www.darkreading.com/risk/the-human-factor-5-reasons-why-cyber-security-is-a-people-problem.
29. https://rocket.chat/blog/it-security.
30. https://www.cybertalk.org/2021/12/02/alarming-cyber-security-facts-to-know-for-2021-and-beyond/.
31. https://www.researchgate.net/publication/325194950_Emerging_Threats_for_the_Human_Element_and_Countermeasures_in_Current_Cyber_Security_Landscape.
32. https://www.semanticscholar.org/paper/Adversarially-Robust-Estimate-and-Risk-Analysis-in-Xing-Zhang/473fd89e58e9bd1ed25b3dc842f2d910c855daf7.
33. https://csrc.nist.gov/Projects/Cybersecurity-Risk-Analytics.
34. https://en.wikipedia.org/wiki/Skunkworks_project.
35. https://www.securitysolutionsmedia.com/2018/11/19/what-socio-technical-system-why-important-risk-management/.
36. A. Jarman (2001), *'Reliability' Reconsidered: A Critique of the Sagan-LaPorte Debate Concerning Vulnerable High-Technology Systems*. Chisholm and Lerner Paper, Canberra 34 M. Landau (1969) Redundancy, rationality, and the problem of duplication and overlap. *Public Administration Review*, 29(4), (July/August), 346–358.
37. https://www.mtu.edu/cls/undergraduate/human-factors/what/.
38. https://en.wikipedia.org/wiki/Technical_debt.

Additional References

Abor, J., Adjasi, C., & Kyereboah-Coleman, A. (2006). Corporate governance and firm performance: Evidence from Ghanaian listed companies. *Corporate Ownership & Control*, 4(2), Winter 2006–2007.

Agrawal, A., & Chadha, S. (2005). Corporate governance and accounting scandals. *Journal of Law and Economics*, 48(2), 371–406.

Akbar, A. (2014). Corporate governance and firm performance: Evidence from textile sector of Pakistan. *Journal of Asian Business Strategy*, 4(12), 200–207.

Akinsulire, O. (2010). *Financial Management* (6th ed.). Lagos: Ceemol Nigeria Ltd.

Al-Baidhani, Prof-Dr-Ahmed. (2014). The Role of Audit Committee in Corporate Governance: Descriptive Study. *SSRN Electronic Journal*. 10.2139/ssrn.2487167.

Ames, D., Hines, C., & Sankara, J. (2018). Board risk committees: Insurer financial strength ratings and performance. *Journal of Accounting and Public Policy*, 37, 130–145.

André, R. (2010). Assessing the accountability of government-sponsored enterprises and quangos. *Journal of Business Ethics*, 97(2), 271–289.

Argento, D., Grossi, G., & Thomasson, A. (2011). Governance and control of externalized water service management: Comparing solutions adopted in Italy and Sweden. *Corporate Ownership & Control*, 188–195.

Armstrong, A., Jia, X., & Totikidis, V. (2005). Parallels in private and public sector governance, GovNet Annual Conference, contemporary issues in governance. *Paper presented to GovNet Annual Conference*, Melbourne, 28–30 November.

Barberis, P. (1998). The new public management and a new accountability. *Public Administration*, 76(3), 451–470.

Basuony, M. A., Mohamed, E. K., Hussain, M. M., & Marie, O. K. (2016). Board characteristics, ownership structure and audit report lag in the Middle East. *International Journal of Corporate Governance*, 7(2), 180–205.

Baxter, P., & Cotter, J. (2009). Audit committees and earnings quality. *Accounting & Finance*, 49(2), 267–290.

Beasley, M. S., Carcello, J. V., Hermanson, D. V., & Lapides, P. D. (2000). Fraudulent financial reporting: Consideration of industry traits and corporate governance mechanisms. *Accounting Horizons*, 14(4), 441–454.

Bedard, J., Chtourou, S. M., & Courteau, L. (2004). The effect of audit committee expertise, independence and activity on aggressive earnings management. *Auditing: A Journal of Practice and Theory*, 23(2), 13–35.

Bevir, M. (2009). *Key Concepts in Governance*. Los Angeles: Sage.

Bhagat, S., & Black, B. (1998). *Board Independence and Long-Term Performance*. University of Colorado and Stanford University Working Paper.

Bhagat, S., & Jefferis, R. H. (2005). *The Econometrics of Corporate Governance Studies*. MIT Press.

Bhattacharya, S. (2012). The effectiveness of the ISM Code: A qualitative enquiry. *Marine Policy*, 36(2), 528–535.

Block, D., & Gerstner, A.-M. (2016, Spring). *One-Tier vs. Two-Tier Board Structure: A Comparison between the United States and Germany*. University of Pennsylvania, Goethe University.

Blue Ribbon Committee. (1999). *Report and Recommendations of the Blue Ribbon Committee on Improving the Effectiveness of Audit Committees*. NYSE and NASD, NY.

Blue Ribbon Committee on Improving the Effectiveness of Corporate Audit Committees. (1999). Report and recommendations of the Blue-Ribbon Committee on improving the effectiveness of corporate audit committees. *The Business Lawyer*, 54(3), 1057–1066.

Bond, J., & Dent, U. (2008). *Auditing: A Nigeria Perspective*. Owerri: Mantle Publisher.

Bouckaert, G. (2017). Taking stock of "governance": A predominantly European perspective. *Governance*, 30(1), 45–52.

Bovens, M. (2005). Public accountability. In *The Oxford Handbook of Public Management*, Ferlie, E., Lynne, L., & Pollitt, C., Eds. Oxford: Oxford University Press.

Bovens, M. (2010). Two concepts of accountability: Accountability as a virtue and as a mechanism. *West European Politics*, 33(5), 946–967.

BraadBaart, O. (2007). Privatizing water: The Jakarta concession and the limits of contract. In *A World of Water*, pp. 297–320.

Bradbury, M. E. (1990). The incentives for voluntary audit committee formation. *Journal of Accounting and Public Policy*, 9, 19–36.

Broadbent, J., Dietrich, M., & Laughlin, R. (2002). The development of principal-agent, contracting and accountability relationships in the public sector. *Public Management: Critical Perspectives*, 2, 107.

Burns, J. E. (2000). The dynamics of accounting change: Interplay between new practices, routines, institutions, power, and politics. *Accounting, Auditing and Accountability Journal*, 13(5), 566–596.

Bushman, R. M., & Smith, A. J. (2001). Financial accounting information and corporate governance. *Journal of Accounting and Economics*, 32(1–3), 237–333.

Bushman, R. M., & Smith, A. J. (2003). Transparency, financial accounting information, and corporate governance. Financial accounting information, and corporate governance. *Economic Policy Review*, 9(1).

Cadbury Committee. (1992). *Financial Aspects of Corporate Governance*. London: Gee Publishing Ltd.

Carcello, J. V., & Neal, T. L. (2003). Audit committee characteristics and auditor dismissals following "new" going-concern reports. *Accounting Review*, 78(1), 95–118.

Chan, K. C., & Li, J. (2008). Audit committee and firm value: Evidence of outside top executive as director corporate governance. *An International Review*, 16(1), 16–31.

Clarke, T. (2004). *Theories of Corporate Governance*. Oxon: The Philosophical Foundations of Corporate Governance.

Clegg, S. (1989). *Frameworks of Power*. London: Sage.

Colley, J. L., Doyle, J., Logan, L. W., & Stettinius, W. (2005). *What is Corporate Governance?* New York: McGrewHill.

Collier, P. (1992). Audit committees in large UK companies.

Collier, P. (1993). Factors affecting the formation of audit committees in major UK listed companies. *Accounting and Business Research*, 23(91A), 421–430.

Collier, P. (1996). The rise of the audit committee in UK quoted companies: A curious phenomenon? *Accounting, Business & Financial History*, 6(2), 121–140.

Collier, P., & Gregory, A. (1999). Audit committee activity and agency costs. *Journal of Accounting and Public Policy*, 18(4–5), 311–332.

Collier, P., & Zaman, M. (2005). Convergence in European corporate governance: The audit committee concept. *Corporate Governance: An International Review*, 13(6), 753–768.

Cybenko, G., Giani, A., & Thompson, P. (2004). Cognitive hacking. *Advances in Computers*, 60, 35–73. https://doi.org/10.1016/S0065-2458(03)60002-1.

Dahya, J., Dimitrov, O., & McConnell, J. J. (2008). Dominant shareholders, corporate boards, and corporate value: A cross-country analysis. *Journal of Financial Economics*, 87(1), 73–100.

Davidson, R., Goodwin-Stewart, J., & Kent, P. (2005). Internal governance structures and earnings management. *Accounting & Finance*, 45(2), 241–267.

Dechow, P. M., Sloan, R. G., & Sweeney, A. P. (1996). Causes and consequences of earning manipulation: An analysis of firms subject to enforcement actions by the SEC. *Contemporary Accounting Research*, 13(2), 1–36.

DeFond, M. L., & Jiambalvo, J. (1991). Incidence and circumstances of accounting errors. *The Accounting Review*, 66(3), 643.

DeFond, M. L., Hann, R. N., & Hu, X. (2005). Does the market value financial expertise on audit committees of boards of directors? *Journal of Accounting Research*, 43(2), 153–193.

Deleon, L. (1998). Accountability in a 'reinvented' government. *Public Administration*, 76(3), 539–558.

DeZoort, F. T., & Salterio, S. E. (2001). The effects of corporate governance experience and financial-reporting and audit knowledge on audit committee members' judgments. *Auditing: A Journal of Practice & Theory*, 20(2), 31–47.

DeZoort, F. T., Hermanson, D. R., Archambeault, D. S., & Reed, S. A. (2002). Audit committee effectiveness: A synthesis of the empirical audit committee literature. *Journal of Accounting Literature*, 21, 38–75.

Dirsmith, M. W., & Covaleski, M. A. (1985). Informal communications, nonformal communications and mentoring in public accounting firms. *Accounting, Organizations and Society*, 10(2), 149–169.

Dubnick, M. (2005). Accountability and the promise of performance: In search of the mechanisms. *Public Performance & Management Review*, 28(3), 376–417.

Dwivedi, O. P., & Jabbra, J. (1988). Introduction: Public service responsibility and accountability. In *Public Service Accountability. A Comparative Perspective*, Jabbra, J., & Dwivedi, O. P., Eds. Hartford: Kumarian Press.

European Commission. (2006). 8th Directive on Statutory Audit of Annual Accounts and Consolidated Accounts. 2006/43/EC.

Fadzil, F. H., Haron, H., & Jantan, M. (2005). Internal auditing practices and internal control system. *Managerial Auditing Journal*, 20, 844–866.

Fligstein, N., & Goldstein, A. (2009). The anatomy of the mortgage securitization crisis. *Paper presented to the Society for the Advancement of Socio-Economics*, Paris, available at: http://www.sase.org/images/SASE09/Fligstein_Subprimes.pdf (accessed August 8, 2010).

Gendron, Y., & Bédard, J. (2006). On the constitution of audit committee effectiveness. *Accounting, Organizations and Society*, 31(3), 211–239.

Gendron, Y., Bedard, J., & Gosselin, M. (2004). Getting inside the black-box: A filed study of practices in "effective" audit committees. *Auditing: A Journal of Practice and Theory*, 23(1), 153–171.

Gilardi, F. (2001). Principal-agent models go to Europe: Independent regulatory agencies as ultimate step of delegation. In *ECPR General Conference*, Canterbury (UK), 6–8.

Gilkison, B. (1999). *Accounting for a Clean Green Environment: Obligations and Opportunities for New Zealand Businesses and their Accountants*, Auckland N.Z.: KPMG.

Gilson, R. J., & Gordon, J. N. (2019). Board 3.0 – An introduction (February 10, 2019). *The Business Lawyer*, 74, Spring, Columbia Law and Economics Working Paper No. 602, Stanford Law and Economics Olin Working Paper No. 531. Available at SSRN: https://ssrn.com/abstract=3332735

Goddard, A. (2005). Accounting and NPM in UK local government–contributions towards governance and accountability. *Financial Accountability & Management*, 21(2), 191–218.

Goodwin-Stewart, J., & Kent, P. (2006). The use of internal audit by Australian companies. *Managerial Auditing Journal*, 21, 81–101.

Gramling, A. A., Maletta, M. J., Schneider, A., & Church, B. K. (2004). The role of the internal audit function in corporate governance: A synthesis of the extant internal auditing literature and directions for future research. *Journal of Accounting Literature*, 23, 194.

Gray, A., & Jenkins, B. (1993). Codes of accountability in the new public sector. *Accounting, Auditing & Accountability Journal*.

Greiling, D., & Spraul, K. (2010). Accountability and the challenges of information disclosure. *Public Administration Quarterly*, 36(3), 338–377.

Guthrie, J., & Turnbull, S. (1995). Audit committees: Is there a role for corporate senates and/or shareholder councils?. *Corporate Governance: An International Review*, 3(2), 78–79.

Hall, R. H. (1999). *Organizations: Structures, Processes and Outcomes*. New Jersey: Prentice-Hall.

Hampel Committee. (1998). *Committee on Corporate Governance: Final Report*. London: Gee Publishing Ltd.

Hardy, C. (1996). Understanding power: Bringing about strategic change. *British Journal of Management*, 7, March, S3–S16.

Hayne, C., & Free, C. (2014). Hybridized professional groups and institutional work: COSO and the rise of enterprise risk management. *Accounting, Organizations and Society*, 39, 309–330.

Heath, J., & Norman, W. (2004). Stakeholder theory, corporate governance, and public management: What can the history of state-run enterprises teach us in the post-Enron era? *Journal of Business Ethics*, 53(3), 247–265.

Hermalin, B. E., & Weisbach, M. S. (2003, April). Boards of directors as an endogenously determined institution: A survey of the economic literature. *Economic Policy Review*, 9(1). Available at SSRN: https://ssrn.com/abstract=794804

Higgs, D. (2002). *Review of the Role and Effectiveness of Non-Executive Directors: Consultation Paper*. London: Department of Trade and Industry.

Higgs, D. (2003). *Review of the Role and Effectiveness of Non-Executive Directors*. London: Department of Trade and Industry.

Holm, C., & Schøler, F. (2010). Reduction of asymmetric information through corporate governance mechanisms—the importance of ownership dispersion and exposure toward the 60 Stratford Peer Reviewed Journals and Book Publishing international capital market. *Corporate Governance: An International Review*, 18(1), 32–47.

Hooks, L., Kaplan, S. E., & Schultz, J. J. (1994). Enhancing communication to assist 27 fraud prevention and detection. *Auditing: A Journal of Practice and Theory*, 13(2), 86–116.

Humphrey, C., & Scapens, R. W. (1996). Theories and case studies of organizational accounting practices: Limitation or liberation? *Accounting, Auditing & Accountability Journal*, 9(4), 86–106.

Iskander, M., & Chamlou, N. (2000). *Corporate Governance: A Framework for Implementation*. Washington, D.C.: World Bank Group. http://documents. worldbank.org/curated/en/810311468739547854/Corporate-governance-a-framework-for-implementation.

Jackson, Sishumba, Loti Saidi, Milupi Nyambe (2022). A Study into the Effects of Internal Audit on the Financial Performance of Commercial Banks in Zambia (A case of Standard Chartered). *International Journal of Current Science Research and Review*, 5(11), 4156–4175.

Kahan, M., & Rock, E. B. (2003). Corporate constitutionalism: Antitakeover charter provisions as precommitment. *University of Pennsylvania Law Review*, 152(2), 473–522.

Kalbers, L. P., & Fogarty, T. J. (1993). Audit committee effectiveness: An empirical investigation of the contribution of power. *Auditing*, 12(1), 24.

Kalbers, L. P., & Fogarty, T. J. (1998). Organizational and economic explanations of audit committee oversight. *Journal of Managerial Issues*, 10, 129–150.

Kasperson, R. E. (2012). The social amplification of risk and low-level radiation. *Bulletin of the Atomic Scientists*, 68(3), 59–66. https://doi.org/10.1177 /0096340212444871.

Kevin, L. (2009). Liability exposures of audit committee chairs. http://www.dan-dodiary.com/2014/04/articles/director-and-officer-liability/liabilityexposures-of-audit-committee-chairs (accessed October 21, 2012).

Klein, A. (2002). Economic determinants of audit committee independence. *Accounting Review*, 77, April, 435–452.

Kooiman, J. (2003). *Governing as Governance*. SAGE Publications Ltd, https:// dx.doi.org/10.4135/9781446215012.

Krishnan, J. (2005). Audit committee quality and internal control: An empirical analysis. *Accounting Review*, 80(2), 649–675.

Laughlin, R. (1995). Empirical research in accounting: Alternative approaches and a case for 'middle-range thinking'. *Accounting, Auditing & Accountability Journal*, 8(1), 63–87.

Mabati, J., Onserio, R., & Mutai, N. (2020). Governance and accountability: The role of audit committee. *Journal of Finance and Accounting* [Stratford Peer Reviewed Journals and Book Publishing], 4(2), 48–62.

Mbaabu, L. M. (2010). *The Relationship between Corporate Governance, Ownership Structure and Financial Performance of Insurance Companies in Kenya* (Doctoral dissertation). University of Nairobi, Kenya.

McMullen, D. A. (1996). Audit committee performance: An investigation of the consequences associated with Audit Committees. *Auditing: Journal of Practice & Theory*, 15(1), 87–103.

McNulty, T., Roberts, J., & Stiles, P. (2005). Undertaking governance reform and research: Further reflections on the Higgs review. *British Journal of Management*, 16, S99–S107.

Medori, D., & Steeple, D. (2000). A framework for auditing and enhancing performance measurement systems. *International Journal of Operations & Production Management*.

Menon, K., & Williams, J. D. (1994). The use of audit committees for monitoring. *Journal of Accounting and Public Policy*, 13(2), 121–139.

Miceli, M. P., & Near, J. P. (1984). The relationships among beliefs, organizational position, and whistleblowing status: A discriminant analysis. *Academy of Management Journal*, 27(4), 687–705.

Millstein, I. M., & MacAvoy, P. W. (1998). The active board of directors and performance of the large publicly traded corporation. *Columbia Law Review*, 98, 1283.

Min, B. S., & Smyth, R. (2012). *Globalisation, Corporate Governance and Firm Productivity*. Monash University, Department of Economics.

Monks, Robert A. G., & Minow, N. (2004). *Corporate Governance*. Malden, MA: Blackwell.

Morin, R. A., & Jarrell, S. L. (2000). *Driving Shareholder Value: Value-building Techniques for Creating Shareholder Wealth*. McGraw Hill Professional.

Mulgan, R. (2000). Accountability': An ever-expanding concept? *Public Administration*, 78(3), 555–573.

Mulgan, R. (2003). One cheer for hierarchy-accountability in disjointed governance. *Political Science*, 55(2), 6–18.

Okaro, S. C., & Okafor, G. O. (2013). Drivers of audit failure in Nigeria- evidence from Cadbury. *Research Journal of Finance and Accounting*, 4(6), 14–17.

Okoye, E., & Cletus, A. (2010). Enhancing the effectiveness of audit committee in Nigerian manufacturing companies. *Journal of Policy and Development Studies*, 4(2), 117–127.

O'Meara, B., & Petzall, S. (2007). How important is the role of the chancellor in the appointment of Australian vice-chancellors and university governance? *International Journal of Educational Management*, 21, 213–231.

Osborne, S. P. (2006). The new public governance? *Public Management Review*, 8(3), 377–387.

Owolabi, A., & Ogbechia, C. (2010). Audit committee reports and corporate governance in Nigeria. *International Journal Critical Accounting*, 2(1), 64–78.

Owolabi, S. A., & Dada, S. O. (2011). Audit committee: An instrument of effective corporate governance. *European Journal of Economics, Finance and Administrative Sciences*, 35(35), 174–183.

Pettigrew, A. (1992). On studying managerial elites. *Strategic Management Journal*, 13(S), 163–182.

Pfeffer, J. (1992). *Managing with Power*. Boston, MA: Harvard Business School Press.

Pincus, K., Rusbarsky, M., & Wong, J. (1989). Voluntary formation of corporate audit committees among NASDAQ firms. *Journal of Accounting and Public Policy*, 8, 239–265.

Pirson, M., & Turnbull, S. (2011). Corporate governance, risk management, and the financial crisis: An information processing view. *Corporate Governance, An International Review*, 19(5), 459–470.

Polidano, C. (1998). Why bureaucrats can't always do what Ministers want: Multiple accountabilities in Westminster democracies. *Public Policy and Administration*, 13(1), 35–50.

Power, M. (2003). Auditing and the production of legitimacy. *Accounting, Organizations and Society*, 28, 379–394.

Price, R., Román, F. J., & Rountree, B. (2011). The impact of governance reform on performance and transparency. *Journal of Financial Economics*, 99(1), 76–96.

Raghunandan, K., Rama, D. V., & Read, W. J. (2001). Audit committee composition, "gray directors," and interaction with internal auditing. *Accounting Horizons*, 15(2), 105–118.

Ramirez, S., & Simkins, B. (Spring 2008). Enterprise-wide risk management and corporate governance. *Loyola University of Chicago Law Journal*, 39, 571.

Ramsay Report. (2001). Independence of Australian company auditors: Review of current Australian requirements and proposals for reform. Dept of Treasury, Commonwealth of Australia, http://www.treasury.gov.au.

Rashid, K., & Islam, S. M. (2008). *Corporate Governance and Firm Value: Econometric Modeling and Analysis of Emerging and Developed Financial Markets*. Emerald Group Publishing.

Rezaee, Z. (2009). *Corporate Governance and Ethics*. Hoboken, NJ, USA: John Wiley & Sons. Inc.

Roberts, J., & Scapens, R. (1985). Accounting systems and systems of accountability — Understanding accounting practices in their organizational contexts. *Accounting, Organizations, and Society*, 10(4), 443–456.

Robinson, D. R., & Owens-Jackson, L. A. (2009). Audit committee characteristics and auditor changes. *Academy of Accounting and Financial Studies Journal*, 13, 117.

Romzek, B. S., & Dubnick, M. J. (1987). Accountability in the public sector: Lessons from the challenger tragedy. *Public Administration Review*, 47(3), 227–238.

Rose-Ackerman, S. (2017). What does "governance" mean? *Governance*, 30(1), 23–27.

Saidin, S. F. B. (2007). *Audit Committee Characteristics and Quality of Unaudited Financial Accounts* (Doctoral dissertation). http://eprints. usm.my/7837/1/a udit_committee_characteristics_and_quality_of_unaudited_financial_acco unts. pdf (accessed March 8, 2012).

Sale, H. A. (2003). Delaware's good faith. *Cornell Law Review*, 89, 456.

Salehi, M., Zanjirdar, M., & Zarei, F. (2012). Factors affecting the quality of audit committee: A study. *Journal of Accounting Research and Audit Practices*, Xi(4), 34–48.

Sandu, C., & Haines, R. (2014). Theory of governance and social enterprise. *The USV Annals of Economics and Public Administration*, 14(2(20)), 204–222.

Sarens, G., & De Beelde, I. (2006). *Internal Audit: The Expert in Providing Comfort to the Audit Committee*. Working Paper, University of Ghent, Belgium.

Scott, W. R. (2001). *Institutions and Organizations* (2nd ed.). Thousand Oaks: Sage Publications.

SEC. (2003). Final rule: Disclosure required by section 406 and 407 of the Sarbanes-Oxley Act of 2002, Release Nos. 33-8177; 34-47235. http://www.sec.gov/rules/final/33-8177.htm.

SEC. (2020). "Modernizing" regulation S-K: Ignoring the elephant in the room. https://www.sec.gov/news/public-statement/lee-mda-2020-01-30.

Securities and Exchange Commission (SEC). (2011). Code of corporate governance in Nigeria. http://www.sec.gov.ng.com/governance.htm.

Shaoul, J., Stafford, A., & Stapleton, P. (2012). Accountability and corporate governance of public private partnerships. *Critical Perspectives on Accounting*, 23(3), 213–229.

Shapira, Z. (2000). Governance in organizations: A cognitive perspective. *Journal of Management and Governance*, 4, 53–67.

Shapiro, E. R. (1994). The practice of group analysis. *Journal of the American Psychoanalytic Association*, 42(3), 955–959. https://doi.org/10.1177/000306519404200330.

Shore, C., & Wright, S. (2004). Whose accountability? Governmentality and the auditing of universities. *parallax*, 10(2), 100–116.

Simkins, B. J., & Ramirez, S. A. (2008). Enterprise-wide risk management and corporate governance (March 1, 2008). *Loyola University Chicago Law Journal*, 39. Available at SSRN: https://ssrn.com/abstract=1657036.

Sinclair, A. (1995). The chameleon of accountability: Forms and discourses. *Accounting, Organizations and Society*, 20(2–3), 219–237.

Slovic, P. (1987). Perception of risk. *Science*, 236, 280–285. https://doi.org/10.1126/science.3563507.

Slovic, P., & Weber, E. (2002). Perception of risk posed by extreme events. *Science*.

Smith Committee. (2003). *Audit Committee Combined Code Guidance*. Financial Reporting Council, London.

Spira, L. (2002). *The Audit Committee: Performing Corporate Governance*. London: Kluwer Academic Publishers.

Thomsen, S. (2008). *An Introduction to Corporate Governance*. Copenhagen: DJOF Publishers.

Tonello, M. (2007, February 1). *Emerging Governance Practices in Enterprise Risk Management*. The Conference Board Research Report No. R-1398-07-WG, available at SSRN: https://ssrn.com/abstract=963221 or http://dx.doi.org/10.2139/ssrn.963221.

Torfing, J., Peters, B. G., Pierre, J., & Sørensen, E. (2012). *Interactive Governance: Advancing the Paradigm*. Oxford, England: Oxford University Press on demand.

Treasury. (2002). *Corporate Disclosure: Strengthening the Financial Reporting Framework*. CLERP9, Department of Treasury, Commonwealth of Australia. http://www.treasury.gov.au.

Turley, S., & Zaman, M. (2003). *Public Policy on Corporate Audit Committees*. London: ACCA Research Paper. Downloadable at: http://www.accaglobal.com/pubs/publicinterest/activities/research/research_archive/orp_035_001.pdf.

Turley, S., & Zaman, M. (2004). Corporate governance effects of audit committees. *Journal of Management & Governance*, 8, 305–332.

Turley, S., & Zaman, M. (2007). Audit committee effectiveness: Informal processes and behavioral effects. *Accounting, Auditing & Accountability Journal,* 20(5), 765–788.

Wally, S., & Baum, J. R. (1994). Personal and structural determinants of the pace of strategic decision making. *The Academy of Management Journal,* 37(4), 932–956.

Williamson, O. E. (1975). Markets and hierarchies: Analysis and antitrust implications: A study in the economics of internal organization. *University of Illinois at Urbana-Champaign's Academy for Entrepreneurial Leadership Historical Research Reference in Entrepreneurship.* Available at SSRN: https://ssrn.com/abstract=1496220

Williamson, O. E. (1979). Transaction-cost economics: The governance of contractual relations. *Journal of Law and Economics,* 22, 233–261. http://doi.org/10.1086/466942.

Williamson, O. E. (2005). Transaction cost economics and business administration. *Scandinavian Journal of Management,* 21(1), 19–40.

Yang, J. S., & Krishnan, J. (2005). Audit committees and quarterly earnings. *International Journal of Auditing,* 9(3), 201–220.

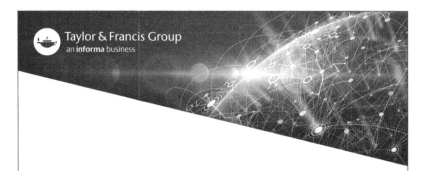

Printed in the United States
by Baker & Taylor Publisher Services